❖ Forbes

TRAVEL GUIDE

Formerly Mobil Travel Guide

NEW YORK

2011

ACKNOWLEDGMENTS

We gratefully acknowledge the help of our representatives for their efficient and perceptive inspections of the lodgings listed. Forbes Travel Guide is also grateful to the talented writers who contributed to this book.

Some of the information contained herein is derived from a variety of third-party sources. Although every effort has been made to verify the information obtained from such sources, the publisher assumes no responsibility for inconsistencies or inaccuracies in the data or liability for any damages of any type arising from errors or omissions.

Neither the editors nor the publisher assume responsibility for the services provided by any business listed in this guide or for any loss, damage or disruption in your travel for any reason.

Front Cover image: ©iStockphoto.com
All maps: Mapping Specialists

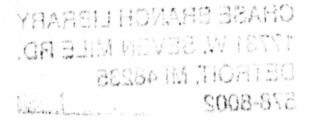

ISBN: 9781936010882
Manufactured in the USA
10 9 8 7 6 5 4 3 2 1

CONTENTS

STAR ATTRACTIONS

If you've been a reader of Mobil Travel Guide, you will have heard that this historic brand partnered in 2009 with another storied media name, Forbes, to create a new entity, Forbes Travel Guide. For more than 50 years, Mobil Travel Guide assisted travelers in making smart decisions about where to stay and dine when traveling. With this new partnership, our mission has not changed: We're committed to the same rigorous inspections of hotels, restaurants and spas—the most comprehensive in the industry with more than 500 standards tested at each property we visit—to help you cut through the clutter and make easy and informed decisions on where to spend your time and travel budget. Our team of anonymous inspectors are constantly on the road, sleeping in hotels, eating in restaurants and making spa appointments, evaluating those exacting standards to determine a property's rating.

What kinds of standards are we looking for when we visit a property? We're looking for more than just high-thread count sheets, pristine spa treatment rooms and white linen-topped tables. We look for service that's attentive, individualized and unforgettable. We note how long it takes to be greeted when you sit down at your table, or to be served when you order room service, or whether the hotel staff can confidently help you when you've forgotten that one essential item that will make or break your trip. Unlike any other travel ratings entity, we visit each place we rate, testing hundreds of attributes to compile our ratings, and our ratings cannot be bought or influenced. The Forbes Five Star rating is the most prestigious achievement in hospitality—while we rate more than 5,000 properties in the U.S., Canada, Hong Kong, Macau and Beijing, for 2011, we have awarded Five Star designations to only 54 hotels, 23 restaurants and 20 spas. When you travel with Forbes, you can travel with confidence, knowing that you'll get the very best experience, no matter who you are.

We understand the importance of making the most of your time. That's why the most trusted name in travel is now Forbes Travel Guide.

STAR RATED HOTELS

Whether you're looking for the ultimate in luxury or the best value for your travel budget, we have a hotel recommendation for you. To help you pinpoint properties that meet your needs, Forbes Travel Guide classifies each lodging by type according to the following characteristics:

★★★★★These exceptional properties provide a memorable experience through virtually flawless service and the finest of amenities. Staff are intuitive, engaging and passionate, and eagerly deliver service above and beyond the guests' expectations. The hotel was designed with the guest's comfort in mind, with particular attention paid to craftsmanship and quality of product. A Five-Star property is a destination unto itself.

★★★★These properties provide a distinctive setting, and a guest will find many interesting and inviting elements to enjoy throughout the property. Attention to detail is prominent throughout the property, from design concept to quality of products provided. Staff are accommodating and take pride in catering to the guest's specific needs throughout their stay.

★★★These well-appointed establishments have enhanced amenities that provide travelers with a strong sense of location, whether for style or function. They may have a distinguishing style and ambience in both the public spaces and guest rooms; or they may be more focused on functionality, providing guests with easy access to local events, meetings or tourism highlights.

Recommended: These hotels are considered clean, comfortable and reliable establishments that have expanded amenities, such as full-service restaurants.

For every property, we also provide pricing information. All prices quoted are accurate at the time of publication; however, prices cannot be guaranteed. Because rates can fluctuate, we list a pricing range rather than specific prices.

STAR RATED RESTAURANTS

Every restaurant in this book has been visited by Forbes Travel Guide's team of experts and comes highly recommended as an outstanding dining experience.

★★★★★Forbes Five-Star restaurants deliver a truly unique and distinctive dining experience. A Five-Star restaurant consistently provides exceptional food, superlative service and elegant décor. An emphasis is placed on originality and personalized, attentive and discreet service. Every detail that surrounds the experience is attended to by a warm and gracious dining room team.

★★★★These are exciting restaurants with often well-known chefs that feature creative and complex foods and emphasize various culinary techniques and a focus on seasonality. A highly-trained dining room staff provides refined personal service and attention.

★★★Three Star restaurants offer skillfully prepared food with a focus on a specific style or cuisine. The dining room staff provides warm and professional service in a comfortable atmosphere. The décor is well-coordinated with quality fixtures and decorative items, and promotes a comfortable ambience.

Recommended: These restaurants serve fresh food in a clean setting with efficient service. Value is considered in this category, as is family friendliness.

Because menu prices can fluctuate, we list a pricing range rather than specific prices. The pricing ranges are per diner, and assume that you order an appetizer or dessert, an entrée and one drink.

STAR RATED SPAS

Forbes Travel Guide's spa ratings are based on objective evaluations of more than 450 attributes. About half of these criteria assess basic expectations, such as staff courtesy, the technical proficiency and skill of the employees and whether the facility is clean and maintained properly. Several standards address issues that impact a guest's physical comfort and convenience, as well as the staff's ability to impart a sense of personalized service. Additional criteria measure the spa's ability to create a completely calming ambience.

★★★★★Stepping foot in a Five Star Spa will result in an exceptional experience with no detail overlooked. These properties wow their guests with extraordinary design and facilities, and uncompromising service. Expert staff cater to your every whim and pamper you with the most advanced treatments and skin care lines available. These spas often offer exclusive treatments and may emphasize local elements.

★★★★Four Star spas provide a wonderful experience in an inviting and serene environment. A sense of personalized service is evident from the moment you check in and receive your robe and slippers. The guest's comfort is always of utmost concern to the well-trained staff.

★★★These spas offer well-appointed facilities with a full complement of staff to ensure that guests' needs are met. The spa facil ties include clean and appealing treatment rooms, changing areas and a welcoming reception desk.

WELCOME TO NEW YORK

THE LARGEST OF THE NORTHEASTERN STATES, New York stretches from the Great Lakes to the Atlantic. The glitter and glamour of New York City—from the skyscrapers in Midtown to the beaches of Coney Island—make America's most populous city a world capital. But New York State has much more to offer than just Gotham. Niagara Falls, the Finger Lakes, the Catskills (where Rip Van Winkle is said to have slept for 20 years), the white-sand beaches of the Hamptons, the lakes and forested peaks of the Adirondacks and the stately bluffs along the Hudson are just a few of the features that attract millions of tourists every year.

When Giovanni da Verrazano entered New York Harbor in 1524, the Native Americans who inhabited the area were at constant war with one another. Around 1570, under Dekanawidah and Hiawatha, they formed the Iroquois Confederacy (the first League of Nations) and began to live in peace. They were known as the Five Nations and called themselves the "Men of Men".

In 1609, Samuel de Champlain explored the valley of the lake that now holds his name, and Henry Hudson sailed up the river that also bears his moniker. New Amsterdam (later called New York City) was founded in 1625. Wars with the Native Americans and the French kept the area in turmoil until after 1763. During the Revolution, eastern New York was a seesaw of military action and occupation. After the war, George Washington was inaugurated as president in 1789 in the federal government's new capital, New York City.

Gov. DeWitt Clinton later envisioned a canal extending from the Hudson River in Albany to the city of Buffalo to develop the state and offer aid to its Western farmers. Constructed from 1817 to 1825, the Erie Canal became the gateway to the West and was one of the greatest engineering feats of its time, reducing the cost of freight between Buffalo and New York City from $100 to $5 a ton. Enlarged and rerouted, it is now part of the New York State Canal system, 527 miles of waterways used predominately today for recreational boating.

New York is a center for modern advancement, from industry to politics to finance. Industry commenced in New York due to its waterpower; trade and

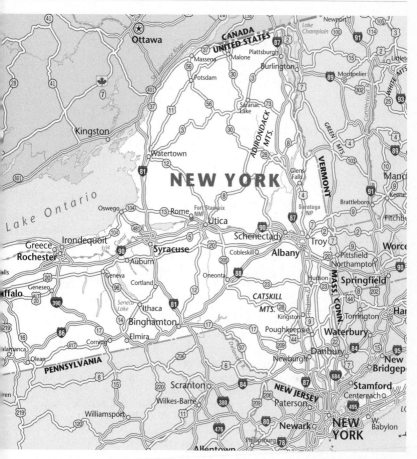

farming flourished thanks to the far-reaching Erie Canal. Optimistic immigrants flooded the eastern shores offering the labor that helped provoke an Industrial Revolution. Four New York natives served as United States presidents (Van Buren, Fillmore and both Roosevelts) and two more built their careers there (Cleveland and Arthur). New York City's Wall Street is central to world economics; there are few states in the country as influential New York.

From the Big Apple to Niagara Falls, from the rolling hills near the Canadian border to the picturesque stretch of Long Island, New York has something for every traveler.

BEST ATTRACTIONS

NEW YORK'S BEST ATTRACTIONS

FINGER LAKES
While most people think of buzzing Manhattan when they conjure up New York, the picturesque Finger Lakes region shows a whole other side to the Empire State. The area offers beautiful lakes, waterfalls and a number of wineries.

GREATER NIAGARA
Niagara Falls gets most of the attention in this area, but the quirky, fun towns that dot the area are worth a visit. You'll find everything from Frank Lloyd Wright homes to museums to great ski spots.

THE HAMPTONS
When the weather turns warm, celebrity city slickers flee crowded Manhattan for the Hamptons' spread-out beaches and soaring summer mansions. The Hamptons are New York's summertime hot spot.

NEW YORK CITY
The city that never sleeps is home to some of the most exceptional attractions anywhere, many of them highly prized for their cultural and historical significance. Besides the world-class museums, shopping, theaters, galleries, music halls, and sports stadiums, you can also stay at some of the most luxurious hotels and dine at some of the finest restaurants in the world.

NIAGARA FALLS
The awe-inspiring Niagara Falls are a must-see for any traveler. Whether you get a glimpse of them during the day or lit-up at night, the robust Falls are a sight. More than 12 million come out each year to marvel at Niagara Falls.

TOP HOTELS, RESTAURANTS AND SPAS

HOTELS

★★★★★FIVE STAR
Four Seasons Hotel New York
(*New York City*)
Mandarin Oriental, New York
(*New York City*)
The Peninsula New York (*New York City*)
The Point (*Saranac Lake*)
The Ritz-Carlton New York, Central Park
(*New York City*)
The St. Regis New York (*New York City*)
Trump International Hotel & Tower
(*New York City*)

★★★★FOUR STAR
The Carlyle, A Rosewood Hotel
(*New York City*)
Lake Placid Lodge (*Lake Placid*)
The Lowell (*New York City*)
Mirbeau Inn & Spa (*Skaneateles*)
The New York Palace (*New York City*)
The Pierre, A Taj Hotel (*New York City*)
The Plaza (*New York City*)
The Ritz-Carlton New York, Battery Park
(*New York City*)

RESTAURANTS

★★★★★FIVE STAR
Daniel (*New York City*)
Eleven Madison Park (*New York City*)
Jean Georges (*New York City*)
Le Bernardin (*New York City*)
Masa (*New York City*)
Per Se (*New York City*)

★★★★FOUR STAR
Adour Alain Ducasse (*New York City*)
Asiate (*New York City*)
Blue Hill at Stone Barns (*Pocantico Hills*)
Bouley (*New York City*)
Del Posto (*New York City*)
The Dining Room at Mirbeau
(*Skaneateles*)
Gilt (*New York City*)
Gordon Ramsay at the London
(*New York City*)
Gotham Bar and Grill (*New York City*)
Gramercy Tavern (*New York City*)
L'Atelier De Joël Rubuchon
(*New York City*)
La Grenouille (*New York City*)
Le Cirque (*New York City*)
Marea (*New York City*)
The Modern (*New York City*)
Picholine (*New York City*)
Sugiyama (*New York City*)

SPAS

★★★★★FIVE STAR
The Peninsula Spa by ESPA (*New York City*)
The Spa at Mandarin Oriental, New York (*New York City*)

★★★★FOUR STAR
The Emerson Spa (*Mount Tremper*)
La Prairie at The Ritz-Carlton Spa (*New York City*)
The Ritz-Carlton Spa, Westchester (*Westchester*)
The Spa at Four Seasons Hotel New York (*New York City*)
Spa Mirbeau (*Skaneateles*)

YOUR QUESTIONS ANSWERED

WHAT'S THE BEST WAY TO SEE NEW YORK CITY IN ONE DAY?

Grab a warm bagel and coffee at **Midtown's H&H Bagels** (*639 W. 46th St., 800-692-2435; www.hhbagels.net*), which many locals consider the best in the city, before heading to Lower Manhattan to hop a Liberty or Ellis Island-bound ferry from **Castle Clinton National Monument** (*Battery Park, 212-344-7220; www. nps.gov/cacl*). Spend a few hours searching Ellis Island's immigrant database for information on your ancestors, perusing its artifact-filled museum, or climbing the pedestal of Lady Liberty.

Head back to Manhattan isle and north to the trendy Soho shopping district for boutique (**Agnes B. Femme & Enfant**, *103 Greene St., 212-925-4649; www. agnesb.us/us*) and department store (**Bloomingdale's**, *504 Broadway, 212-729-5900; www.bloomingdales.com*) goods, plus treats ranging from T-shirts to original pieces of art from street vendors.

Leave enough time to enjoy a meal at the ever-popular French bistro **Balthazar**. You won't go wrong with the steak frites, and be sure to buy a buttery pastry from the bakery before hopping a cab back to Midtown for a Broadway show. (Check out the TKTS Discount Booth in Times Square for same-day show discounts, but plan ahead for the perennially long lines.)

For one last nightcap (or the first of many in the city that never sleeps), take a cab downtown and step into one of the many lounges that fill the gritty streets of the Lower East Side, now one of New York's favorite after-dark destinations. Or join the crowds in the Meatpacking District, where the The Standard hotel has rejuvenated the nightlife scene. Its beer garden, located under the High Line, is an ideal warm-weather spot, as is the **Standard Grill**, which serves bistro classics until 4 a.m.

WHAT'S THE BEST WAY TO SEE NEW YORK CITY IN THREE DAYS?

Start the morning of your second day lazing and gazing in lush Central Park; depending on the season and your tastes, you can ice skate, visit the zoo or go for a bike ride before heading to nearby Museum Mile.

Two possibilities: the **American Museum of Natural History** where you can stroll among the famed dinosaur fossils, or the Metropolitan Museum of Art, which houses some two million works that cover everything from ancient Egyptian artifacts to modern American masterpieces.

Cap off your day with a Ning Sling cocktail (orange vodka mixed with lychee and passion-fruit juices) at **The Peninsula Hotel**'s rooftop bar Salon de Ning. For something a little more low-key and substantial, grab a couple of slices at retro-styled **Big Nick's Burger and Pizza Joint** (*2175 Broadway, 212-362-9238; www.bignicksnyc.com*).

Spend your third day exploring one of New York's outer boroughs. In Brooklyn, enjoy a fragrant morning stroll through the 52-acre **Brooklyn Botanic Garden** (*900 Washington Ave., Brooklyn, 718-623-7200; www.bbg.org*), where the Cranford Rose Garden has more than 5,000 rosebushes spanning almost 1,400 varieties. Or make friends with Paul Cezanne, Edgar Degas and Georgia O'Keeffe at the **Brooklyn Museum of Art** (*200 Eastern Parkway, Brooklyn, 718-638-5000; www.brooklynmuseum.org*). It's the second-largest art museum in the city, after the Met. Spend the afternoon catching rays or raising the hairs on the back of your neck at the beaches and amusement parks of Coney Island where you can ride the iconic Cyclone, one of the country's oldest (and most rickety) wooden roller coasters in operation. Then grab a hot dog at the original **Nathan's Famous** (*1310 Surf Ave., Brooklyn, 718-946-2705; www.nathansfamous.com*).

If you decide to head north from Manhattan and spend the day in the Bronx, you can ride a camel or take the Wild Asia Monorail to see tigers and elephants at the Bronx Zoo. If you'd rather see fly balls than fur balls, head to New Yankee Stadium for a baseball game at the Bronx Bombers' brand-new field.

End your trip with dinner on Arthur Avenue, this borough's answer to Manhattan's Little Italy. After a day game, stop by family-run **Mike's Deli** (*2344 Arthur Ave., Bronx, 718-295-5033; www.arthuravenue.com*), located in the Arthur Avenue Retail Market, for some large and delicious sandwiches, with names such as the Godfather, Michelangelo and Sophia Loren. Or choose from pastas, salads and other platters. One favorite is the eggplant parmigiana. For a heartier meal, bring your culinary imagination because there aren't any menus at **Dominick's Restaurant** (*2335 Arthur Ave., Bronx, 718-733-2807*)—the waiters recite the menu aloud and you order. Or just tell them what you're in the mood for ("How about the catch of the day over some linguini?") and they might bring it out specially made to order.

WHAT ARE THE BEST DAY TRIPS OUTSIDE OF NEW YORK CITY?

Sure, you can get a taste of minimalism at one of Manhattan's many contemporary museums or galleries. But less than an-hour-and-a-half outside of the city limits sits **Dia:Beacon** (*3 Beekman St., Beacon, New York, 845-440-0100; www.diabeacon.org; admission: adults $10, students and seniors $7, children under 12 free*), one of the largest modern art museums in the world—and arguably one of the best. The

YOUR QUESTIONS ANSWERED *continued*

300,000-square-foot museum, opened in May 2003, is actually housed in three brick buildings originally built in 1929 as a box printing factory for the snack giant Nabisco. The extensive galleries and gardens, designed by Robert Irwin in collaboration with OpenOffice (a Manhattan architectural firm), are more intimate than imposing, with the enormous space feeling more like the halls of a private home (no small feat, considering the epic proportions of some of the masterpieces on display). Dia founders (then a husband-and-wife team) Heiner Friedrich and Philippa de Menil collected much of their art during the 1960s and 1970s, though the collection now runs through the present. Much of it is conceptual, and some of it is positively monumental in both size and scope. Among the pieces hang 72 canvases from Andy Warhol's Shadows, several large-scale sheet metal sculptures by Richard Serra, the graphite wall drawings of Sol LeWitt, and the abstract paintings of Agnes Martin. The museum is perched on the eastern bank of the Hudson River; with its rolling green hills and soaring blue skies, it's the perfect setting for a picnic lunch and an easy place to forget that you're just a short train ride from the bustle of New York City.

WHERE IS THE BEST SHOPPING IN MIDTOWN?

Home to Broadway theaters, media powerhouses and much of the city's commerce, Midtown is quite literally the center of New York City and boasts some of its toniest emporiums. Time-pressed office workers jostle for elbow room with gaggles of tourists on the well-trodden sidewalks of Fifth and Madison avenues.

Start your spree at Bloomingdale's sprawling flagship, which takes up an entire city block (*1000 Third Ave., 212-705-2000; www.bloomingdales.com*). Bloomies offers more democratically priced items than the next few department stores on your list. It also has a huge selection of jeans on the second floor, great men's formalwear and loads of shoes for brides.

Your next stop is hip department store Barneys New York (*660 Madison Ave., 212-826-8900; www.barneys.com*), where creative director Simon Doonan's over-the-top, often humorous windows have featured a live actor playing Sigmund Freud and a mannequin of Margaret Thatcher in dominatrix garb. Inside, the loot is less risqué but equally attention-grabbing, ranging from Stella McCartney to Manolo Blahnik. Don't even think about skipping the shoe department; locals love to lunch at Fred's, up on the ninth floor, where the chicken soup will keep you fortified.

Get ready to drop a bundle at luxe Bergdorf Goodman (*754 Fifth Ave. at East 58th Street, 212-753-7300; www.bergdorfgoodman.com*). Ladies can peruse Valentino gowns and Prada clutches or the pieces inside specialty designer boutiques within the store for Chanel, Armani and other high-end labels. Gents get their due just across the street at Bergdorf Goodman Men's (*745 Fifth Ave.*), three entire floors devoted to men with John Varvatos jackets and William Rast jeans.

Nearby lies a trinity of goodies for accessory fiends at leather-good icon Louis Vuitton (*1 E. 57th St., 212-758-8877; www.louisvuitton.com*), bastion of the iconic little blue box Tiffany & Co. (*727 Fifth Ave., 212-755-8000; www.tiffany.com*) and diamond king Harry Winston (*718 Fifth Ave., 212-245-2000; www.harrywinston. com*). Label hounds can then hit the Trump Tower for Gucci (*725 Fifth Ave., 212-826-2600; www.gucci.com*) before heading down to trendy Henri Bendel (*712 Fifth Ave., 212-247-1100; www.henribendel.com*), which draws in young ladies craving makeup, gorgeous lingerie and designs by the next big things in fashion. Bendel's also offers a slew of fun gifts up on the second floor, from picture frames to key chains.

Start praying to the retail gods for heavy markdowns as you head a block-and-a-half farther south to the name-sake flagship of Saks Fifth Avenue (*611 Fifth Ave., 212-753-4000; www.saksfifthavenue.com*), whose shoe department nearly boasts its own zip code. Then, walk the 11 blocks from Saks to mainstay Lord & Taylor (*424 Fifth Ave., 212-391-3344; www.lordandtaylor.com*).

End your day by heading five blocks further south and an avenue west to behemoth Macy's (*151 W. 34th St., Herald Square, 212-695-4400; www.macys. com*). The enormous department store stays open late on weekends.

ADIRONDACKS

Northern New York's Adirondacks offer gorgeous scenery, with abundant lakes and ponds, forests and those majestic mountains. It draws sporty types and outdoor enthusiasts alike. Bolton Landing, on the shores of Lake George, earned the nickname "Millionaires Row" after an influx of wealthy urbanites chose to summer here in the 1800s. Today, most of the waterfront mansions have been converted into resorts, but the cultural atmosphere lives on. While Bolton Landing attracts fewer tourists than nearby Lake George village, summers can still be quite crowded.

The Lake George area is a traveler's dream: You'll find everything from lakeside fun to quiet mountain retreats. In the foothills of the Adirondacks, the area is a center for winter as well as summer sports; there are many miles of snowmobile trails.

Mount Marcy, the highest mountain in New York State (5,344 feet), rises from the Adirondack peaks that surround Lake Placid. Resting on its namesake lake, the village also partly surrounds Mirror Lake, which makes for a scenic setting. This is one of the most famous all-year vacation centers in the East and the site of the 1932 and 1980 Winter Olympics.

Surrounded by Adirondack Park, the village of Saranac Lake was first settled in 1819 when Jacob Moody, who had been injured in a sawmill accident, retired to the wilderness, built a log cabin at what is now Pine and River streets and raised a family of mountain guides. The qualities that attracted Moody and made the town a famous health resort in the 19th century continue to lure visitors who come for the fresh mountain air and a relaxing environment.

WHAT TO SEE

BOLTON LANDING
BOLTON HISTORICAL MUSEUM
4924 Main St., Bolton Landing, 518-644-9960; www.boltonhistorical.org

Housed in a former church, this small museum explores the historical past of the Lake George region with a collection of ice boats, a Smith-Granger rowboat built in Bolton around 1900, antique photographs of lakeside mansions and antique farming equipment.

Admission: adults $10, seniors and students $5. July-August, daily 9 a.m.-2 p.m., 7-9 p.m. Closed Sunday evening. Spring and fall, Saturday-Sunday 9 a.m.-2 p.m.

MARCELLA SEMBRICH OPERA MUSEUM
4800 Lake Shore Drive, Bolton Landing, 518-644-9839; www.operamuseum.com

Metropolitan Opera diva Marcella Sembrich used this studio in the early 20th century to teach piano, violin and vocals to promising pupils from Juilliard and the Curtis Institute. The studio was part of her summer lakeside mansion, named Bay View. Today, the museum displays operatic memorabilia from throughout Sembrich's career, including opera costumes, paintings and sculptures, and autographed photographs from her contemporaries, such as Brahms and Puccini. Be sure to explore the grounds, which exhibit great views of Lake George.

Admission: $2 suggested donation. Mid-June-mid-September, daily 10 a.m.-12:30 p.m., 2-5:30 p.m.

LAKE GEORGE

FORT WILLIAM HENRY MUSEUM
48 Canada St., Lake George, 518-668-5471; www.fwhmuseum.com

A 1755 fort rebuilt from original plans, the complex includes dungeons, army barracks and an example of an Iroquois longhouse. The onsite museum hosts exhibits involving relics from the French and Indian War. Get a taste of battle in the 18th century as costumed guides provide demonstrations of typical military drills, musket firings, bullet molding and cannons. A replica of the fort was used in the filming of the movie *The Last of the Mohicans*.

Admission: adults $14.95, seniors and military $12.95, children 3-11 $7.95, children under 3 free. May-mid-October, daily 9 a.m.-6 p.m.

THE GREAT ESCAPE AND SPLASHWATER KINGDOM FUN PARK
1172 State Route 9, Queensbury, 518-792-3500; www.sixflags.com

New York's largest theme park has more than 120 rides, live shows and attractions, including numerous roller coasters, the Raging River Raft Ride, the All-American High-Dive Show and a Storytown-themed children's area. Splashwater Kingdom waterpark features a giant wave pool, waterslides, Adventure River and kiddie pools.

Admission: prices vary. Mid-May-mid-September, daily 11 a.m.-6 p.m.

LAKE GEORGE BATTLEFIELD PICNIC AREA
139 Beach Road, Lake George Village, 518-668-3352

Grab a blanket and bring a picnic to the site of the Battle of Lake George. There are ruins of the original Fort William Henry as well as a monument to French missionary Isaac Jogues.

Admission: $7 per vehicle. Mid-June-August, daily.

LAKE PLACID

JOHN BROWN FARM HISTORIC SITE
115 John Brown Road, Lake Placid, 518-523-3900; www.nysparks.state.ny.us

This historic site marks abolitionist John Brown's final home and burial place. In 1859, Brown attempted to lead a slave revolt at Harper's Ferry. Two of his sons and 10 others died in the struggle. Brown was tried and executed. There are nice hiking trails throughout the 244-acre grounds.

Admission: adults $2, seniors and children 13-18 $1, children under 12 free. May-October, Wednesday-Monday 10 a.m.-5 p.m.

LAKE PLACID CENTER FOR THE ARTS
17 Algonquin Drive, Lake Placid, 518-523-2512; www.lakeplacidarts.org

Concerts, films, dance performances and art exhibits come through this large art center year round. It is home to the Lake Placid School of Ballet and the LPCA Children's Theatre.

Prices and showtimes vary.

MACKENZIE-INTERVALE SKI JUMPING COMPLEX
Route 73, Lake Placid, 518-523-2202; www.orda.org

Though these towering structures may seem awkward against the landscape, the view from the top is extraordinary. Take a glass elevator up the 26 stories

HIGHLIGHT

WHAT ARE THE TOP THINGS TO DO IN THE ADIRONDACKS?

LEARN MORE ABOUT DIVA MARCELLA SEMBRICH AT THE OPERA MUSEUM

Met Opera star Sembrich used to give lessons at this studio, which now displays costumes, paintings and more from her illustrious career.

RIDE COASTERS AT THE GREAT ESCAPE AND SPLASHWATER KINGDOM FUN PARK

You have your choice of more than 120 rides at New York's largest theme park. And when you need to cool off, head over to Splashwater Kingdom.

CHECK OUT OLYMPIC CENTER

The center hosted the famous 1980 Winter Games, when the underdog U.S. hockey team beat the favored Soviets. The upset was immortalized in the film *Miracle*.

VISIT ROBERT LOUIS STEVENSON MEMORIAL COTTAGE

If you're a fan of the *Treasure Island* author, see where the writer lived for a year as well as memorabilia from his life.

for vistas of Lake Placid and the surrounding mountains, and a sense of what these skiers experience before every jump.

Admission: adults $10, children and seniors $7. Mid-October-mid-December, Thursday-Sunday 9 a.m.-4 p.m. Mid-December-mid-March, Wednesday-Sunday 9 a.m.-4 p.m.

OLYMPIC CENTER

218 Main St., Lake Placid, 518-523-1655; www.orda.org

Built for the 1932 Winter Olympics and renovated for the 1980 Winter Games, this arena hosts winter and summer skating shows, hockey games and concerts. It was made famous in the 1980 Olympics as the place where the U.S. hockey team beat the seemingly invincible Soviets, an account reenacted in the Hollywood movie *Miracle*. The center also includes a museum with Olympic paraphernalia.

Admission: Rink: adults $7, seniors and children $5. Museum: adults $5, seniors and children $3. Rink: daily 7 p.m.-9 p.m. Museum: daily 10 a.m.-5 p.m.

PLATTSBURGH
ALICE T. MINER COLONIAL COLLECTION
9618 Main St., Chazy, 518-846-7336; www.minermuseum.org

Housed in a 19th-century colonial home, this museum has a collection of household furnishings including a 17th-century table, oil lamps and antique quilts. Explore the Lincoln room, which keeps books and letters relating to past presidents and others.

Free. April, by appointment; May-December, Tuesday-Saturday 10 a.m.-4 p.m.

KENT-DELORD HOUSE MUSEUM
17 Cumberland Ave., Plattsburgh, 518-561-1035; www.kentdelordhouse.org

This historic 1797 house served as British officers' quarters during the Battle of Plattsburgh in the War of 1812. Inside, there is a collection of period furnishings and an apothecary.

Admission: adults $5, students $3, children under 12 $2. Tuesday-Friday, 9 a.m.-3:15 p.m.

SARANAC LAKE
ROBERT LOUIS STEVENSON MEMORIAL COTTAGE
11 Stevenson Lane, Saranac Lake, 518-891-1462; www.adirondacks.com

This modest farmhouse is where Robert Louis Stevenson lived while undergoing treatment for what is believed to have been tuberculosis from 1887 to 1888. Today, the building contains a collection of photographs, letters and memorabilia from Stevenson's life.

Admission: $5. July-mid-September, Tuesday-Sunday 9:30 a.m.-noon, 1-4:30 p.m.

SIX NATIONS INDIAN MUSEUM
Adirondack Park, Buck Pond Road, Onchiota, 518-891-2299

Indoor and outdoor exhibits portray the life of Native Americans. You'll see a council ground, a display on the types of fires, and ancient and modern articles. There are also frequent lectures on the culture and history of the Iroquois Confederacy.

Admission: adults $2, children $1. July-August, daily 10 a.m.-6 p.m.

WHERE TO STAY

BOLTON LANDING
★★★THE SAGAMORE
110 Sagamore Road, Bolton Landing, 518-644-9400, 866-385-6221; www.thesagamore.com

This historic resort reigns over its own private 72-acre island in Lake George. From golf, tennis and water sports to myriad winter activities, this resort is a year-round destination. Two types of accommodations offer you the choice of comfortable rooms at the historic hotel or cabin retreats in spacious lodges. Dining at any of the six restaurants comes with a view; meals are even served aboard the resort's own replica of a 19th-century touring vessel.

350 rooms. Restaurant, bar. Fitness center. Pool. Spa. Beach. Golf. Tennis. $251-350

LAKE GEORGE

★★FORT WILLIAM HENRY RESORT

48 Canada St., Lake George, 518-668-3081, 800-234-0267; www.fortwilliamhenry.com

With a spectacular setting in the Adirondacks—along with courteous service and elegant accommodations—visitors are easily attracted to this Lake George resort, the oldest in the area. Guest rooms vary by size and, depending on type, include king beds, full-size sleeper sofas, microwaves, refrigerators, whirlpool tubs and executive desks with workstations. Grab a bite at the resort's onsite restaurants, the White Lion, where breakfast is served with a spectacular lake view, and J.T. Kelly's Steak and Seafood, a casually elegant haven serving classic American and Italian cuisines.

193 rooms. Restaurant, bar. Business center. Fitness center. Pool. Spa. $151-250

LAKE PLACID

★★★LAKE PLACID LODGE

144 Lodge Way, Lake Placid, 877-523-2700; www.lakeplacidlodge.com

This charming resort, situated on the edge of Lake Placid in the heart of the Adirondacks, was rebuilt after a 2005 fire destroyed the original, historic main lodge. Its arts and craft style remains true to the original spirit of the lodge. The interior is a luxurious take on rustic Americana, with warm colors and traditional furnishings dressed up with proper plaids, animal prints and florals. The lodge features two restaurants: a casual pub where you can sip a hot toddy while playing a game of chess, and an upscale dining room, Artisans, which serves masterfully presented takes on fresh, organic American cuisine.

30 rooms. Restaurant, bar. Complimentary breakfast. $351 and up

★★MIRROR LAKE INN RESORT AND SPA

77 Mirror Lake Drive, Lake Placid, 518-523-2544; www.mirrorlakeinn.com

Located on a hilltop at the edge of Lake Placid's downtown, this resort overlooks Mirror Lake as well as a stunning mountain range on the horizon. The lake can be seen from many of the guest rooms and the resort's restaurants, where the décor mixes a mission-style sensibility with walnut floors, marble, antiques and stone fireplaces.

129 rooms. Restaurant, bar. Fitness center. Pool. Spa. Beach. Tennis. $251-350

SARANAC LAKE

★★★★THE POINT

Highway 30, Saranac Lake, 518-891-5674, 800-255-3530; www.thepointresort.com

Exceptionally well-heeled travelers seeking a glamorous stay in the wilderness head straight for the Point. This former great camp of William Avery Rockefeller revives the spirit of the early 19th-century Adirondacks, when the wealthy came to rusticate in this sylvan paradise. No signs direct visitors to this intimate camp, and a decidedly residential ambience is maintained. The resort has a splendid location on a 10-acre peninsula on Upper Saranac Lake. Rooms feature Adirondack twig furnishings, stone fireplaces, elegant bathrooms and luxe antiques. From snowshoeing and cross-country skiing to water sports, trail hikes and croquet, you'll find a variety of outdoor activities. All guest requests are well catered to. Will you be in the mood for champagne and truffle popcorn at 4 a.m.? At your service. Gourmet dining figures largely in the experience and with a nod to the patrician past, guests don black-tie attire twice weekly at the communal dining table in the resort's great room.

11 rooms. Restaurant, bar. Spa. No children allowed. Beach. Tennis. $351 and up.

WARRENSBURG

★★★FRIENDS LAKE INN

963 Friends Lake Road, Chestertown, 518-494-4751; www.friendslake.com

A stay at this restored 19th-century inn offers cross-country skiing, a private beach and canoeing on Friends Lake. Many of the Adirondack-style rooms feature soaring ceilings, river rock-enclosed fireplaces and whirlpool tubs. The inn's contemporary American menu features dishes such as braised Chilean sea bass with a tomato fennel broth and ancho-rubbed lamb chops with a minted pea purée.

17 rooms. Restaurant, bar. Pool. $251-350

RECOMMENDED

BOLTON LANDING

MELODY MANOR RESORT

4610 Lakeshore Drive, Bolton Landing, 518-644-9750; www.melodymanor.com

On the shores of Lake George amid the Adirondack Mountains, the Melody Manor certainly has a winning locale. The rooms are bland apart from their scenic lake views, but with amenities including a beach with rowboats and paddleboats, a swimming pool and clay tennis courts, there is no reason to stay inside. The onsite Italian restaurant serves simple hearty cuisine.

40 rooms. Restaurant, bar. Pool. Beach. Tennis. Closed November-April. $151-250

LAKE GEORGE

BEST WESTERN OF LAKE GEORGE

Exit 21 and I-H 87, Lake George, 518-668-5701, 800-582-5540; www.bestwestern.com

An Adirondack-style look brings this chain motel up a notch, as some of the rooms offer sloped wood ceilings and fireplaces. Request a room with scenic mountain views (as opposed to poolside). Lake George beaches are just a mile down the road.

87 rooms. Complimentary breakfast. Pool. $151-250

WHICH HOTELS IN THE ADIRONDACKS HAVE THE BEST VIEW?

Fort William Henry Resort:
Situated on 18 acres at the head of Lake George, this resort offers a lovely vista of the water and the surrounding Adirondack Mountains.

Lake Placid Lodge:
This luxurious resort is the only resort actually on Lake Placid and offers beautiful views of the Adirondacks.

Mirror Lake Inn Resort and Spa:
The resort rests at the top of a hill and overlooks Mirror Lake. Plus, you'll get a glimpse of the gorgeous mountain range in the backdrop.

The Point:
Surrounded by water, this luxurious hotel and spa is on a picturesque 10-acre peninsula on Upper Saranac Lake.

The Sagamore:
You'll see water everywhere you turn at this resort, since it sits on a private 72-acre island in Lake George. Admire the view from your room or at one of the restaurants.

THE GEORGIAN

384 Canada St., Lake George, 518-668-5401, 800-525-3436; www.georgianresort.com

The rooms need a face-lift, but the views of Lake George and the Adirondacks from the lakeside property compensate for it. There is a private beach and marina. Ask for a room with a private balcony.

162 rooms. Restaurant, bar. Pool. Beach. $61-150

ROARING BROOK RANCH & TENNIS RESORT

Route 9N South, Lake George, 518-668-5767, 800-882-7665; www.roaringbrookranch.com

Two miles from Lake George, this resort offers three pools, five tennis courts with tennis pros, 25 horses for wilderness riding, golf nearby, and so much more. The resort's conference center makes it attractive for meetings and special events. Guest rooms are plain but roomy, and a stay here includes two meals a day.

142 rooms. Restaurant, bar. Business center. Fitness center. Pool. Tennis. Closed March-mid-May, November-December. $61-150

THE TIKI RESORT

2 Canada St., Lake George, 518-668-5744, 800-446-4656; www.tikiresort.com

If you've never bathed in a red heart-shaped bathtub, now is your chance (in the Honeymoon Suite). This resort with views of Lake George is a tad cheesy with its Polynesian-themed dinner theater, but the rooms are updated with large picture windows and many have balconies overlooking the Adirondacks.

110 rooms. Restaurant, bar. Fitness center. Pool. Closed November-April. $151-250

LAKE PLACID

ADIRONDACK INN BY THE LAKE

2625 Main St., Lake Placid, 518-523-2424, 800-556-2424; www.adirondack-inn.com

Situated across the street from the Olympic Arena and Mirror Lake, this hotel is within walking distance to all that Lake Placid has to offer. Guests can find a nice spot to relax at the back of the property, where a lovely lily pond and brick patio can be found. Guest rooms are basic and most have exterior entries.

49 rooms. Restaurant. Complimentary breakfast. Business center. Fitness center. Pool. Beach. $61-150

CROWNE PLAZA RESORT AND GOLF CLUB LAKE PLACID

101 Olympic Drive, Lake Placid, 518-523-2556, 877-570-5891; www.lakeplacidcp.com

Situated on a hilltop, this resort offers an incredible view of the town of Lake Placid and Mirror Lake. Guest rooms in the Adirondack wing of the hotel are full of luxurious amenities such as granite countertops, full kitchens, antler light fixtures, mission-style furniture and white bed linens and duvets. The beach is a few blocks away, and complimentary paddle and rowboats are available to guests.

245 rooms. Restaurant, bar. Fitness center. Pool. Pets accepted. Beach. Golf. Ski in/ski out. Tennis. $61-150

GOLDEN ARROW LAKESIDE RESORT

2559 Main St., Lake Placid, 518-523-3353, 800-582-5540; www.golden-arrow.com

The lobby of this lakeside resort is housed in a large A-frame building with a magnificent view of Mirror Lake and a wood-burning fireplace. Each guest room is decorated in gold tones with Broyhill or Thomasville furniture. You can enjoy the hotel's beach, complete with paddleboats, rowboats, kayaks, canoes and a swimming area.

150 rooms. Restaurant, bar. Fitness center. Pool. Pets accepted. Beach. $151-250

SARANAC LAKE

THE HOTEL SARANAC

100 Main St., Saranac Lake, 518-891-2200, 800-937-0211; www.hotelsaranac.com

This historic red brick hotel is in the heart of downtown Saranac Lake. There is a country-like feeling to the décor, and basic guest rooms feature bedspreads similar to hand-sewn quilts. Many of the rooms also offer a lovely city view. The hotel is the tallest building in downtown, and a large sign with the hotel's name sits on top so it's never hard to find.

86 rooms. Restaurant, bar. Business center. $61-150

SARANAC INN GOLF & COUNTRY CLUB

125 County Route 46, Saranac Lake, 518-891-1402; www.saranacinn.com

For basic and no-frills accommodations, Saranac Inn Golf & Country Club offers a comfortable stay. Situated off Highway 30, it is approximately 30 minutes from Lake Placid and close to the shores of Upper Saranac Lake. The property sits on more than 350 acres of rolling hills and a sea of trees. Duffers can enjoy a round on the beautiful 18-hole golf course.

10 rooms. Restaurant, bar. Golf. Mid-October-April. $61-150

WHERE TO EAT

BOLTON LANDING

★★★TRILLIUM

110 Sagamore Road, Bolton Landing, 518-644-9400; www.thesagamore.com

This restaurant boasts some of the most majestic views of Lake George in the area and is pleasantly paired with a casual, stylish atmosphere and a professional staff that provides unsurpassed service. Organic and local ingredients fill the imaginative menu, including Kobe steak sandwiches and honey-and-paprika-glazed duck. The wine list is also impressive.

American. Dinner. Reservations recommended. $16-35

LAKE GEORGE

★★★MONTCALM

1415 Highway 9, Lake George Village, 518-793-6601

Rich American classics such as roasted rack of lamb and veal Oscar are the mainstay of this resort-town restaurant where the reasonable prices attract a loyal following. Salads are prepared tableside by an attentive waitstaff.

American. Lunch, dinner. Reservations recommended. Children's menu. Bar. $16-35

LAKE PLACID

★★★ARTISANS

Lake Placid Lodge, Whiteface Inn Road, Lake Placid, 518-523-2700; www.lakeplacidlodge.com

At this much-lauded restaurant located in the cozy Lake Placid Lodge, you will find anything from duck consommé to lobster and sweetbread ravioli paired with stunning lake vistas. There are also three- and four-course prix fixe menus from which to choose. Diners are required to be over age 12.

American. Dinner. Reservations recommended. Outdoor seating. Bar. $36-85

WHICH ADIRONDACK RESTAURANTS HAVE THE BEST VIEWS?

Artisans:
You'll gaze at stunning panoramas of Lake Placid at Artisans. For an up-close view of the water, opt to dine in the covered balcony during warmer weather.

Trillium:
This restaurant offers some of the most breathtaking vistas of Lake George in the area. Take in the water with your honey-and-paprika-glazed duck.

PLATTSBURGH

★★★ANTHONY'S
538 Route 3, Plattsburgh, 518-561-6420; www.anthonysrestaurantandbistro.com

An elegant candlelit setting and unobtrusive, crisp service round out the dining experience at Anthony's, where the menu includes such continental fare as grilled lamb sausage with an apple-mango chutney and broiled sea scallops with an herb butter.

American. Lunch, dinner. Children's menu. Bar. $16-35

WARRENSBURG

★★★GRACE'S RESTAURANT AND LOUNGE
Griffin House Bed & Breakfast, 3 Hudson St., Warrensburg, 518-623-2449; www.merrillmageehouse.com

Situated in the heart of the Adirondack Mountains, the Griffin House Bed & Breakfast offers comfortable, relaxed accommodations—and delicious dining. The inn's dinner menu includes such tasty dishes as New York strip steak with mushroom and tomato ragu and shrimp Florentine, and jumbo shrimp sautéed with bacon, garlic and spinach.

Continental. Lunch (Sunday) dinner. Closed Tuesday-Wednesday. Reservations recommended. Outdoor seating. Bar. $16-35

RECOMMENDED

BOLTON LANDING

FREDERICK'S RESTAURANT
4970 Lake Shore Drive, Bolton Landing, 518-644-3484; www.fredericksrestaurant.com

This casual hot spot draws locals and tourists year-round with live music and a stellar raw bar on Sundays in summer and cozy fireside dining during the winter.

Seafood. Lunch, dinner. Outdoor seating. Bar. $16-35

VILLA NAPOLI
Melody Manor Resort, 4608 Lakeside Drive, Bolton Landing, 518-644-9047; www.melodymanor.com

Located within the Melody Manor Resort, the main dining room is inspired by Italy with a hand-carved Carrera marble fireplace, Venetian plaster walls and original hand-painted murals. The fare is equally authentic and includes wild boar sausage over slow-cooked peperonata and stuffed eggplant in a red pepper sauce.

Italian. Breakfast, dinner. Closed mid-October-mid-May. Reservations recommended. Outdoor seating. Children's menu. Bar. $16-35

LAKE GEORGE
LOG JAM
1484 Highway 9, Lake George Village, 518-798-1155; www.logjamrestaurant.com

You may feel like you're stepping back in time at this log cabin-like eatery with heavy wood furniture and fireplaces galore. Rest assured that the seafood is some of the freshest around. For a regional twist, try the maple-syrup-glazed salmon.

American. Lunch, dinner. Bar. Reservations recommended. Children's menu. $16-35

WARRENSBURG
FRIENDS LAKE INN
963 Friends Lake Road, Chestertown, 518-494-4751; www.friendslake.com

With its original tin ceiling and rustic wood beams, this restaurant exudes country charm. Yet the food is anything but simple. Standout dishes include Hudson Valley duck breast in a mandarin-thyme reduction atop orzo and spinach, and caramelized sea scallops with ginger polenta cake and roasted red peppers.

American, seafood. Lunch, dinner. Reservations recommended. Outdoor seating. Children's menu. Bar. $36-85

CAPITAL DISTRICT/SARATOGA SPRINGS

The big city in this region is the state capital, Albany. Politics is a colorful part of the business in New York's capital city. Located on the western bank of the Hudson River and at the crossroads of several major state highways, Albany is a center for democracy, transportation, business, in-dustry and culture.

Saratoga Springs is a resort city that is rural yet decidedly cos-mopolitan. Much of the town's Victorian architecture has been restored. The city boasts the natural springs, geysers and mineral baths that first made the town famous, as well as internationally recognized harness and thoroughbred racing and polo, respected museums and the Saratoga Performing Arts Center.

WHAT TO SEE

ALBANY
ALBANY INSTITUTE OF HISTORY & ART
125 Washington Ave., Albany, 518-463-4478; www.albanyinstitute.org

Founded in 1791, the Albany Institute is the second-oldest museum in the United States. It specializes in the history and art of the Upper Hudson Valley spanning the last four centuries. The curatorial collection is extensive with more than 30,000 pieces, including paintings, prints, sculptures, furnishings, textiles, silver and more. If you're traveling with kids, check the website for the many family-friendly activities.

Admission: adults $10, seniors and students $8, children 6-13 $6, children 5 and under free. Wednesday-Saturday 10 a.m.-5 p.m., Sunday noon-5 p.m.

AUSABLE CHASM
2144 Route 9, Ausable Chasm, 518-834-7454; www.ausablechasm.com

Located in the beautiful Champlain Valley, this sandstone gorge often referred to as the "Little Grand Canyon of the East" plummets 150 feet to the Au Sable River. Stroll through the Adirondack Forest, float along the river in a raft or

WHAT ARE THE REGION'S TOP MUSEUMS?

Albany Institute of History & Art:
At the second-oldest museum in the United States, you can peruse paintings, sculptures, prints and more of the Upper Hudson Valley from the last four centuries.

National Museum of Dance:
This museum honors professional dance with displays of photos, costumes and videos. Check out the Hall of Fame, which features twinkle toes such as Fred Astaire.

National Museum of Racing and Hall of Fame:
Before heading to Saratoga Race Course, make a stop across the street at this museum to learn the history of thoroughbred racing.

New York State Museum:
The free museum examines the geology, biology and anthropology of the Big Apple, from Manhattan to Upstate New York.

tube, or follow a guide into the chasm at dusk on a "lantern tour."

Admission: adults $16, children 5-13 $9, children under 5 free. Mid-May-October, daily.

CRAILO STATE HISTORIC SITE

9½ Riverside Ave., Rensselaer, 518-463-8738; www.nysparks.state.ny.us

This 18th-century Dutch house is now a museum of Dutch culture in the Hudson Valley. Exhibits highlight the history and development of Dutch settlements in America.

Admission: adults $5, seniors and students $4, children under 13 free. Mid-April-May and September-October, Wednesday-Sunday 11 a.m.-5 p.m.; June-August, Tuesday-Sunday 11 a.m.-5 p.m.; November-March, Monday-Friday 11 a.m.-4 p.m.

NEW YORK STATE MUSEUM

Cultural Education Center of the Empire State Plaza, Madison and State streets, Albany, 518-474-5877; www.nysm.nysed.gov

The scientific fields of geology, biology and anthropology are promoted at this educational center. Life-size dioramas, photomurals and thousands of artifacts illustrate the past, present and future relationship between people and nature in New York State. Three major halls detail life in metropolitan New York, the Adirondacks and Upstate New York. Be sure to visit the working carousel and the memorial to the World Trade Center.

Admission: free. Daily 9:30 a.m.-5 p.m.

SCHUYLER MANSION STATE HISTORIC SITE

32 Catherine St., Albany, 518-434-0834; www.nysparks.state.ny.us

This Georgian mansion, built in 1761, was the home of Philip Schuyler, a general of the Revolutionary War and U.S. senator. Alexander Hamilton married Schuyler's daughter Elizabeth here in 1780, and other prominent early leaders visited the estate.

Admission: adults $4, seniors and students $3, children under 12 free. Mid-May-October, Wednesday-Sunday 11 a.m.-5 p.m.; November-mid-May, by appointment only.

SHAKER HERITAGE SOCIETY

875 Watervliet Shaker Road, Albany, 518-456-7890; www.shakerheritage.org

As the first Shaker settlement in America, the site includes a museum located in the original 1848 Shaker Meeting House, a barnyard, an orchard and an herb garden. Stroll around the Ann Lee Pond nature preserve and the Shaker Cemetery, where founder Mother Ann Lee is buried.

Admission: free. February-October, Tuesday-Saturday 9:30 a.m.-4 p.m.; November-December, Monday-Saturday 10 a.m.-4 p.m.

STATE CAPITOL
Empire State Plaza, State and Swan streets, Albany, 518-474-2418; www.assembly.state.ny.us

The New York State capitol took four decades to construct and the result was a $25 million granite chateau. Legislative session begins on the Wednesday after the first Monday in January.

SARATOGA SPRINGS
HISTORIC CONGRESS PARK
Canfield Casino and Union Ave., Saratoga Springs, 518-584-6920

Both the Museum of the Historical Society and the Walworth Memorial Museum are housed in the historic 1870 Canfield Casino on the grounds of Congress Park. The museums trace the history of the city's growth. Exhibits change frequently, but often include gambling paraphernalia, antique photographs and negatives, and period furnishings.

Admission: adults $5, seniors and students $4, children under 12 free. June-August, Monday-Saturday 10 a.m.-4 p.m., Sunday 1-4 p.m.; September-May, Wednesday-Saturday 10 a.m.-4 p.m., Sunday 1-4 p.m.

NATIONAL BOTTLE MUSEUM
76 Milton Ave., Ballston Spa, 518-885-7589; www.nationalbottlemuseum.org

Glass in all shapes and for all purposes, including antique bottles, jars and dinnerware, are on display. There is even a miniature model of a glass furnace, as it would have appeared in the 1800s. Classes in flameworking and lamp-working are offered weekly.

Admission: by donation. June-September, daily 10 a.m.-4 p.m.; October-May, Monday-Friday 10 a.m.-4 p.m.

NATIONAL MUSEUM OF DANCE
99 S. Broadway, Saratoga Springs, 518-584-2225; www.dancemuseum.org

Dedicated to American professional dance, the museum boasts an impressive collection of photographs, costumes, artifacts and videos immortalizing the art of dance. The only permanent exhibit here is the Hall of Fame, which has honored such greats as Fred Astaire, George Balanchine and Martha Graham. Kids will enjoy the Discovery Room, where a stage and wearable costumes allow children to put on their own dance performances.

Admission: adults $6.50, seniors and students $5, children 3-12 $3, children under 3 free. Mid-March-December, Tuesday-Sunday 10 a.m.-4 p.m.

NATIONAL MUSEUM OF RACING AND HALL OF FAME
191 Union Ave., Saratoga Springs, 518-584-0400, 800-562-5394; www.racingmuseum.org

This museum is appropriately situated across from historic Saratoga Race Course, the oldest-operating thoroughbred racetrack in the country. Exhibitions on the history and mechanics of thoroughbred racing include the stories of racing champs Man o' War, Secretariat, Seattle Slew and Affirmed. The building also contains displays on Saratoga's gambling heyday. There are training track tours in summer.

Admission: adults $7, seniors and students $5, children under 6 free. November-December, Tuesday-Saturday 10 a.m.-4 p.m., Sunday noon-4 p.m.; January-March, Wednesday-Saturday

10 a.m.-4 p.m., Sunday noon-4 p.m.; April-October, Monday-Saturday 10 a.m.-4 p.m., Sunday noon-4 p.m.

SARATOGA PERFORMING ARTS CENTER
108 Avenue of The Pines, Saratoga Springs, 518-587-3330; www.spac.org

The SPAC is one of the premier performing arts venues in the region, drawing diverse art and theater acts from near and far. There is a majestic amphitheater with seats for 5,000 under cover and a sprawling lawn beyond, as well as the Little Theatre, a 500-seat indoor showcase for chamber music. Bring a picnic and make an afternoon of it.

Prices and showtimes vary.

SARATOGA SPA STATE PARK
19 Roosevelt Drive, Saratoga Springs, 518-584-2535; www.saratogaspastatepark.org

This 2,200-acre park is home to the performing arts center, mineral bath houses, Saratoga Automobile Museum and the Saratoga Spa Golf Course, among other recreational outlets. Trails snake throughout the natural preserve, and wide-open meadows become prime snowshoeing and cross-country skiing spots in winter.

YADDO GARDENS
Union Avenue, Saratoga Springs, 518-584-0746; www.yaddo.org

An artists' retreat since 1926, this Victorian Gothic mansion has hosted such famous residents as Flannery O'Connor, Leonard Bernstein and John Cheever. The mansion is closed to the public, but the landscaped gardens are open year round.

Admission: free. Tours: $5. Daily 8 a.m.-dusk. Tours: Late-June-early September, Saturday-Sunday 11 a.m.

WHERE TO STAY

ALBANY
★★★ALBANY MARRIOTT
189 Wolf Road, Albany, 518-458-8444, 800-443-8952; www.marriott.com

Convenience is king at this seven-story brick hotel: It is within two miles of the Albany International Airport; downtown Albany is approximately 10 miles away; and Sarasota Springs is a 30-minute drive to the north. If you're looking to stay put, there is an indoor and outdoor pool, a sizeable fitness center and a patio that receives great afternoon sun.

359 rooms. Restaurant, bar. Business center. Fitness center. Pool. $151-250

★★★CROWNE PLAZA HOTEL ALBANY-CITY CENTER
40 Lodge St., Albany, 518-462-6611, 877-227-6963; www.ichotelsgroup.com

Catering to business travelers and politicos, this hotel is located in historic downtown Albany, across from the Capitol Building and near the Empire State Plaza and Times Union Center, and is within walking distance of the city's top attractions. Guest rooms feature Crowne Plaza Sleep Advantage bedding with triple-sheeted pillow-top mattresses and the pillow of your choice. Book a room on the club floor for access to executive lounge services, including a business center, complimentary snacks and happy hour cocktails.

386 rooms. Restaurant, bar. Business center. Fitness center. Pool. $151-250

★★★DESMOND HOTEL AND CONFERENCE CENTER

660 Albany Shaker Road, Albany, 518-869-8100, 800-448-3500; www.desmondhotels.com

With indoor courtyards and elegantly decorated rooms, the Desmond feels more like an 18th-century village than a hotel. The location is within minutes of downtown and Albany International Airport. Guest rooms are full of Old World charm with large fireplaces, original oil paintings and classic furnishings. Business travelers are equally catered to with writing desks in the rooms and a large conference center and amphitheater with state-of-the-art digital technology.

324 rooms. Restaurant, bar. Business center. Fitness center. Pool. $151-250

★★★GREGORY HOUSE COUNTRY INN

3016 Highway 43, Averill Park, 518-674-3774; www.gregoryhouse.com

This country inn, located near Albany and Troy, offers 12 rooms and a restaurant that specializes in high-end Italian fare. Each guest room is decorated differently with antique furniture, French doors and original artwork. The inn is the perfect accommodation for those planning to visit nearby Tanglewood in Lenox, Mass., the summer home of the Boston Symphony.

12 rooms. Restaurant, bar. Complimentary breakfast. $61-150

RECOMMENDED

ALBANY
CENTURY HOUSE HOTEL

997 New Loudon Road (Route 9), Latham, 518-785-0931, 888-674-6873; www.thecenturyhouse.com

Originally purchased by the Rensselaer family in 1790, this hotel is rich with history. Today, the property offers modern, basic accommodations and a convenient location near the Albany airport and the Capital District. Feast on the complimentary country breakfast, and you will be reminded that you are far from Manhattan. If the weather permits, enjoy the outdoor pool and seasonal tennis courts. This is one of the best options in Albany if you're looking for extended-stay accommodations.

68 rooms. Restaurant, bar. Complimentary breakfast. Fitness center. Pool. Pets accepted. Tennis. $151-250

COURTYARD BY MARRIOTT ALBANY AIRPORT

168 Wolf Road, Albany, 518-482-8800, 866-541-6400; www.marriott.com

Business travelers in for a quick visit to the state capital will find this hotel convenient and reliable with complimentary Internet access, two-line phones and well-appointed conference rooms. The indoor pool and hot tub are relaxing year round and the fitness center, though small, is an added perk. The hotel offers free shuttle service to the Albany International Airport and an onsite convenience market for any forgotten necessities.

78 rooms. Restaurant, bar. Business center. Fitness center. Pool. $151-250

HOLIDAY INN ALBANY

205 Wolf Road, Albany, 518-458-7250, 888-465-4329; www.hialbanywolf.com

For business travelers visiting General Electric, IBM, Verizon or one of the other big Tech Valley businesses, this suburban Albany hotel is as convenient as it gets, especially since it is equipped with a 24-hour business center with printing and fax capabilities. If you find yourself with downtime, all guest rooms are outfitted with flat-screen TVs. There is also an outdoor pool and sauna, as well as a 24-hour fitness center.

312 rooms. Restaurant, bar. Business center. Fitness center. Pool. Pets accepted. $151-250

SARATOGA SPRINGS
GIDEON PUTNAM RESORT AND SPA
24 Gideon Putnam Road, Saratoga Springs, 518-584-3000; www.gideonputnam.com

Built in 1930 and located in Saratoga Spa State Park, this Georgian Revival structure greets guests with beautifully landscaped grounds and an expansive, marble-tiled lobby. In addition to bike rentals, cross-country skiing, tennis, golf, swimming and ice skating, guests can indulge in numerous relaxing treatments and the rejuvenating mineral springs at the adjacent Roosevelt Baths and Spa.

120 rooms. Restaurant, bar. Business center. Fitness center. Spa. $251-350

GRAND UNION MOTEL
120 S. Broadway, Saratoga Springs, 518-584-9000; www.grandunionmotel.com

Guests looking for a nice place to stay without the frills and huge dollar signs will find the Grand Union Motel to be a good choice. It's conveniently near the downtown shopping district of Saratoga Springs, Saratoga Spa State Park and the Saratoga Springs Race Track. The Crystal Spa is also on the premises. Guest rooms are small and bland but clean with access from the exterior.

64 rooms. Pool. Spa. Pets accepted. $61-150

THE INN AT SARATOGA
231 Broadway, Saratoga Springs, 518-583-1890, 800-274-3573; www.theinnatsaratoga.com

The Inn at Saratoga is a 150-year-old Victorian home with a large covered porch and a lot of character. It is the oldest-operating hotel in Saratoga Springs and only a short stroll from downtown. Guest rooms are bright and airy with plush bedding and upscale furnishings. The onsite restaurant serves exceptional American fare.

42 rooms. Restaurant, bar. Complimentary breakfast. $61-150

THE SARATOGA HILTON
534 Broadway, Saratoga Springs, 518-584-4000, 888-866-3591; www.thesaratogahotel.com

The expansive public space of this high-rise building has a contemporary feel. Huge fresh flowers and leather furniture with sleek lines decorate the lobby. Guest rooms are spacious and updated with soothing tones and luxury bedding. Located adjacent—and almost connecting to—the City Center, the hotel is on the edge of the charming downtown shopping district, so it is accessible to all the town has to offer. Take in horse races, music, museums, performing arts, nature walks, mineral baths and more.

242 rooms. Restaurant, bar. Business center. Fitness center. Pool. $151-250

WHERE TO EAT

ALBANY

★★★JACK'S OYSTER HOUSE

42 State St., Albany, 518-465-8854; www.jacksoysterhouse.com

This downtown landmark—a two-block walk from the State Capitol and just across from the city's former 19th-century train station—has been dishing seafood to local politicians, businessmen and families since 1913. Enormous photos of historic Albany hang above elegant black-leather booths and tabletops adorned with flowers and candles. Renowned for its impressive oyster selection, Jack's also serves superb steaks.

American. Lunch, dinner. Reservations recommended. Children's menu. Bar. $16-35

★★★LA SERRE

14 Green St., Albany, 518-463-6056; www.laserrealbany.com

Located in a historic building that dates to the 1840s, La Serre, "the greenhouse" in French, features vintage-looking light fixtures and a gas fireplace that add to its cultivated décor. The continental-style menu features standouts such as Angus beef and New Zealand lamb. This is a great choice if you're following dinner with a show at the Palace or Capital Repertory theaters, which are only a short walk from La Serre.

Continental. Lunch, dinner. Closed Sunday. Reservations recommended. Outdoor seating. Bar. $16-35

★★★MANSION HILL

115 Philip St., Albany, 518-465-2038, 888-299-0455; www.mansionhill.com

This charming inn bills itself as Albany's best-kept secret, and indeed meals at this downtown bed and breakfast are top notch. The menu, which might include homemade ravioli, pan-roasted half duckling or chicken tenderloins, emulates the traditionally elegant décor with hardwood furnishings and bouquets of fresh flowers. In warmer weather, a spot at one of the outdoor tables is perfect for laid-back people-watching.

American. Breakfast, dinner. Closed Sunday. Reservations recommended. Outdoor seating. $16-35

★★★SCRIMSHAW

Desmond Hotel and Conference Center, 660 Albany Shaker Road, Albany, 518-452-5801, 800-448-3500; www.desmondhotels.com

Elegance is paramount at this 18th-century-style eatery within the Desmond Hotel where the fish—brought in daily from Boston—takes the spotlight. Specialties include oysters on the half-shell, cedar-plank salmon, several surf-and-turf dishes and the signature Scrimshaw potato, whipped potatoes served within a puff pastry shell.

American. Dinner. Closed Sunday. Reservations recommended. Children's menu. Bar. $16-35

SARATOGA SPRINGS

★★★CHEZ PIERRE

979 Route 9, Gansevoort, 518-793-3350, 800-672-0666; www.chezpierrerestaurant.com

Joe and Pierrette Baldwin's romantic French restaurant serves inspired cooking—like the classic steak au poivre flambé and veal Oscar, a veal cutlet

WHICH CAPITAL DISTRICT RESTAURANTS HAVE THE BEST SEAFOOD?

Jack's Oyster House: This family-owned eatery has been serving seafood since 1913. Obviously, oysters are the menu headliners; have them raw or in oysters Rockefeller.

Scrimshaw: This restaurant in the Desmond Hotel has fish flown in daily from Boston. Try the fresh cedar-plank salmon or go a different route with oysters on the half-shell.

topped with crabmeat, asparagus and hollandaise sauce—in a setting accented with murals painted by local artists and framed pictures of the owners' homeland. If you're in the mood for seafood, opt for the lobster Newburg or filet of sole Marguery with white wine and a mussel and shrimp cream sauce.

French. Dinner. Closed Monday. Reservations recommended. Bar. $36-85

RECOMMENDED

ALBANY
BONGIORNO'S RESTAURANT
23 Dove St., Albany, 518-462-9176; www.bongiornositalianrestaurant.com

Family-owned and -operated since 1978, Bongiorno's is a local favorite for the authentic Southern Italian cuisine made from fresh local ingredients. Don't let the aging country décor fool you; the dishes are inventive and tasty. Try the scaloppine biancaneve, which are veal medallions sautéed with brandy and mushrooms.

Italian. Lunch, dinner. Closed Sunday. Outdoor seating. Bar. $16-35

SARATOGA SPRINGS
OLDE BRYAN INN
123 Maple Ave., Saratoga Springs, 518-587-2990; www.oldebryaninn.com

Built in 1832, this restaurant was originally a log cabin and still retains the original wood floors and brick walls, making for a rustic and unique setting. Booths and tables are available, and the lounge has many personalized pewter mugs hanging above the bar for frequent visitors. The menu offers something for everyone, including sandwiches, salads, seafood and steak. Fill up on hearty fare like apple cider-pepper pork chops or chicken with a pumpkin-walnut sauce.

American. Lunch, dinner. Outdoor seating. Children's menu. Bar. $16-35

PRIMO'S RESTAURANT
The Inn at Saratoga, 231 Broadway, Saratoga Springs, 518-583-1890, 800-274-3573; www.theinnatsaratoga.com

The atmosphere is casual and welcoming at this small yet charming restaurant located within the Inn at Saratoga. There are 15 tables inside and a covered porch with a few additional dining tables. The romantic Victorian décor includes ornate chandeliers, vintage light fixtures, arched doorways and chairs upholstered in a floral pattern. Many pictures of historic Saratoga

Springs adorn the walls and a gas fireplace makes the room cozy in winter. To make your dining experience even cozier, order comfort food like beef brisket with pan gravy and potato pancakes or lobster macaroni and cheese.
American. Dinner. Reservations recommended. Outdoor seating. Bar. $16-35

CATSKILLS

Easily accessible from New York City, the Catskills are made up of lush, postcard-worthy valleys and quiet towns. Hunter is in the area known as "the mountaintop"—a stretch of land in the picturesque northern Catskills. Hunter Mountain is the second tallest peak in the Catskills and boasts the oldest ski resort in the range. There is plenty to do off the mountain as well, thanks to the thriving art scene and seasonal festivals.

The beautiful valley of Mount Tremper is not far from the free love and artists' haven of Woodstock, while Shandaken is the home of the highest peak in the Catskills, Slide Mountain. Skiing, hiking and hunting are popular in this area of mountains and streams.

Woodstock has traditionally been known as an art colony. In 1902, Englishman Ralph Radcliffe Whitehead came from California to set up a home and handicraft community (Byrdcliffe, north of town). The Art Students' League of New York established a summer school here a few years later, and in 1916 Hervey White conceived the Maverick Summer Music Concerts, the oldest chamber concert series in the country. Woodstock was the original site chosen for the famous 1969 Woodstock Music Festival. When the event grew bigger than anyone imagined, it was moved 60 miles southwest to a farmer's field near Bethel, New York. Nevertheless, the festival gave Woodstock much notoriety.

WHAT TO SEE

HUNTER
HUNTER MOUNTAIN SKI RESORT
Highway 23A, Hunter, 518-263-4223, 800-486-8376; www.huntermtn.com
Once winter strikes, Hunter Mountain becomes the go-to spot for skiing and snowboarding in the Catskills. There are more than 52 trails, a well-established ski-school and rental outfitters.
Admission: adults $35-63, children 13-18 $35-57, seniors and children 7-12 $35-43, children under 7 free-$10. November-mid-April, daily.

SHANDAKEN
BELLEAYRE MOUNTAIN
Route 28, Shandaken, 845-254-5600, 800-942-6904; www.belleayre.com
Cherished wilderness since the 1880s, this ski mountain boasts steep inclines, varied terrain and a comfortable mountainside resort. There are 41 runs and a half-pipe, as well as cross-country trails.
Admission: prices vary. November-mid-April, daily.

HIGHLIGHT

WHAT ARE THE TOP THINGS TO DO IN THE CATSKILLS?

CHECK OUT ART IN QUAINT WOODSTOCK

Visit the Woodstock Artists Association Gallery to see artwork from local and regional artists.

SPEND THE DAY ON THE SLOPES

Head to one of the ski resorts in the area, either Hunter Mountain Ski Resort or Belleayre Mountain, and enjoy a day of skiing.

WOODSTOCK

WOODSTOCK ARTISTS ASSOCIATION GALLERY

28 Tinker St., Woodstock, 845-679-2940; www.woodstockart.org

This gallery has been at the heart of the Woodstock community since 1920. Organized into three spaces, the building showcases constantly changing group exhibits, solo shows and a nationally recognized permanent collection. Many of the works displayed here are by local and regional artists and represent all mediums.

Friday-Saturday noon-6 p.m., Sunday noon-5 p.m.

WHERE TO STAY

HUNTER

★★★SCRIBNER HOLLOW LODGE

Route 23A, Hunter, 518-263-4211, 800-395-4683; www.scribnerhollow.com

This resort has a classical mountain lodge atmosphere with modern hotel conveniences. The lodge has custom-decorated guest rooms, many with exposed wood beams, river-stone fireplaces and balconies with mountain views. Be sure to check out the unique cave-like underground pool and hot tub with seven waterfalls.

37 rooms. Restaurant, bar. Pool. Tennis. Closed April-mid May. $151-250

MOUNT TREMPER

★★★EMERSON RESORT & SPA

5340 Route 28, Mount Tremper, 877-688-2828; www.emersonresort.com

A country retreat with a Zen feel, rooms at this resort are available in the rustic lodge or the adults-only inn, which has 25 comfortable suites with fireplaces and whirlpool tubs. The Phoenix restaurant serves sophisticated dishes with an Asian flair, while the Spa Café delivers food as soothing and delicious as a day at the resort's onsite spa.

53 rooms. Restaurant, bar. Complimentary breakfast. Fitness center. Pool. Spa. Pets accepted. No children allowed. $251-350

SHANDAKEN
★★★THE COPPERHOOD INN & SPA
70-39 Route 28, Shandaken, 845-688-2460; www.copperhood.com

This European-style oasis with elegant, inviting rooms and a helpful staff overlooks the rushing waters of the Esopus Creek. Guests can take advantage of an extensive range of spa services and recreational activities, or simply enjoy nature. The inn's menu includes such dishes as free-range chicken with sun-dried tomatoes and tarragon purée.

15 rooms. Restaurant, bar. Fitness center. Pool. Spa. Tennis. $251-350

RECOMMENDED

MOUNT TREMPER
KATE'S LAZY MEADOW MOTEL
5191 Highway 28, Mount Tremper, 845-688-7200; www.lazymeadow.com

Owned by Kate Pierson of B-52s fame, this small single story motel offers far more than what meets the eye upon seeing the exterior. The décor is funky to say the least, with mini kitchenettes, custom wallpaper and vintage furnishings. Family cabins, lodges and airstream trailers are also available.

10 rooms. No children under 14. $151-250

WHERE TO EAT

RECOMMENDED
WOODSTOCK
BEAR CAFÉ
295A Tinker St., Woodstock, 845-679-5555; www.bearcafe.com

The outdoor patio is only a few feet from bubbling Saw Kill stream, and the indoor space is just as charming with wood paneled walls and a large stone fireplace. The authentic American fare is skillfully executed with such standout dishes as New Zealand King salmon with a chili lime barbecue glaze, stir-fried shitake mushrooms and vegetables, and housemade pumpkin ravioli with butternut squash, portobello mushrooms, pearl onions and aged provolone.

American. Dinner. Closed Tuesday. Outdoor seating. Bar. $36-85

VIOLETTE RESTAURANT & WINE BAR
85 Mill Hill Road, Woodstock, 845-679-5300; www.violettewoodstock.com

Brightly colored mismatched chairs and intimate table settings give a sense of simple elegance to this local favorite where a mother-and-son team churn out inventive cuisine including butternut squash crepes and mussels steamed in a tomato and basil broth.

American. Lunch, dinner, Sunday brunch. Closed Wednesday. Reservations recommended. Outdoor seating. Bar. $16-35

SPA

★★★★THE EMERSON SPA
5340 Route 28, Mount Tremper, 877-688-2828; www.emersonresort.com

This Indian-influenced Upstate spa features 10 treatment rooms perfect for sampling a variety of Eastern-inspired treatments. Indian head massages, Dosha balancing massages and Abhyanga massages, involving two therapists in unison, are some of the bodywork offerings, while shirodhara and bindi herbal body treatments round out the Ayurvedic menu. From aromatherapy facials and sea salt body scrubs to warm mud wraps, many of the treatments use natural ingredients for cleansing, detoxifying and healing the skin.

CENTRAL NEW YORK

In the heart of the state, you'll encounter amazing natural beauty and rich history. Binghamton lies at the junction of the Chenango and Susquehanna rivers. Greater Binghamton is home to Binghamton University, which brings a youthful academic energy to the city. Other claims to fame include the fifth-oldest zoo in the nation and the world's largest collection of functioning antique carousels, which explains its nickname "Carousel Capital of the World". Another college town, home to a branch of the State University College of New York, Oneonta lies deep in the hills at the western edge of the Catskills.

Founded by James Fenimore Cooper's father, Judge William Cooper, Cooperstown is in the center of "Leatherstocking" country. Legend has it that here in 1839, on the south end of Otsego Lake, Abner Doubleday devised modern baseball. The National Baseball Hall of Fame and Museum is located on Main Street and draws more than 300,000 avid baseball fans each year.

WHAT TO SEE

BINGHAMTON
BINGHAMTON ZOO AT ROSS PARK
60 Morgan Road, Binghamton, 607-724-5461; www.rossparkzoo.com

Officially opened in 1875, the Binghamton Zoo is the fifth-oldest zoological institution in the country behind those in Philadelphia, Chicago, Cincinnati and Buffalo. Wealthy businessman Erastus Ross donated the 90-acre plot to the city of Binghamton. The zoo includes several botanical gardens and a new outdoor exhibit featuring snow leopards and cougars.

Admission: adults $7, seniors and students $6, children 3-11 $4.50, children under 3 free. April-November, daily 10 a.m.-5 p.m.

DAY OF A PLAYWRIGHT
The Forum, 236 Washington St., Binghamton, 607-778-2480;

"Day of a Playwright" is a permanent exhibit at the Forum Theatre for the Performing Arts. This theater has an exhibit honoring Syracuse-born Rod Serling, who grew up in Binghamton and created *The Twilight Zone* TV series. It includes photos and documents highlighting his career in television and film.

Admission: Donation accepted. September-May, Monday-Friday 8 a.m.-4 p.m.

DISCOVERY CENTER OF THE SOUTHERN TIER

60 Morgan Road, Binghamton, 607-773-8661; www.thediscoverycenter.org

Kids love this hands-on museum that includes a life-sized fire truck (with dress-up fireman uniforms), a simulated news television studio with video monitor, and imitation hospital and dentist offices. The interactive educational opportunities are endless. Exhibits change regularly.

Admission: adults $5, children 1-16 $6, children under 1 free. Tuesday-Friday 10 a.m.-4 p.m., Saturday 10 a.m.-5 p.m., Sunday noon-5 p.m.

COOPERSTOWN

THE FARMERS' MUSEUM AND VILLAGE CROSSROADS

5775 State Highway 80, Cooperstown, 607-547-1450, www.farmersmuseum.org

An outdoor museum of rural life, this sprawling 10-acre site showcases craftspeople presenting printing, weaving and blacksmithing in a historic setting. The famous "Cardiff Giant," a 10-foot statue presented to the public in 1869 as a petrified prehistoric man, is here. Kids will adore the Empire State Carousel, which boasts 25 hand-carved animals.

Admission: Mid-May-mid-October: adults $11, seniors $9.50, children 7-12 and students $5, children under 7 free. April-mid-May, mid-October-late-October: adults $9, seniors $8, students $5, children 7-12 $4, children under 7 free. April-mid-May, Tuesday-Sunday 10 a.m.-4 p.m.; mid-May-mid-October, daily 10 a.m.-5 p.m.; mid-October-late-October, Tuesday-Sunday 10 a.m.-4 p.m. Closed November-March.

FENIMORE ART MUSEUM

5798 State Highway 80, Cooperstown, 607-547-1400; www.fenimoreartmuseum.org

This museum doubles as the headquarters of the New York State Historical Association and is filled with exhibits of Native American art and artifacts, academic and decorative arts of the Romantic Era, a research library and a large American folk art collection. The permanent exhibit on the Cooper family is particularly interesting.

Admission: adults $11, seniors $9.50, students and children 7-12 $5, children under 7. April-mid-May, Tuesday-Sunday 10 a.m.-4 p.m.; mid-May-mid-October, daily 10 a.m.-5 p.m.; mid-October-December, Tuesday-Sunday 10 a.m.-4 p.m.

GLIMMERGLASS STATE PARK

1527 County Highway 31, Cooperstown, 607-547-8662; www.nysparks.com

The same Glimmerglass mentioned in James Fenimore Cooper's Leatherstocking Tales, this park overlooks Ostego Lake. Plenty of outdoor activities are available, including swimming, fishing, hiking, biking, cross-country skiing and picnicking.

Admission: free. Daily.

NATIONAL BASEBALL HALL OF FAME AND MUSEUM

25 Main St., Cooperstown, 607-547-7200, 888-425-5633; www.baseballhalloffame.org

This nationally known museum is dedicated to the game and its players. The Hall of Fame Gallery contains plaques honoring the game's all-time greats. The museum also features displays on baseball's best moments, the World Series, All-Star Games, ballparks and a complete history of the game. New Hall of Famers are inducted annually (between June and August). If you're in the area

HIGHLIGHT

WHAT ARE THE TOP THINGS TO DO IN CENTRAL NEW YORK?

BRING THE BROOD TO DISCOVERY CENTER OF THE SOUTHERN TIER
The kids will have a ball climbing the life-size fire truck, making news reports in the television studio or playing doctor in the re-created hospital.

TAKE THEM OUT TO THE NATIONAL BASEBALL HALL OF FAME AND MUSEUM
This is a must-see for baseball fans. The Hall of Fame Gallery honors the game's best players, and the museum features exhibits on World Series, ballparks and more.

RUN OVER TO THE NATIONAL SOCCER HALL OF FAME
The displays at the Hall of Fame honor the game with trophies, mementos, uniforms and more. A theater screens soccer flicks dating from the 1930s.

GET A PINT AT THE F.X. MATT BREWING COMPANY
Tour one of the few remaining regional breweries in the country. Then taste the favorite Saranac India Pale Ale or seasonal suds like the Pumpkin Ale.

or a baseball junkie, the induction ceremony is worth the stop, plus it's free.
Admission: adults $16.50, seniors $11, children 7-12 $6, military and children under 7 free. September-May, daily 9 a.m.-5 p.m.; June-August, daily 9 a.m.-9 p.m.

ONEONTA
HANFORD MILLS MUSEUM
County Routes 10 and 12, East Meredith, 607-278-5744, 800-295-4992; www.hanfordmills.org
Originating as a mill built in 1840, this museum examines the evolution of technology and power generation. The original water-powered sawmill, gristmill and woodworking complex are all onsite and demonstrations of antique machinery occur regularly.
Admission: adults $8.50, seniors $5, children under 13 free. Mid-May-mid-October, Tuesday-Sunday 10 a.m.-5 p.m.

HARTWICK COLLEGE
5200 South Park Ave., Hamburg, 607-431-4200; www.hartwick.edu
This rural college boasts an archived collection of works by Willard Yager, Judge

William Cooper and John Christopher Hartwick. The Hall of Science displays fresh and saltwater shells and the Yager Museum contains more than 10,000 Native American artifacts as well as the Van Ess Collection of Renaissance and Baroque Art.

Admission: free. Daily.

NATIONAL SOCCER HALL OF FAME

Wright National Soccer Campus, 18 Stadium Circle, Oneonta, 607-432-3351; www.soccerhall.org

Whether you refer to it as soccer or football, you'll be at home among the sports paraphernalia at this Hall of Fame. Displays and exhibits on "the beautiful game" range from youth, amateur and collegiate to professional soccer. On display are trophies, mementos, historical items and uniforms. Real soccer addicts will enjoy the video theater, where they can watch soccer films dating from 1930s.

Admission: adults $12.50, seniors $8.50, students $9.50, children 6-12 $7.50, children under 6 free. April-June, daily 10 a.m.-5 p.m.; July-August, daily 9 a.m.-6 p.m.; September-March, Wednesday-Sunday 10 a.m.-5 p.m.

UTICA

CHILDREN'S MUSEUM

311 Main St., Utica, 315-724-6128; www.museum4kids.net

One of the nation's oldest children's museums includes hands-on exhibits teaching history, natural history and science. Highlights include an Iroquois exhibit with a section of Long House, a well-stocked dress-up area and an outdoor railroad display.

Admission: adults $9, seniors $8, children 2-17 $7, children under 2 free. Monday-Tuesday, Thursday-Friday 9:30 a.m.- 3 p.m., Saturday 9:45 a.m.-3:15 p.m.

F.X. MATT BREWING COMPANY

830 Varick St., Utica, 315-642-2480; www.saranac.com

Started by a German-born immigrant in 1885, this is one of only a few regional breweries left in the country. Get a plant tour, ride a trolley and then visit the 1888 Tavern for free beer or root beer samples (for those under 21).

Admission: adults $5, children under 12 free. June-August, Monday-Saturday 1-4 p.m., Sunday 1-3 p.m.; September-May, Friday-Saturday 1 p.m., 3 p.m.

MUNSON-WILLIAMS-PROCTOR ARTS INSTITUTE

310 Genesee St., Utica, 315-797-0000; www.mwpai.org

This institute comprises a museum, performing arts center and well-regarded art school. The Museum of Art boasts a sizeable collection of 18th-, 19th- and 20th-century American and European paintings and sculpture displayed throughout 20 galleries. Adjacent to the main building is Fountain Elms, a Victorian house museum, with five mid-19th-century rooms and various changing exhibits. It's worth visiting the art school galleries to observe up-and-coming talent.

Admission: free. Tuesday-Saturday 10 a.m.-5 p.m., Sunday 1-5 p.m.

UTICA ZOO

99 Steele Hill Road, Utica, 315-738-0472; www.uticazoo.org

More than 250 exotic and domestic animals roam this 80-acre zoo. You'll spot

WHICH IS THE
MOST HISTORIC
HOTEL IN CENTRAL
NEW YORK?

The Otesaga Resort
has been hosting
travelers in its Federalist-
style building since
1909. A member of
the Historic Hotels of
America, the lakeside
resort retains its
grandeur with stately
white columns and
brick facade.

Siberian tigers, red pandas and Burmese pythons.
There is also a small children's zoo.

*Admission: adults $6.75, seniors $5.75, children 4-12 $4.25,
children under 4 free. Daily 10 a.m.-5 p.m.*

WHERE TO STAY

COOPERSTOWN
★★★OTESAGA RESORT
60 Lake St., Cooperstown, 607-547-9931, 800-348-6222;
www.otesaga.com

The elegant accommodations and lovely surroundings
of this grand lakeside resort have been a draw for visitors
since 1909. The Federalist-style building, with its large
wood-columned portico and stunning veranda that
overlooks Lake Otsego, is part of the Historic Hotels
of America. Spacious guest rooms feature a charming,
antique feel, yet include amenities such as wireless Internet
access. The championship 18-hole Leatherstocking Golf
Course is adjacent, and tennis, fishing, jogging, biking and
horseback riding are also available.

*135 rooms. Restaurant, bar. Complimentary breakfast. Closed
December-mid-April. $250-350*

ONEONTA
★★★CATHEDRAL FARMS COUNTRY INN
4158 Highway 23, Oneonta, 607-432-7483, 800-327-6790

This country inn—a servants' house built in the
1930s—is a convenient 20 minutes from Cooperstown
and the Baseball Hall of Fame. The property offers
rooms and suites, an outdoor heated pool and Jacuzzi
and an onsite restaurant.

19 rooms. Restaurant. Pool. $151-250

RECOMMENDED

BINGHAMTON
CLARION COLLECTION GRAND ROYALE HOTEL
80 State St., Binghamton, 607-722-0000, 888-242-0323;
www.grandroyalehotel.com

Formerly a city hall, this historic Beaux Arts building
boasts 20-foot ceilings and a beautiful lobby fireplace.
This hotel is conveniently located near the Binghamton
Zoo, Binghamton University and the Discovery Center.
Complimentary Internet access and an onsite business
center make this a good choice for business travelers. If
you need to get in a workout during your travels, you
can use the fitness center at the nearby YMCA for free.

*61 rooms. Restaurant, bar. Complimentary breakfast. Business
center. Pets accepted. $61-150*

UTICA
RADISSON HOTEL-UTICA CENTRE
200 Genesee St., Utica, 315-797-8010; www.radisson.com

This chain hotel is a pleasant surprise. The lobby and public areas are bright and tastefully decorated. The soothing décor carries into the guest rooms, where large picture windows and contemporary furnishings provide an updated atmosphere. Additional perks include a large fitness facility, an indoor pool and a hot tub.

158 rooms. Restaurant, bar. Business center. Fitness center. Pool. $61-150

WHERE TO EAT

UTICA
★★★HORNED DORSET
Horned Dorset Inn, Highway 8, Leonardsville, 315-855-7898

Apple orchards and farmland create a bucolic backdrop for the first-class contemporary American cooking and warm European service found at this historic inn with its charming, expansive dining rooms. There are rooms in the inn should you wish to stay longer and savor the rural setting, which is just a half hour south of Utica.

French. Dinner. $36-85

RECOMMENDED

BINGHAMTON
THE NEW ARGO
117 Court St., Binghamton, 607-724-4692

This restaurant maintains its classic Greek diner atmosphere, though with a cleaner, brighter appeal. The menu is extensive and the portions are hefty. Be sure to save room for dessert—it's made fresh daily by the owner's mother.

Greek. Breakfast, lunch, dinner. Children's menu. $15 and under

NUMBER FIVE
33 S. Washington St., Binghamton, 607-723-0555; www.number5restaurant.com

Operating in a fire station built in 1897, this American steak and seafood house has been open since 1978. Located on the south side of downtown Binghamton and convenient to hotels, the antique-filled, fine dining atmosphere is warm and romantic. Try the stuffed Greek tenderloin or the jumbo crab

---

WHICH RESTAURANTS ARE LOCAL FAVORITES IN CENTRAL NEW YORK?

Farmhouse:
An actual restored 1780s farmhouse, the restaurant cooks up Maryland blue crab cakes and chicken Parmesan that draw in the locals.

Number Five:
Locals fill the romantic dining room to order from the award-winning wine list and to gorge on the Greek tenderloin and jumbo crab cakes.

cakes, both local favorites. It also offers an award-winning wine list and live music on weekends.

American, seafood. Dinner. Children's menu. Bar. $16-35

ONEONTA

CHRISTOPHER'S

Route 23, Southside Oneonta, 607-432-2444;
www.christopherslodging.com

For a casual meal, Christopher's is a good pick. Portions are enormous and the rustic lodge-like ambiance is complete with stuffed moose heads and field-stone fireplaces. Try the New York strip with bleu cheese crumbles or the slow-cooked barbecue pork ribs slathered with housemade barbecue sauce. Finish with a sweet slice of coconut cream pie.

American. Lunch, dinner. Children's menu. Bar. $16-35

FARMHOUSE

5649 State Highway 7, Oneonta, 607-432-7374; www.farmhouserestaurant.com

This restored farmhouse from the 1780s offers a quaint country atmosphere to enjoy simple American fare. The Maryland blue crab cakes are popular among locals, as is the chicken Parmesan.

American, seafood. Lunch (Monday-Friday), dinner. Closed Tuesday. Children's menu. Bar. $16-35

FINGER LAKES

Scientists say glaciers scooped out the Finger Lakes, resulting in one of the most delightful landscaping jobs in America. There are 11 lakes in all, and Canandaigua, Keuka, Seneca, Cayuga, Owasco and Skaneateles are the largest. The smaller lakes also have the characteristic finger shape. Seneca is the deepest at 630 feet and Cayuga the longest at 40 miles. The region has many glens and gorges with plunging streams. Hundreds of recreation spots dot the shores, offering every imaginable sport. The famous New York State wine grapes grow in the many miles of vineyards in the area.

On Owasco Lake, Auburn is one of the largest cities in the Finger Lakes region. Harriet Tubman, whose home was a link in the Underground Railroad, lived here.

The world glassmaking center of Corning began to grow when completion of the Chemung Canal brought in shipments of Pennsylvania anthracite, a type of coal. In 1868, lower fuel and material costs attracted the Brooklyn Flint Glass Works, incorporated in 1875 as the Corning Glass Works. Mass production of bulbs for Thomas A. Edison's electric light soon began, lending the city the nickname Crystal City. The central shopping district has been restored to its 1890s appearance and has some worthwhile restaurants and shops to visit.

Rochester is a high-tech industrial and cultural center and the third-largest city in the state. Its educational institutions include the University of Rochester and the Rochester Institute of Technology. Rochester has had its share of famous citizens, too: Susan B. Anthony, champion of women's rights; Frederick Douglass, black abolitionist and statesman; George Eastman, inventor of flexible film and founder of Kodak; Hiram Sibley, founder of Western Union; and musicians Mitch

Miller, Cab Calloway and Chuck Mangione.

Another college town is Syracuse. It began as a trading post at the mouth of Onondaga Creek, but now it's home to Syracuse University and is full of restaurants and cultural sites.

Located at the southern tip of Keuka Lake, Hammondsport is the center of the New York State wine industry. The grape growers are mainly of German and Swiss origin and they have more than a century of viticulture in New York State behind them. What's more, Glenn H. Curtiss, a pioneer aviator, was born here, and most of his early experimental flights took place in this area. The town is also known for its antique shops.

At the south end of Canandaigua Lake is another grape-growing, winemaking area, Naples. Many of its residents are descendants of Swiss and German winemakers. Artists also flock to this picturesque village, especially in fall when the foliage is at its peak.

WHAT TO SEE

AUBURN
CAYUGA MUSEUM/CASE RESEARCH LAB
203 Genesee St., Auburn, 315-253-8051; www.cayuganet.org

The Cayuga Museum, housed in a Greek Revival Willard-Case Mansion built in 1836, explores the industrial history of Cayuga County. A large emphasis is given to the Auburn Correctional Facility, the oldest continually operating prison in the nation. Other highlights include original 19th-century furnishings and a Civil War exhibit. Behind the museum is the Case Research Lab where T.W. Case and E.I. Sponable invented sound film in 1926, putting an end to the silent-movie era.

Admission: $3 suggested donation. Cayuga Museum: Tuesday-Sunday noon-5 p.m. Case Research Lab: Tuesday-Sunday noon-4:30 p.m. Closed January.

FORT HILL CEMETERY
19 Fort St., Auburn, 315-253-8132

Fort Hill Cemetery was incorporated on May 15, 1851, under its official name: "Trustees of the Fort Hill Cemetery Association of Auburn." But it once was used by Native Americans for burial mounds as early as A.D. 1100. Today the cemetery consists of 83 acres, more than 10,000 burial sites and remains one of the most beautiful landscapes in Auburn. Many famous historical Auburn residents, including William H. Seward and Harriet Tubman, rest here.

Admission: free. Daily dawn-dusk.

HARRIET TUBMAN HOME
180 South St., Auburn, 315-252-2081

Born as a slave, Harriet Tubman escaped in 1849 and rescued more than 300 slaves via the Underground Railroad. She assisted the Union Army during the Civil War and, after settling in Auburn after the war, continued to pursue other humanitarian endeavors.

Admission: $4. Tuesday-Friday 11 a.m.-4 p.m.

HIGHLIGHT

WHAT ARE THE TOP THINGS TO DO IN THE FINGER LAKES?

SEE AN EXTENSIVE COLLECTION AT THE CORNING MUSEUM OF GLASS

This museum isn't just for admiring glass, though there are more than 25,000 pieces on display. You can touch the work and see glassblowing demonstrations.

GET TIPSY AT WIDMER'S WINE CELLARS

Tour one of the largest wineries on the East Coast. The winery also produces bottles under the labels Brickstone Cellars and Manischewitz.

TAKE SOME PHOTOS AT THE GEORGE EASTMAN HOUSE

Visit Kodak founder George Eastman's mansion. Adjacent is a building that houses 19th- and 20th-century photos from major photographers.

LET THE KIDS FROLIC AT THE STRONG MUSEUM

The Strong is the second-largest children's museum in the country. Let the kids see the 3-D Sesame Street exhibit and play with toys, dolls and more.

HONOR A PIONEER AT THE SUSAN B. ANTHONY HOUSE

The women's rights godmother was arrested here for voting in a presidential election. The house now contains artifacts from the women's suffrage movement.

PAY A VISIT TO THE EVERSON MUSEUM OF ART

I.M. Pei designed this striking contemporary building, and it was the noted architect's first museum. Inside is art from Jackson Pollock and more.

SEWARD HOUSE

33 South St., Auburn, 315-252-1283; www.sewardhouse.org

This building was the home of William Henry Seward, whose resume includes posts as governor of New York, U.S. senator, and Abraham Lincoln and Andrew Johnson's secretary of state. Seward was instrumental in bringing California into the Union as a free state and later in purchasing Alaska. The house is stocked with antique furniture, decorative arts, photographs and family documents.

Admission: adults $7, seniors $6, students $2, children under 10 free. Tuesday-Saturday 10 a.m.-4 p.m.

WILLARD MEMORIAL CHAPEL AND WELCH MEMORIAL BUILDING

17 Nelson St., Auburn, 315-252-0339; www.willardchapel.org

A National Historic Landmark, these gray-and-red stone Romanesque Revival buildings were once part of the Auburn Theological Seminary in the early 1800s. The chapel's interior was designed and handcrafted by the Tiffany Glass and Decoration Company and is the only complete and unaltered Tiffany chapel known to exist. A Tiffany Concert Series in the chapel takes place every summer at lunchtime.

Admission: $3 suggested donation. Tuesday-Friday 10 a.m.-4 p.m.

CORNING

BENJAMIN PATTERSON INN MUSEUM COMPLEX

59 W. Pulteney St., Corning, 607-937-5281; www.pattersoninnmuseum.org

The central attraction at this complex is a restored and furnished 1796 inn, originally built to encourage settlement here. The two-story structure includes a public room and kitchen on the first floor and a ballroom and two bedrooms on the second floor. The DeMonstoy Log Cabin, Browntown one-room schoolhouse and Starr Barn with agricultural exhibit and blacksmith shop are also onsite.

Admission: adults $4, seniors $3.50, students $2. Monday-Friday 10 a.m.-4 p.m.

CORNING MUSEUM OF GLASS

1 Museum Way, Corning, 607-937-5371, 800-732-6845; www.cmog.org

More than 25,000 objects are on display in this real-life glass menagerie, including outstanding pieces of both antique and modern Steuben glass and an 11-foot-high leaded glass window designed by Tiffany Studios in 1905. The library has the most complete collection of materials on glass in the world. The Steuben Factory, the only factory in the world that produces Steuben crystal, features skilled craftsmen transforming hot molten glass into fine crystal.

Admission: adults $12.50, seniors and students $11.25, local residents $5, children under 19 free. June-August, daily 9 a.m.-8 p.m.; September-May, daily 9 a.m.-5 p.m.

ROCKWELL MUSEUM OF WESTERN ART

111 Cedar St., Corning, 607-937-5386; www.rockwellmuseum.org

Along with antique firearms and changing exhibits, this museum contains the largest collection of American Western art in the East, including paintings by Remington, Russell, Bierstadt, Catlin and others. The museum also offers a combination ticket in conjunction with the Corning Glass Museum. Afterward, grab a bite at the onsite Southwestern restaurant Catalina.

Admission: adults $6.50, seniors and students $5.50, children under 19 free. June-August, daily 9 a.m.-8 p.m.; September-May, daily 9 a.m.-5 p.m.

HAMMONDSPORT
GLENN H. CURTISS MUSEUM
8419 State Route 54, Hammondsport, 607-569-2160; www.glennhcurtissmuseum.org

Like the Wright brothers, local aviator Glenn H. Curtiss owned a bicycle shop. His invention of the first flying boat, which took off over Lake Keuka, gave him the nickname "the father of naval aviation." The museum displays the Curtiss bicycle shop and a Dawn of Aviation Gallery.

Admission: adults $7.50, seniors $6, children 7-18 $4.50, children under 7 free. May-October, Monday-Saturday 9 a.m.-5 p.m., Sunday 10 a.m.-5 p.m.; November-April, Monday-Saturday 10 a.m.-4 p.m., Sunday 10 a.m.-4 p.m.

WINE AND GRAPE MUSEUM OF GREYTON H. TAYLOR/BULLY HILL VINEYARDS
8843 Greyton H. Taylor Memorial Drive, Hammondsport, 607-868-3610; www.bullyhill.com

Learn about the wine-making techniques of the 18th century at this museum. There are exhibits on early champagne and brandy production. Be sure to see the presidential wine glass collection.

Admission: Tour: free. Tasting: $2. May-October, Monday-Saturday 9 a.m.-4 p.m., Sunday 11:30 a.m.-4 p.m. Visitor Center: May-October, Monday-Thursday 9 a.m.-6 p.m., Friday-Saturday, 9 a.m.-8 p.m., Sunday 10 a.m.-6 p.m.; November-April, Monday-Saturday 9 a.m.-5 p.m., Sunday 10 a.m.-5 p.m.

NAPLES
CUMMING NATURE CENTER OF THE ROCHESTER MUSEUM AND SCIENCE CENTER
6472 Gulick Road, Naples, 585-374-6160; www.rmsc.org

A 900-acre living museum, the center has nature trails, natural history programs and a conservation trail with an operating sawmill. In winter, there are 15 miles of groomed trails for cross-country skiing and snowshoeing.

Admission: $3 suggested donation. Late December-mid-November, Wednesday-Friday 9 a.m.-3:30 p.m., Saturday-Sunday 9 a.m.-4:30 p.m.

WIDMER'S WINE CELLARS
1 Lake Niagara Lane, Naples, 585-374-6311; www.widmerwine.com

If the name Widmer doesn't ring a bell, how about Brickstone Cellars or Manischewitz? Widmer's is one of the largest wineries on the East Coast, and produces wines under many label titles. Tours take you though the wine-making process from start to finish, and free tastings are available in the gift shop. Rabbis are also onsite to explain the process of making Kosher wine.

Tours: $2. Tasting: free. May-December, daily 10 a.m.-5 p.m.; January-April, daily noon-4 p.m.

ROCHESTER
GENESEE COUNTRY VILLAGE & MUSEUM
1410 Flint Hill Road, Mumford, 585-538-6822; www.gcv.org

This 19th-century working village has 68 restored and furnished buildings, where locals in period costumes teach you about what life in this part of the country was like more than 150 years ago. The village also boasts an art gallery, a "base ball" (it was spelled as two words in the 19th century) park, a nature center and heirloom gardens.

Admission: adults $15, seniors and students $12, children 4-16 $9, children under 4 free. Mid-May-mid-October, Tuesday-Friday 10 a.m.-4 p.m., Saturday-Sunday 10 a.m.-5 p.m.

GEORGE EASTMAN HOUSE

900 East Ave., Rochester, 585-271-3361; www.eastmanhouse.org

Kodak founder George Eastman's 50-room mansion and gardens contain restored rooms with their original 1920s furnishings and décor. Adjacent to the house is the archive building; eight exhibit spaces display an extensive collection of 19th- and 20th-century photography representing major photographers of the past 150 years, as well as a chronological display of the evolution of photography.

Admission: adults $10, seniors $8, students $6, children 5-12 $4, children under 5 free. Tuesday-Wednesday, Friday-Saturday 10 a.m.-5 p.m., Thursday 10 a.m.-8 p.m., Sunday 1-5 p.m.

HIGH FALLS IN THE BROWN'S RACE HISTORIC DISTRICT

Visitor Center, 60 Brown's Race, Rochester, 585-325-2030; www.cityofrochester.gov

One of Rochester's earliest industrial districts has been renovated to preserve the area where flour mills and manufacturers once operated and Eastman Kodak and Gleason Works originated. Today, the district still houses businesses in renovated historic buildings, such as the Eastman Technologies Building. Center at High Falls, on Brown's Race Street, is an interpretive museum with hands-on interactive exhibits on the history of the area, as well as information on other attractions to visit in Rochester. Brown's Race Market has been transformed from a maintenance facility of the Rochester Gas and Electric Corporation into three levels of attractions, including a nightclub, jazz club and restaurant. A laser light show can be viewed at dusk from the pedestrian bridge that crosses the Genesee River. The area is between the Inner Loop and Platt and State streets, along the Genesee River Gorge.

MEMORIAL ART GALLERY (UNIVERSITY OF ROCHESTER)

500 University Ave., Rochester, 585-276-8900; www.mag.rochester.edu

The permanent collection has more than 12,000 pieces of art spanning 50 centuries and includes works by Monet, Matisse and Homer. In addition to its well-balanced permanent stock, the gallery offers a year-round schedule of temporary exhibitions, lectures, concerts, tours and family activities.

Admission: adults $10, students, seniors and military $6, children 6-18 $4, children under 6 free. Wednesday, Friday-Sunday 11 a.m.-5 p.m., Thursday 11 a.m.-9 p.m.

ROCHESTER HISTORICAL SOCIETY

485 East Ave., Rochester, 585-271-2705; www.rochesterhistory.org

The Rochester Historical Society, the brainchild of anthropologist Louis Henry Morgan, was established in 1860 only to languish as the Civil War loomed over Rochester and the nation. In 1887, Caroline Perkins, philanthropist and wife of businessman Gilman H. Perkins, revived the society and led it to local prominence. For decades the society has collected and preserved what today amounts to more than 200,000 objects and documents. The headquarters for the society is Woodside, a Greek Revival mansion dating back to 1839, which contains a collection of portraits and memorabilia, costumes, a reference library and a manuscript collection.

Admission: free. Monday-Friday 9 a.m.-3 p.m.

ROCHESTER INSTITUTE OF TECHNOLOGY

1 Lomb Memorial Drive, Rochester, 585-475-2411; www.rit.edu

It's not just about techies here. This prestigious university covers everything from photography to computer science, criminal justice to bioinformatics. The National Technical Institute for the Deaf is also located here. When visiting, be sure to stop by the Bevier Gallery or grab your skates and head to the Frank Ritter Memorial Ice Arena.

Admission: free. Daily.

ROCHESTER MUSEUM & SCIENCE CENTER

657 East Ave., Rochester, 585-271-4320; www.rmsc.org

Kids will love this hands-on museum where science and nature come to life. Local history is explored through exhibits such as "Flight to Freedom: Rochester's Underground Railroad" and Rochester's 1873 time capsule. The onsite Strasenburgh Planetarium hosts astronomy and laser-light shows.

Admission: adults $10, seniors and students $9, children 3-18 $8, children under 3 free. Monday-Saturday 9 a.m.-5 p.m., Sunday 11 a.m.-5 p.m.

SENECA PARK ZOO

2222 St. Paul St., Rochester, 585-336-7200;
www.senecaparkzoo.org

Animals from all over the world reside at this zoo, including African elephants, penguins, orangutans and polar bears. Aviary fans might enjoy the free-flight bird room (just watch for dive-bombs). The Rocky Coasts features underwater viewing of polar bears and seals.

Admission: adults $7-9, seniors $6-8, children 3-11 $4-6, children under 3 free. January-March, daily 10 a.m.-4 p.m.; April-October, daily 10 a.m.-5 p.m.; November-December, daily 10 a.m.-4 p.m.

STRONG MUSEUM

1 Manhattan Square, Rochester, 585-263-2700;
www.strongmuseum.org

As the second-largest children's museum in the U.S., the Strong features a myriad of exhibits; 25,000 toys, dolls, miniatures; and more. There is also an interactive 3-D exhibit based on the Children's Television Workshop program Sesame Street. The glass atrium features a street scene with an operating 1956 diner and a 1918 carousel.

Admission: adults $10, seniors $9, children 2-15 $8, children under 2 free. Monday-Thursday 10 a.m.-5 p.m., Friday-Saturday 10 a.m.-8 p.m., Sunday noon-5 p.m.

SUSAN B. ANTHONY HOUSE

17 Madison St., Rochester, 585-235-6124; www.susanbanthonyhouse.org

Susan B. Anthony lived here for 40 years and was arrested at her house in 1872 for voting illegally in the presidential election. The Victorian brick building contains mementos of the women's suffrage movement and antique furnishings.

Admission: adults $6, seniors $5, students and children under 13 $3. Tuesday-Sunday 11 a.m.-5 p.m.

SKANEATELES
MID-LAKES NAVIGATION BOAT TRIPS
11 Jordan St., Skaneateles, 315-685-8500, 800-545-4318; www.midlakesnav.com

Choose among 32-mile cruises along the shoreline of Skaneateles Lake.

Admission: prices vary. July-August, Monday-Saturday.

SYRACUSE
BEAVER LAKE NATURE CENTER
8477 E. Mud Lake Road, Baldwinsville, 315-638-2519

This 600-acre nature preserve with 10 miles of trails and boardwalks also has a 200-acre lake that serves as a rest stop for migrating ducks and geese and a visitor center. In the winter, the preserve is popular with cross-country skiers and snow-shoers. Other programs include maple sugaring and guided canoe tours.

Daily 7:30 a.m.-dusk.

ERIE CANAL MUSEUM
318 Erie Blvd. E., Syracuse, 315-471-0593; www.eriecanalmuseum.org

Indoor and outdoor exhibits detail the construction and operation of the Erie Canal, including a 65-foot reconstructed canal boat from which exhibits are seen. A re-created general store and post office are other interesting stops within the museum.

Admission: free. Tuesday-Saturday 10 a.m.-5 p.m., Sunday 10 a.m.-3 p.m.

EVERSON MUSEUM OF ART
401 Harrison St., Syracuse, 315-474-6064; www.everson.org

The first I.M. Pei-designed museum houses a permanent collection of American art and a collection of American ceramics, with changing exhibits. Look for the works of such familiar masters as Jackson Pollock and Andrew Wyeth. It is also the home of the Syracuse China Center for the Study of American Ceramics.

Admission: $5. Tuesday-Friday, Sunday noon-5 p.m., Saturday 10 a.m.-5 p.m.

LANDMARK THEATRE
362 S. Salina St., Syracuse, 315-475-7980; www.landmarktheatre.org

This historic theater was built in 1928 as Loew's State Theatre in the era of vaude-ville movie houses. The interior architecture is filled with carvings, chandeliers and ornate gold decorations. Concerts, plays, dance recitals and classic movies are hosted there frequently. Check the website for specific dates and showtimes.

Prices and showtimes vary.

ONONDAGA HISTORICAL ASSOCIATION MUSEUM
321 Montgomery St., Syracuse, 315-428-1864; www.cnyhistory.org

Examining the history of Syracuse and the Onondaga County region is the aim here, with changing and permanent exhibits ranging from architecture to transportation to cultural diversity. Those with an interest in beer will enjoy the small collection of artifacts depicting the history of brewing in Syracuse.

Admission: $7. Wednesday-Friday 10 a.m.-4 p.m., Saturday-Sunday 11 a.m.-4 p.m.

ROSAMOND GIFFORD ZOO AT BURNET PARK

1 Conservation Place, Syracuse, 315-435-8511; www.rosamondgiffordzoo.org

This small zoo traces the origin of life from 600 million years ago, with exhibits on animals' unique adaptations and animal/human interaction. Such exotic animals as the red panda, the white-spotted bamboo shark and the Madagascar hissing cockroach all call the zoo home.

Admission: adults $6.50, seniors and students $4.50, children 3-15 $4, children under 3 free. Daily 10 a.m.-4:30 p.m.

ST. MARIE AMONG THE IROQUOIS

Syracuse, 315-453-6767; www.onondagacountyparks.com

St. Marie Among the Iroquois is a re-creation of a 17th-century French mission that once occupied a place on the shores of Onondaga Lake. The onsite museum explores the history of the Iroquois and their interaction with the French. Blacksmithing, cooking, carpentry and gardening demonstrations take place as well.

Admission: adults $3, seniors $2.50, children 6-17 $2, children under 6 free. May-mid-October, Tuesday-Friday 9:30 a.m.-2:30 p.m., Saturday-Sunday noon-5 p.m.

SYRACUSE UNIVERSITY

University Avenue at University Place, Syracuse, 315-443-1870; www.syr.edu

Founded in 1870, this private research university is most noted for the Maxwell School of Citizenship and Public Affairs, Newhouse School of Public Communications, College of Engineering and 50,000-seat Carrier Dome where football, basketball and lacrosse all draw students and area locals.

WHERE TO STAY

AURORA
★★★AURORA INN

391 Main St., Aurora, 315-364-8888, 866-364-8808; www.aurora-inn.com

A perfectly charming 1833 Federal-style structure perched on the banks of Cayuga Lake, this Finger Lakes-area inn offers rooms with beds covered in Frette linens and contemporary touches, such as flat-screen TVs and whirlpool baths. Public rooms are cozy and inviting with oriental rugs and antique furnishings. The onsite restaurant is a local favorite and features a large outdoor patio with views of the lake for memorable dining in warm weather.

10 rooms. Restaurant. Complimentary breakfast. $251-350

ROCHESTER
★★★CROWNE PLAZA

70 State St., Rochester, 585-546-3450, 866-826-2831; www.rcpny.com

This Crowne Plaza offers a convenient location in the center of downtown Rochester. Airport shuttle service, a concierge, same-day laundry service and a business center with an array of offerings provide convenience, while a well-equipped fitness facility and an outdoor heated pool offer onsite recreation.

362 rooms. Restaurant, bar. Business center. Fitness center. Pool. Pets accepted. $61-150

★★★HYATT REGENCY ROCHESTER
125 E. Main St., Rochester, 585-546-1234, 800-492-8804;
www.hyatt.com

A skywalk connects the hotel to the convention center, which is near shopping, entertainment, wineries and the airport. You will find well-appointed rooms in browns and orange-reds with 42-inch flat-screen televisions, iPod docking stations and granite vanities. The hotel also offers a health club, extraordinary meeting spaces and a friendly staff.

338 rooms. Restaurant, bar. Business center. Fitness center. Pool. $151-250

★★★STRATHALLAN HOTEL
550 East Ave., Rochester, 585-461-5010, 800-678-7284;
www.strathallan.com

This European-style hotel offers warm and spacious studios and one-bedroom suites. Located in a stately residential neighborhood, the property is convenient to area attractions such as the Rochester Museum & Science Center. The restaurant offers dishes such as sweet potato-crusted Hawaiian snapper served in a country club setting, and the bar is a quiet place to relax.

156 rooms. Restaurant, bar. Business center. Fitness center. $151-250

SKANEATELES
★★★★MIRBEAU INN & SPA
851 W. Genesee St., Skaneateles, 315-685-5006, 877-647-2328;
www.mirbeau.com

This 12-acre Finger Lakes country estate, filled with ponds, gardens and woodlands, seems to have leapt off Claude Monet's canvases. Delightful Provençal fabrics and French country furnishings make the rooms cozy and comfortable while fireplaces and soaking tubs add romance. The friendly staff is available when you need it and unobtrusive when you don't. With winsome views of the lily pond and footbridge and the fresh-from-the-garden taste of the dishes, the restaurant truly transports diners. The European-style spa is both modern and charming.

34 rooms. Restaurant, bar. Fitness center. Spa. $251-350

★★★SHERWOOD INN
26 W. Genesee St., Skaneateles, 315-685-3405, 800-374-3796;
www.thesherwoodinn.com

Beautifully furnished with an aura of refinement,

this 1807 inn, a former stagecoach stop, has fantastic views of Clift Park and Skaneateles Lake. Guest rooms are tastefully decorated with wood furniture and antiques. Some rooms even boast canopy beds and fireplaces. Stop in at the inn's tavern to enjoy a pint at the original bar, which dates back to 1807.

25 rooms. Restaurant, bar. Complimentary breakfast. Business center. $151-250

SYRACUSE

★★★DOUBLETREE HOTEL SYRACUSE
6301 Highway 298, Syracuse, 315-432-0200; www.doubletree.com

This comfortable hotel caters to the business travelers who visit the corporate park in which it is located and the area's surrounding businesses. Amenities include signature Sweet Dreams beds, MP3 docking stations and Herman Miller work chairs.

250 rooms. Restaurant, bar. Business center. Fitness center. Pool. $61-150

★★★GENESEE GRANDE HOTEL
1060 E. Genesee St., Syracuse, 315-476-4212, 800-365-4663;www.geneseegrande.com

Located in the University Hill section of downtown Syracuse, this hotel is a convenient spot for those visiting campus. Rooms have soft, comfortable beds, flat-screen TVs and Brazilian granite baths, and service is friendly.

159 rooms. Restaurant, bar. Complimentary breakfast. Fitness center. $61-150

★★★THE MARX HOTEL AND CONFERENCE CENTER
701 E. Genesee St., Syracuse, 315-479-7000, 877-843-6279; www.marxsyracuse.com

Located in downtown Syracuse, this chic, contemporary hotel has rooms featuring desks with ergonomic seating and high-speed Internet access. There's also a fully equipped fitness center. Those on a working vacation can order room service for breakfast, lunch or dinner, and the complimentary van service transports sightseers.

279 rooms. Restaurant, bar. Business center. Fitness center. Spa. Pets accepted. $61-150

★★★SHERATON UNIVERSITY HOTEL AND CONFERENCE CENTER
801 University Ave., Syracuse, 315-475-3000, 800-395-2105; www.sheratonsyracuse.com

Bordering Syracuse University and the surrounding hospitals, this hotel is within walking distance of downtown civic centers, restaurants, entertainment arenas and other attractions. Service is friendly, and rooms have comfortable beds. The 24-hour business center is ideal for business travelers in a last minute scramble.

236 rooms. Restaurant, bar. Business center. Fitness center. Pool. $151-250

RECOMMENDED

AURORA

SPRINGSIDE INN
6141 W. Lake Road, Auburn, 315-252-7247; www.springsideinn.com

This country clapboard inn dating back to 1851 is charming and well-managed. Each room is unique, but all include private baths, Victorian antiques and views of the pond, outdoor fountain or gazebo. Locals come for the lavish Sunday brunch, which includes a heavenly cheese soufflé.

7 rooms. Restaurant, bar. Complimentary breakfast. $151-250

CORNING

DAYS INN

23 Riverside Drive, Corning, 607-936-9370, 800-329-7466; www.daysinn.com

Whether you're in Corning for a visit or just passing through, this ideally located motel has everything to make your stay comfortable and enjoyable. It's set next to the Museum of Glass among the shops and restaurants of charming downtown Corning, so you'll have good reason to venture beyond your basic room.

56 rooms. Restaurant. Complimentary breakfast. Pool. $61-150

RADISSON HOTEL CORNING

125 Denison Parkway E., Corning, 607-962-5000, 800-333-3333; www.radisson.com

This hotel is all about location. The Rockwell Museum of Art is next door, while the Museum of Glass and area shopping and dining are also steps away. The lobby has a spacious, natural feel, with many trees and foliage and the calming sound of running water coming from an impressive waterfall fountain. Guest rooms are bright with Sleep Number beds and luxurious down comforters.

177 rooms. Restaurant, bar. Fitness center. Pool. Pets accepted $61-150

ROCHESTER

RADISSON HOTEL ROCHESTER RIVERSIDE

120 E. Main St., Rochester, 585-546-6400, 800-395-7046;www.radisson.com

This large chain hotel is on the banks of the Genesee River in downtown Rochester and is directly connected to the Rochester Riverside Convention Center. Guest rooms were recently remodeled to include data ports and upgraded bathrooms.

465 rooms. Restaurant, bar. Fitness center. Pool. Pets accepted. $61-150

HOLIDAY INN HOTEL & SUITES MARKETPLACE

800 Jefferson Road, Rochester, 585-475-9190, 888-465-4329; www.hirochesterairport.com

From the free airport shuttle service to the free DVD rentals, there are numerous perks at this chain property. Rooms have refrigerators, microwaves and work stations, which are helpful for business travelers.

120 rooms. Restaurant, bar. Complimentary breakfast. Business center. Fitness center. Pool. $61-150

SYRACUSE

COURTYARD SYRACUSE CARRIER CIRCLE

6415 Yorktown Circle, East Syracuse, 315-432-0300; www.marriott.com

This Marriott provides guest rooms with luxury bedding, complimentary Internet access, new furniture and sizeable work stations for business travelers. The hotel is only minutes from Syracuse University.

149 rooms. Restaurant. Business center. $61-150

EMBASSY SUITES SYRACUSE

6646 Old Collamer Road, Syracuse, 315-446-3200, 800-362-2779; www.embassy-suites.com

For a little extra room with an affordable price tag, this is a good option. All guest rooms include a private bedroom and separate living space with two flat-screen TVs, a refrigerator, a microwave and a dining table.

215 rooms. Restaurant, bar. Complimentary breakfast. Business center. Fitness center. Pool. $61-150

HOLIDAY INN

6555 Old Collamer Road S., East Syracuse, 315-437-2761, 800-465-4329; www.holiday-inn.com

This chain hotel is conveniently located near Syracuse University and the Carrier Dome, as well as many corporate headquarters. The indoor pool is a nice amenity for kids.

203 rooms. Restaurant, bar. Complimentary breakfast. Fitness center. Pool. $61-150

WHERE TO EAT

AURBURN

★★★AURORA INN DINING ROOM

Aurora Inn, 391 Main St., Aurora, 315-364-8888, 866-364-8808; www.aurora-inn.com

Located in the Aurora Inn, this comfortable restaurant offers perfectly prepared versions of American classics with a lakefront setting. Dishes include traditional recipes such as lobster Newburg, Waldorf salad and a traditional pot roast, slow-cooked and served with roasted fingerling potatoes and vegetables. Pair your meal with one of the many local Finger Lakes wines on offer for an added indulgence.

American. Breakfast, lunch, dinner. $16-35

ROCHESTER

★★★THE GRILL AT STRATHALLAN

550 East Ave., Rochester, 585-461-5010; www.strathallan.com

This sophisticated yet casual Mediterranean dining room serves fresh, creative and elegantly prepared food paired with selections from an extensive wine cellar. Seafood dishes, such as sesame-crusted tuna with bok choy, are a great choice. There are also a number of tasty vegetarian options, like a vegetable Napoleon with zucchini, heirloom tomatoes, eggplant and fresh mozzarella.

American. Breakfast, lunch (Monday-Friday), dinner. Closed Sunday. Jacket required. $36-85

★★★MARIO'S ITALIAN STEAKHOUSE

2740 Monroe Ave., Rochester, 585-271-1111; www.mariosviaabruzzi.com

This charming villa is built and decorated in authentic central Italian style. Mario's unique Italian cuisine includes signatures like steak Diane, and pork loin with fig chutney. The Sunday buffet brunch is very popular.

Italian. Dinner, Sunday brunch. Outdoor seating. Children's menu. Bar. $16-35

★★★ROONEYS

90 Henrietta St., Rochester, 585-442-0444; www.rooneysrestaurant.com

This atmospheric downtown spot, with intimate mood lighting and white tablecloths, is housed in an 1860 tavern and the original bar is still in use. Many of the meat dishes are wood-grilled, and there's often venison, though the menu changes daily.

Continental. Dinner. Bar. $16-35

SKANEATELES

★★★★THE DINING ROOM AT MIRBEAU

Mirbeau Inn & Spa, 851 W. Genesee St., Skaneateles, 315-685-1927, 877-647-2328; www.mirbeau.com

This elegant and newly reconcepted dining room takes the form of a French steakhouse in the evening and delivers the best of French country-style cooking in a cozy, romantic setting. Executive chef Stephen Landon features comfort foods on his menus with items such as steak frittes, a pan-grilled sirloin with french fries and meatloaf with mashed potatoes and gravy. The wine list includes selections from around the world, and around the corner, with local Finger Lakes wineries highlighted.

American, French. Breakfast, lunch, dinner, Sunday brunch. Reservations recommended. Outdoor seating. Bar. $36-85

SYRACUSE
★★★PASCALE
204 W. Fayette St., Syracuse, 315-471-3040;
www.pascalerestaurant.com
Centrally located in Armory Square, a revitalized sector of downtown Syracuse, this restaurant features eclectic international food served in a contemporary setting. The menu changes seasonally, but the mixed grill is a top option year-round. The wines-by-the-glass list is extensive and affordable.

American. Dinner. Closed Sunday. Outdoor seating. Children's menu. Bar. $36-85

RECOMMENDED

AURBURN
LASCA'S
252-258 Grant Ave., Auburn, 315-253-4885; www.lascas.com
A local staple for 20 years, this casual eatery serves up consistently good American fare at reasonably low prices. House specialties include the veal piccata and filet n' tail, which comprises Australian lobster tail and mushroom-topped filet mignon.

Italian, American. Dinner. Closed Monday, first two weeks in February. Children's menu. Bar. $36-85

CORNING
LONDON UNDERGROUND CAFÉ
69 E. Market St., Corning
If the name doesn't tip you off, this eatery is all about British influence. The décor is dominated by artwork depicting London's subway, and the three-level space does gives a sense of being underground at times. The menu includes great salads and pasta dishes. The signature fish and chips is light and tasty. Give any of the desserts a go; they are all made in house.

American. Lunch, dinner. Closed Sunday. Children's menu. $16-35

NAPLES
NAPLES HOTEL
111 S. Main St., Naples, 585-374-5630
Housed in an 1895 Federal-style building, this restaurant is full of antiques and Victorian flair, including lace curtains and plush furnishings. German dishes are the focus. If you're looking for a more casual atmosphere, head to the tap room next door.

German. Lunch, dinner. Children's menu. Bar. $16-35

WHAT IS THE BEST PLACE FOR BRUNCH IN THE FINGER LAKES?

On Sundays, locals head to **Mario's Italian Steakhouse** for brunch. The buffet features made-to-order waffles and Nutella crêpes; a carving station with lamb and salmon; and flowing chocolate and caramel fountains for dessert.

ROCHESTER

DINOSAUR BAR-B-QUE

99 Court St., Rochester, 585-325-7090;
www.dinosaurbarbque.com

It's all about meat at this casual smoke shack. Housed in a turn-of-the-century railroad station adjacent to the Genesee River, this local favorite offers chicken, beef and pork in Cuban, Cajun, jerk and just about any other style of barbecue that you can imagine. Live blues is performed Monday through Saturday nights.

Barbecue. Lunch, dinner. Bar. $36-85

SYRACUSE

BROOKLYN PICKLE

2222 Burnet Ave., Syracuse, 315-463-1851

If you want to relive your college days, when enormous slapdash sandwiches constituted a high-end meal, stop for a sub at Brooklyn Pickle. The restaurant is clean and the young staff is friendly. Your best bet is to order the sub for which the restaurant was named.

Deli. Lunch, dinner. Closed Sunday. Outdoor seating. $15 and under.

COLEMAN'S

100 S. Lowell Ave., Syracuse, 315-476-1933;
www.colemansirishpub.com

St. Patrick's Day is a daily celebration at this Tipperary Hill restaurant. A tribute to everything Irish in Syracuse, the menu is packed with winning classics like corned beef and cabbage and juicy Reuben sandwiches. Weekend evening diners are treated to live Irish music.

Irish. Lunch, dinner. Outdoor seating. Children's menu. Bar. $15 and under

GLEN LOCH MILL

4626 North St., Jamesville, 315-469-6969; www.glenloch.net

Housed in a mill dating back to 1827, the restaurant has a rustic appeal. The fresh seafood is the main attraction with dishes like coconut-crusted tilapia and deep-fried haddock.

Seafood, steak. Dinner, Sunday brunch. Closed Monday. Outdoor seating. Children's menu. Bar. $16-36

SPA

SKANEATELES
★★★★SPA MIRBEAU

Mirbeau Inn & Spa, 851 W. Genesee St., Skaneateles, 315-685-1927, 877-647-2328;
www.mirbeau.com

Fourteen thousand square feet of tranquility await at the Spa Mirbeau, whose beautiful natural surroundings serve as the inspiration for everything from the herbal-infused steam rooms to body wraps and facials. After some pre-treatment relaxation in the resting area—complete with heated foot pools—you're ready to head to one of 18 treatment rooms. More than just a rubdown, the Monet's Favorite Fragrance massage blends essential oils of herbs and flowers from the Finger Lakes region to create an aromatherapy treatment that stimulates the senses. The expansive fitness center offers everything from meditation to Pilates.

THE HAMPTONS

When moneyed Manhattanites and New York City celebs want an escape from the concrete jungle—especially in the summer—they pack up their beach gear and head to the sandy shores of the Hamptons. The hamlet of Amagansett dates back to the 1680s and offers all the natural beauty of the region. Adore its bays, natural beaches and rolling dunes, as well as its charming seaside cafes and boutiques. Keep your eyes peeled for celebrities; Amagansett is a favorite promenade for Billy Joel, Jerry Seinfeld, Gwyneth Paltrow, Sarah Jessica Parker and Matthew Broderick, among others. East Hampton is another star magnet of a resort town.

The small community of Bridgehampton hosts the **Hampton Classic**, an annual summer horse show, and the **Mercedes-Benz Polo Challenge**. It's also home to several palatial estates situated along the sandy coastline. The village is clustered with antique shops, art galleries and upscale restaurants. Wine is a burgeoning business in this region with boutique wineries arriving on nearly every corner.

Southampton is the most formal of the fabled Hamptons, attracting the high society that summer here in vast mansions overlooking Lake Agawam and the Atlantic dunes. The village center boasts terrific shopping in the form of **Saks Fifth Avenue**, **Ralph Lauren** and more. And the town's **Parrish Art Museum** is a terrific spot to browse the ever-changing collections.

Montauk is a lively, somewhat honky-tonk fishing town at the far eastern end of Long Island, with a big business in deep-sea fishing. Boats can be rented, and there are miles of uncrowded beaches for sunning and surfing. Of course, there is also a glittering summer community here, too, but residents such as Ralph Lauren tend to be more low-key than the denizens of other nearby Hamptons communities.

Sag Harbor, a great whaling town of the 19th century, provided prototypes from which author James Fenimore Cooper created characters for his sea stories. Sheltered in a cove of Gardiner's Bay, the economy of Sag Harbor is still fueled by the sea, attracting wealthy New Yorkers who come to retreat and relax in this chic summertime community by the beach.

WHAT TO SEE

AMAGANSETT
MISS AMELIA'S COTTAGE MUSEUM
Montauk Highway 27A and Windmill Lane, Amagansett, 631-267-3020

This original home, built in 1725, is part of Amagansett history. Mary Amelia Schellinger was a descendant of Jacob Schellinger, the founder of Amagansett. As the last of her family to live in the house, she went without electricity and running water for years, passing away in 1930. The cottage features its original furnishings and depicts life in Amagansett through the colonial period. Throughout the summer, there are weekend pony rides and an antique sale.

Admission: $2, pony ride $5. June-September, Friday-Sunday 10 a.m.-4 p.m.

TOWN MARINE MUSEUM
301 Bluff Road, Amagansett, 631-267-6544; www.easthamptonhistory.org

Offering a history lesson on Long Island's East End community, this museum includes three floors of exhibits on commercial and sports fishing, local shipwrecks and underwater archaeology. The permanent collection of artifacts, photographs and displays on the offshore whaling industry from colonial times to the present is a highlight.

Admission: adults $4, seniors $3, students $2. June-mid-October, Saturday 10 a.m.-5 p.m., Sunday noon-5 p.m.; July-August, Friday, Monday 10 a.m.-5 p.m.

BRIDGEHAMPTON
CHANNING DAUGHTERS WINERY
1927 Scuttlehole Road, Bridgehampton, 631-537-7224;
www.channingdaughters.com

This 28-acre winery produces a host of hand-picked varieties, such as pinot grigio, chardonnay, pinot noir and merlot. Although small, Channing Daughters poses special offerings like a discounted wine club and a wood sculpture garden that showcases the art of owner Walter Channing. The winery gives out wine tastings from May to October.

Admission: Tasting: $5. May-September, daily 11 a.m.-5 p.m.; October-April, Thursday-Monday 11 a.m.-5 p.m.

WÖLFFER ESTATE VINEYARD
139 Sagg Pond Road, Sagaponack, 631-537-5106; www.wolffer.com

This Tuscan-style winery is more reminiscent of an enchanted European estate than a vineyard in the Hamptons, but the harvests are decidedly American. The local soil acts as the perfect host for Wölffer's slow-growing vines, and the cool climate, thanks in part to the close proximity of the Atlantic, allows for late harvests and strong, natural acidity. A visit to the estate is a special affair: Immaculately manicured grounds and a trickling, circular fountain greet you as you make your way into the impressive 12,000-square-foot winery. While the winemaking facilities make their home on the lower level, the main floor impresses with terracotta tiling, antique stained-glass windows and massive French doors that open onto the vineyards. Sit, imbibe a glass of crisp chardonnay, take in the spectacular view and you'll forget that you're farther from Italy than it seems.

November-March, Sunday-Wednesday 11 a.m.-5 p.m., Thursday 11 a.m.-7:30 p.m.,

HIGHLIGHT

WHAT ARE THE TOP THINGS TO DO IN THE HAMPTONS?

GO WINE TASTING AT WÖLFFER ESTATE VINEYARD
Long Island is like the Napa of the East Coast. Taste some of the best wine at this Tuscan-style winery, which boasts immaculate, picturesque grounds.

VISIT THE POLLOCK-KRASNER HOUSE AND STUDY CENTER
Art aficionados will want to make a trip to this East Hampton site to see artist Jackson Pollock's home and paint-covered studio.

CAMP OUT IN HITHER HILLS STATE PARK
This state park offers some of the best beachside camping in the country. Plus, it has lots of hiking and biking trails.

CHECK OUT THE MONTAUK LIGHTHOUSE
George Washington commissioned this lighthouse, which is the oldest in the state. To get great ocean views, be sure to climb up to the top of the lighthouse.

PERUSE THE COLLECTION AT THE PARRISH ART MUSEUM
The Parrish features works from top artists who have lived or worked in the region, including Jackson Pollock, Lee Krasner, Willem de Kooning and Dan Flavin.

Friday-Saturday 11 a.m.-6 p.m.; April-October, Sunday-Wednesday 11 a.m.-6 p.m., Thursday 11 a.m.-7:30 p.m., Friday-Saturday 11 a.m.-7 p.m.

EAST HAMPTON
GUILD HALL MUSEUM
158 Main St., East Hampton, 631-324-0806; www.guildhall.org

This small museum features regional art exhibits and seasonally changing shows. There are also interesting art and poetry lectures and classes. Film festivals and concerts often take place at the John Drew Theater.

Admission: free. June-August, Monday-Saturday 11 a.m.-5 p.m., Sunday noon-5 p.m.; September-May, Friday-Saturday 11 a.m.-5 p.m., Sunday noon-5 p.m.

HISTORIC CLINTON ACADEMY
151 Main St., East Hampton, 631-324-6850; www.easthamptonhistory.org

The first preparatory school in New York is now a museum housing a collection of Eastern Long Island artifacts. The Georgian-style building was restored in 1921 and boasts beautiful gardens throughout the property.

Admission: adults $4, seniors $3, students $2. June-mid-October, Saturday 10 a.m.-5 p.m., Sunday noon-5 p.m.; July-August, Friday 10 a.m.-5 p.m.

HISTORIC MULFORD FARM

10 James Lane, East Hampton, 631-324-6850; www.easthamptonhistory.org

This living history museum and farm features 18th-century New England architecture, colonial history, period rooms and costumed interpreters. The property includes the Mulford House, constructed in 1680, and the Mulford Barn, which was built in 1721 and remains one of the best examples of an early-18th-century English barn plan.

Admission: adults $4, seniors $3, students $2. June-mid-October, Saturday 10 a.m.-5 p.m., Sunday noon-5 p.m.; July-August, Friday 10 a.m.-5 p.m.

"HOME SWEET HOME" HOUSE

14 James Lane, East Hampton, 631-324-0713; www.easthampton.com

Named after the popular 19th-century song Home, Sweet Home, written by John Howard Payne, this house was originally owned by Payne's grandfather, Aaron Isaacs (the first Jewish person to settle in the area). The historic lean-to house features a stunning collection of antiques and china and is dedicated to Payne, who was also an actor, playwright and diplomat.

Admission: adults $4, seniors $3, students $2. May-September, Monday-Saturday 10 a.m.-4 p.m., Sunday 2-4 p.m.; April, October-November, Friday-Saturday 10 a.m.-4 p.m., Sunday 2-4 p.m.

MAIN BEACH

101 Ocean Ave., East Hampton

Beautiful white-sand Main Beach is set against the backdrop of mansions. It is one of the nation's top-rated beaches and a big draw for summertime crowds. Visitors must pay a $20 daily parking permit that is only valid on weekdays; the permit is not available on weekends or holidays for nonresidents.

POLLOCK-KRASNER HOUSE AND STUDY CENTER

830 Fireplace Road, East Hampton, 631-324-4929; http://naples.cc.sunysb.edu

Abstract Expressionist Jackson Pollock's studio and house, plus a reference library on 20th-century American art, are open to the public and worth a trip. Inside the unassuming circa 1879 house remains much of the furniture used by Pollock, as well as a collection of jazz records and a personal library. Don't miss Pollock's paint-covered studio floor.

Admission: $5. May, September-October, Thursday-Saturday 11 a.m.-4 p.m.; June-August, Thursday-Saturday noon-4 p.m.

MONTAUK

HITHER HILLS STATE PARK

50 S. Fairview Ave., Montauk, 631-668-2554

The 1,755-acre park has hiking and biking trails, pine forests and some of the best beachside camping in the country. The "walking dunes" are on the eastern boundary of the park, so named because powerful northwest winds cause the mammoth dunes to shift nearly three feet every year.

Admission: $8 per vehicle. Daily dawn-dusk.

MONTAUK LIGHTHOUSE

Montauk Point, Montauk, 631-668-2544; www.montauklighthouse.com

You've come as far east as you can on Long Island. In fact, Montauk Point is called "The End" by locals. What better way to end a trip on Long Island than with a visit to this historic lighthouse that was commissioned by George Washington and completed in 1796? It's the oldest lighthouse in the state, featuring 137 winding narrow steps to the top and views of the ocean from any angle. The lighthouse beacon still rotates and can be seen for 19 nautical miles.

Admission: adults $8, seniors $7, children under 13 $4. May-October, daily 10:30 a.m.-4:30 p.m.; closing and off-season times vary.

MONTAUK POINT STATE PARK

50 S. Fairview Ave., Montauk, 631-668-3781; www.nysparks.state.ny.us

Surrounding Montauk Lighthouse, this park is filled with barren moors and grassy dunes. Rip tides prevent swimming, but surf-casting (fishing near the shoreline) is popular here. Beachcombing and bird-watching are also favored pastimes at this park.

Admission: $6 per vehicle. Daily dawn-dusk.

SAG HARBOR
CUSTOM HOUSE

Main and Garden streets, Sag Harbor, 631-692-4664; www.splia.org

This building served as a custom house and post office during the late 18th and early 19th centuries. Antique furnishings and historic documents are on exhibit in the converted museum.

Admission: adults $3, seniors and children $2. June-mid-October, Saturday-Sunday 1-5 p.m.

ELIZABETH A. MORTON NATIONAL WILDLIFE REFUGE

784 Noyac Road, Sag Harbor, 631-286-0485; www.fws.gov

At one time, Native American tribes inhabited this 187-acre plot. Today, a variety of birds—some endangered—call it home at different times of the year. Bring your binoculars; you're likely to see osprey, terns and water birds.

Daily dawn-dusk.

SAG HARBOR WHALING AND HISTORICAL MUSEUM

200 Main St., Sag Harbor, 631-725-0770; www.sagharborwhalingmuseum.org

Listed on the National Register of Historic Places, this museum, housed in a mansion, celebrates Sag Harbor's long history of whaling. It features items such as the tools used to harpoon whales, a replica of a whaleboat, whale teeth and bones and other materials associated with whaling.

Admission: adults $5, seniors and students $3, children under 12 free. Mid-May-October, daily 10 a.m.-5 p.m., Sunday 1-5 p.m.

SOUTHAMPTON
COOPERS BEACH

268 Meadow Lane, Southampton

Southampton offers seven miles of white sand, but the most coveted spot is Coopers Beach. Coopers consistently ranks in the top of every nation's-best-beaches list, and it's usually the only New York spot to do so. It's also one of a few beaches in this tony portion of Long Island where the public can enjoy the pristine sandy shores. But it'll cost you to sunbathe there; nonresidents must purchase a $40 daily parking permit.

OLD HALSEY HOUSE

249 S. Main St., Southampton, 631-283-2494

This 1648 structure is the oldest English frame house in the state. Once the head-quarters for English General William Erskine during the American Revolution, the house is now a museum exhibiting furniture from the 17th and 18th centuries.

Admission: $3. Mid-July-mid-September, Tuesday-Sunday 11 a.m.-5 p.m.

PARRISH ART MUSEUM

25 Jobs Lane, Southampton, 631-283-2118; www.parrishart.org

One of the top museums on eastern Long Island, the Parrish is most well-known for its collection of 19th- and 20th-century American paintings and prints by local artists. There is also a sizeable display of Japanese woodblock prints. The museum was built in 1898 as a repository for Samuel Longstreth Parrish's Italian Renaissance art collection. The museum often hosts lectures, workshops and children's programs.

Admission: adults $7, seniors and students $5, children under 18 free. June-mid-September, Monday-Saturday 11 a.m.-5 p.m., Sunday 1-5 p.m.; mid-September-May, Monday, Thursday-Saturday 11 a.m.-5 p.m., Sunday 1-5 p.m.

SOUTHAMPTON HISTORICAL MUSEUM

17 Meeting House Lane, Southampton, 631-283-2494; www.southamptonhistoricalmuseum.org

This mansion, built in 1843, depicts Southampton's colorful history. It has original furnishings, photos and quilts, as well as Montauk and Shinnecock Indian artifacts on display. The museum's grounds include a one-room school-house, drugstore, paint shop, blacksmith shop and carpentry store.

Admission: adults $4, children under 17 free. Tuesday-Saturday 11 a.m.-5 p.m., Sunday 1-5 p.m.

WHERE TO STAY

EAST HAMPTON

★★★THE 1770 HOUSE

143 Main St., East Hampton, 631-324-1770; www.1770house.com

This restored 18th-century house proffers antique furnishings and a prime location near East Hampton's top-notch shopping and dining. The rooms are elegant with Frette linens and flat-screen televisions. Some of the rooms also have fireplaces.

7 rooms. Restaurant, bar. Complimentary breakfast. No children under 12. $151-250

★★★C/O THE MAIDSTONE

207 Main St., East Hampton, 631-324-5006; www.maidstonearms.com

The Osborne family—no, not Ozzy and Sharon Osbourne—built this estate as a private residence in the 1750s, and the terrifically situated property has been operating as an inn since the 1870s. Enjoy the bustle of the Hamptons during the summer months or settle in by the fireplaces during cozy winter stays. The rooms have Scandinavian furnishings and perks like Bodum French presses, aromatherapy burners and essential oils, Malin + Goetz toiletries, Hästens beds, WiFi and compli-mentary hand-painted Swedish clogs for you to wear. The back garden becomes vibrant with flowers in spring, and it's the perfect setting for the free yoga sessions.

19 rooms. Restaurant, bar. Complimentary breakfast. $151-250

MONTAUK

★★★GURNEY'S INN RESORT AND SPA
290 Old Montauk Highway, Montauk, 631-668-2345, 800-445-8062; www.gurneys-inn.com

This sprawling resort facing the Atlantic Ocean provides a peaceful escape. Once here, head to the beautiful beach, take a sunrise walk or participate in activities like volleyball or yoga. The Seawater Spa offers body wraps and scrubs, massage therapy, facials and salon services. The indoor heated pool, which features seawater drawn from the resort's own wells, has views of the Atlantic from its floor-to-ceiling windows. Contemporary elegance is the theme of guest rooms.

109 rooms. Restaurant, bar. Spa. Beach. $251-350

★★★MONTAUK YACHT CLUB
32 Star Island Road, Montauk, 631-668-3100, 888-692-8668; www.montaukyachtclub.com

The resort's 60-foot lighthouse replica, built in 1928, is still a focal point at this elegant retreat overlooking Lake Montauk. The numerous activities include volleyball, charter fishing, the La Bella Vita Spa and a fitness center with saunas. Guest rooms have floor-to-ceiling windows and private balconies. You might run into former *Real Housewives of New York City* funnywoman Bethenny Frankel here; it's one of her favorite Hamptons hotels.

107 rooms. Restaurant, bar. Fitness center. Pool. Spa. Beach. Tennis. Closed December-March. $251-350

RECOMMENDED

AMAGANSETT

SEA CREST ON THE OCEAN
2166 Montauk Highway, Amagansett, 631-267-3159, 800-732-3297

This family-friendly resort offers direct beach access and spacious one- and two-bedroom units, many with in-suite kitchens. While the décor is basic, the rooms are airy and bright. There are barbecue pits near the dunes for evening bonfires.

66 rooms. Pool. Beach. Tennis. $151-250

SOUTHAMPTON

SOUTHAMPTON INN
91 Hill St., Southampton, 631-283-6500, 800-732-6500; www.southamptoninn.com

Situated on 5 acres of rolling lawns, this Tudor-style inn offers rooms with classic country furnishings, Tempur-Pedic mattresses and toiletries by Gilchrist & Soames. The activity options are endless with biking, kayaking, fishing, tennis and a pool only a few steps away.

90 rooms. Restaurant, bar. Business center. Pool. Pets accepted. Tennis. $151-250

WHERE TO EAT

EAST HAMPTON

★★★DELLA FEMINA
99 N. Main St., East Hampton, 631-329-6666; www.dellafemina.com

The celebrity caricatures that line the walls of this contemporary American eatery hint at the see-and-be-seen reputation that it carries during summer months. The

WHICH HAMPTONS HOTEL HAS THE MOST UNUSUAL AMENITIES?

C/O The Maidstone offers a slew of out-of-the-ordinary amenities, including vintage Scandinavian bikes, butlers for hire and picnic baskets filled with slow-food options. It's probably the only place that provides hand-painted clogs.

off-season welcomes a more mellow atmosphere where good food and prix fixe menus dominate the scene. Go local and choose the roasted Montauk striped bass with littleneck clams or sea scallops with scallions in a coconut-milk broth.

American. Dinner, Sunday brunch (November-April). Closed Wednesday (November-April). Outdoor seating. Bar. $36-85

★★★EAST HAMPTON POINT

295 Three Mile Harbor Road, East Hampton, 631-329-2800; www.easthamptonpoint.com

With stunning waterfront and sunset vistas overlooking Three Mile Harbor, East Hampton Point has a subtle nautical décor. The skilled kitchen turns out dishes such as roasted Scottish salmon with asparagus, morel risotto with a truffle-leek sauce and Maine halibut with black olives, tomatoes, fennel and baby artichokes.

American. Lunch, dinner. Closed September-March. Reservations recommended. Outdoor seating. Children's menu. Bar. $36-85

★★★THE LIVING ROOM RESTAURANT

C/O The Maidstone, 207 Main St., East Hampton, 631-324-5440; www.alisonrestaurant.com

The Living Room Restaurant serves chef James Carpenter's take on slow food, with a Swedish twist. Try the Scandinavian Toast Skagen with baby shrimp, lemon scented crème fraiche, and dill from the garden. The menu changes often based on what is local and in season, but rest assured all is freshly prepared. Can't decide what you're in the mood for? Try the new five-course tasting menu.

Contemporary Swedish. Breakfast, lunch, dinner. Bar. $36-85

SAG HARBOR

★★★AMERICAN HOTEL

American Hotel, 49 Main St., Sag Harbor, 631-725-3535; www.theamericanhotel.com

Located in the American Hotel is an elegant and romantic restaurant filled with Empire and Victorian antiques and furnishings. The menu offers American and French classics, and an excellent wine list. Seafood is a good choice here, from the Atlantic lobster to the pan-seared diver scallops.

American, French. Lunch, dinner. Reservations recommended. Outdoor seating. Bar. $36-85

RECOMMENDED

AMAGANSETT
LOBSTER ROLL
1980 Montauk Highway, Amagansett, 631-267-3740; www.lobsterroll.com

This local dive is little more than a shack by the sea, but few seem to mind once they taste the creamy New England clam chowder and fresh lobster rolls. The booths and outdoor picnic tables are packed all summer with hungry locals and tourists taking breaks from the beach.

Seafood. Lunch, dinner. Closed November-April. Outdoor seating. Children's menu. $15 and under

BRIDGEHAMPTON
BOBBY VAN'S STEAKHOUSE
2393 Montauk Highway, Bridgehampton, 631-537-0590; www.bobbyvans.com

Named after Bobby Van, a local piano player and actor who entertained his well-heeled friends at his area Hamptons home, this restaurant attracts a crowd of Manhattanites enjoying an escape. French doors and polished wood paneling give the space a masterful look and the waitstaff is without flaw. Seafood is the specialty here, with dishes such as miso-steamed black sea bass and crispy skin-on salmon with morel mushrooms and fava beans. Steak-seekers should also bring their appetites. The restaurant also offers perfectly done steak-house classics.

Seafood, steak. Lunch, dinner. Bar. $16-35

EAST HAMPTON
NICK & TONI'S
136 N. Main St., East Hampton, 631-324-3550; www.nickandtonis.com

The décor of the dining room is simple, bright and colorful with a mosaic wood-burning brick oven and an open-air patio. The wood-roasted chicken is a good bet, as are any of the oven-charred pizzas. Arrive early in summer and be prepared to wait, as this is easily one of East Hampton's most popular restaurants.

Mediterranean. Dinner, Sunday brunch. Bar. $36-85

PALM
94 Main St., East Hampton, 631-324-0411; www.thepalm.com

This restaurant serves consistently delicious American fare in a charming old-fashioned setting. The prime rib is fantastic, as is the lobster.

Seafood, steak. Dinner. Bar. $36-85

MONTAUK
CROW'S NEST RESTAURANT & INN
4 Old West Lake Drive, Montauk, 631-668-2077; www.crowsnestinn.com

Though the nautical décor is slightly kitschy, the fresh seafood is anything but. The clam chowder is thick and creamy and the lobsters are sweet and delicious. Kids will love the 14-foot aquarium filled with exotic tropical fish and the shark tank.

Seafood. Lunch, dinner. Children's menu. Bar. $16-35

DAVE'S GRILL

468 W. Lake Drive, Montauk, 631-668-9190; www.davesgrill.com

This no-nonsense spot on the Montauk fishing docks serves fresh seafood, including clams casino, stuffed lobster and Dave's famous fish stew. Don't leave without indulging in the signature chocolate bag dessert, a playful take on a sundae.

Seafood. Dinner. Closed Wednesday; also November-April. Outdoor seating. Bar. $16-35

GOSMAN'S RESTAURANT

500 W. Lake Drive, Montauk, 631-668-5330; www.gosmans.com

A dockside hangout popular with locals, Gosman's is a good spot for anything seafood. The Montauk lobsters are brought in daily.

Seafood. Lunch, dinner. Closed mid-October-mid-April. Outdoor seating. Children's menu. Bar. $16-35

HARVEST ON FORT POND

11 S. Emery St., Montauk, 631-668-5574;
www.harvest2000.com

Family-style portions and breathtaking sunset views are the draw at this waterfront restaurant. In warm weather, ask to dine in the herb garden. Order the pork tenderloin with apricot-apple chutney with a salad of watercress, pine nuts and Spanish prosciutto. Then follow it up with the cream puffs stuffed with vanilla gelato.

Mediterranean. Dinner. Closed February. Outdoor seating. Bar. $36-85

SECOND HOUSE TAVERN

161 Second House Road, Montauk, 631-668-2877;
www.secondhousetavern.com

Situated on Fort Pond, this large airy restaurant keeps a casual atmosphere with farmstand tables and lofted ceilings. The grilled Australian lamb chops with mustard spaetzle and the seared sea scallops are specialties of the house.

Dinner. Outdoor seating. Children's menu. Bar. $16-35

SAG HARBOR

ESTIA'S LITTLE KITCHEN

1615 Sag Harbor, Sag Harbor, 631-725-1045;
www.eatshampton.com

This local roadside hangout takes the "little" in its name seriously. Space is limited and the décor isn't much, but the kitchen serves up fresh inventive American dishes, and service is friendly and low-key. Start off with the crab and sweet corn Napoleons, and then move onto the potato-crusted flounder or the braised lamb shank with butternut squash.

American. Breakfast, lunch, dinner. Reservations recommended. Closed Tuesday. $16-35

IL CAPUCCINO

30 Madison St., Sag Harbor, 631-725-2747; www.ilcapuccino.com

This charming Italian restaurant is a satisfying place for dinner after a day at the beach. The menu is filled with straightforward dishes like lasagna and homemade ravioli that are consistently delicious. There's a nice wine list, and make-you-drool desserts include the housemade Italian cheesecake and cannoli.

Italian. Dinner. Children's menu. Bar. $16-35

SPINNAKER'S

63 Main St., Sag Harbor, 631-725-9353

Located in the heart of downtown Sag Harbor, this local spot provides fresh seafood and burgers. The lobster salad is a must.

American, International. Lunch, dinner, Sunday brunch. Reservations recommended. Children's menu. Bar. $16-35

SOUTHAMPTON
COAST GRILL

1109 Noyack Road, Southampton, 631-283-2277; www.therestaurantsweb.com

This cute local eatery overlooks Wooley Pond and draws quite a crowd during peak season. The kitschy décor includes pink walls and hanging painted fish. The food is always good and the portions are generous. The signature clam chowder is a standout.

American, seafood. Dinner. Closed Wednesday. Bar. $16-35

GOLDEN PEAR

99 Main St., Southampton, 631-283-8900; www.goldenpearcafe.com

If you're looking for the local spot to scarf down a bowl of chili or laze over a hot cup of coffee, the Golden Pear is it. Choose a seat at the counter to get in on any Hampton gossip. The restaurant is small, so don't be surprised if you have to wait for a table during summer.

American. Breakfast, lunch. $16-35

JOHN DUCK JR.

15 Prospect St., Southampton, 631-283-0311

Located in a converted farmhouse, this restaurant has been a family affair for more than a century. The country ambiance is in full swing throughout the five separate dining rooms, including a glassed-in porch. Sunday brunch here is a treat.

American, German. Lunch, dinner, Sunday brunch. Closed Monday. Children's menu. Bar. $16-35

LE CHEF

75 Jobs Lane, Southampton, 631-283-8581; www.lechefbistro.com

Le Chef brings a touch of France to the east end of Long Island. The baby rack of lamb with mint and pan-roasted potatoes is particularly good, as is the nut-crusted local flounder. Save room for dessert; the signature French vanilla crêpes are (not surprisingly) delicious.

French. Lunch, dinner, brunch. Bar. $16-35

WHICH HAMPTONS RESTAURANTS SERVE THE BEST SEAFOOD?

Dave's Grill:
Head to the Montauk docks to try Dave's famous fish stew, which is cioppino with fish reduction, orzo, English peas, herbs and a dash of cream.

Gosman's Restaurant:
Locals dine at this restaurant to have lobster, fried fish and yellowtail flounder with a view overlooking the water.

Lobster Inn:
This Southampton restaurant serves the freshest lobster in town. The succulent critters always taste like they are fresh off of the boat.

Lobster Roll:
This place may be a dive, but locals tolerate it for its wonderful bowls of New England clam chowder and fresh namesake lobster rolls.

LOBSTER INN

162 Inlet Road, Southampton, 631-283-1525

Locals come more for the fresh-off-the-boat seafood than the rustic interior. Nevertheless, it's hard to find a fresher lobster in town. In summer, the outdoor tables are a nice spot to while away the afternoon.

American, seafood. Lunch, dinner. Outdoor seating. Children's menu. Bar. $16-35

MIRKO'S

Water Mill Square, Water Mill, 631-726-4444; www.mirkosrestaurant.com

Professionally run by a husband-and-wife team, this small American bistro is off the beaten path and all the more charming because of it (especially during the summer months when Main Street can feel more like Manhattan). While the ambience is charming, the food is decidedly sophisticated, with dishes like spice-rubbed roasted duck breast with a wild rice griddle cake, Bing cherry compote and orange-honey-pomegranate sauce.

American. Dinner. Reservations recommended. Outdoor seating. Bar. $36-85

WHERE TO SHOP

BRIDGEHAMPTON COMMONS

Montauk Highway, Bridgehampton, 631-537-2174

Get out the credit cards and do a little damage. Actually, prices aren't as bad as you'd think at this retail outpost, with brand-name stores like Banana Republic, Victoria's Secret and Williams-Sonoma.

Daily.

SHINNECOCK INDIAN OUTPOST

Old Montauk Highway, Southampton, 631-283-8047; www.shinnecocktradingpost.com

This funky shop sells Native American crafts, clothes and glassware. There's also an onsite moccasin store that proclaims itself the home of America's original shoe. If you're hungry, the deli is a good bet for a quick morning coffee and bagel.

June-August, daily 6:30 a.m.-7 p.m.; September-May, daily 6:30 a.m.-6 p.m.

NEW YORK CITY

Only in New York. It's a refrain you'll often hear echoed throughout the city's streets and corridors. The city that never sleeps is home to some of the most exceptional attractions anywhere, many of them highly prized for their cultural and historical significance. Besides the world-class museums, shopping and entertainment venues New York offers, there's another attraction that can't be replicated elsewhere: the colorful cast of characters who give the city its soul. After you've spent a day touring the city's top sights, take a seat in Central Park or at a café in Union Square and participate in the city's best free attraction: people watching. Without the intangible energy of New York's residents, the Statue of Liberty becomes just another heap of scrap metal and the lights of Times Square go dark. It's more than just iconic landmarks that make this city one of a kind. New York has a pulsing electricity all its own—something that has to be experienced to be understood.

As the culture capital of the world, there is no place like New York City for a big dose of art, theater, music and more. Every year, people arrive in the city hoping to make it here on account of their ceaseless creativity and limitless drive. See what's happening in the city's galleries, music halls, theaters and sports stadiums. If it's happening here, you can bet it will be good, or at the very least, interesting, thought-provoking and inspiring.

New York City may never sleep, but at some point, you have to. You'll find everything from white glove butler service to cutting edge interior design at New York's hundreds of hotels, which means you can choose one that seems almost tailor made for your tastes. Rooms in Manhattan might be small, and bathrooms even smaller, but this city also has some of the most storied, trend-setting, luxurious hotels in the world. Who hasn't dreamed of living at The Plaza (like Eloise) or thirsted to mingle with the in-crowd in one of the city's top hotels? Just try to get at least some sleep while you're in town.

And what's not to love about New York dining? There's the depth, breadth and height of the many options, from $400 dinners in a glassy skyscraper at Masa in Columbus Circle to the $4.75 burger at Danny Meyer's Shake Shack. There's the longevity—restaurants like Le Bernardin and Gotham Bar and Grill that wowed in the 1980s and continue to impress. There are ethnic eats and underground supper clubs, global-fusion flavors, dark and moody dining rooms (Minetta Tavern) and fluorescently lit delis (Barney Greengrass). There's the trend toward farmers market fare—any chef worth his or her (artisanal or kosher) salt cooks with the seasons in mind and uses local purveyors to do so. The personalities of the star chefs and knowing that for every superstar chef such as Daniel's Daniel Boulud, there's a talented, young go-getter like Daniel Humm of Eleven Madison Park striving to be the Next Big Thing makes the city's dining scene dynamic. There's just so much to adore, consume and explore in New York City.

Finally, there is perhaps no better place than New York City for serious shopping. You can spend days walking up and down Fifth Avenue, starting at Bergdorf's and ending up at Saks. Then you'll want to head downtown, where many of the stores are show-stoppers themselves (Prada, Dolce & Gabbana).

No other city in the U.S. has the nerve-rattling energy that New York does. Just the sheer act of walking down the street is an exercise in evading too-busy-to-mind locals and navigating traffic. Don't even start on trying to catch a taxi or negotiating a multi-train transfer. That's why some of the best spas in the world call the Big Apple home. If it's good enough for frazzled New Yorkers, you bet it'll be good enough for you.

YOUR QUESTIONS ANSWERED

WHAT IS THE BEST WAY TO GET TO MANHATTAN FROM THE AIRPORTS?

The quickest option to get to Manhattan or other points from either LaGuardia, JFK or Newark airports is to take a city-licensed yellow taxi for a zoned fee. (Avoid the car-service drivers and unlicensed drivers who often lurk near the baggage area, and head to a designated taxi stand instead). Not including tolls—which are the passengers' responsibility—or tip, the ride to Midtown Manhattan from JFK is around $45, from LaGuardia between $25 and $30, and from Newark about $60-75. Public transportation from the airports can be time-consuming, but it's definitely the cheapest option. From JFK, take the AirTrain ($5) to the Z, E, J or A subway line ($2.25) (*visit www.airtrainjfk.com for more info*). From LaGuardia, the M60 bus ($2.25) runs from the airport through Harlem and to the Upper West Side in Manhattan. From Newark, take a New Jersey Transit train ($15) from the airport to Penn Station in Manhattan. A good alternative is a shuttle service, which generally costs $12-$25 depending on your starting and ending points. SuperShuttle (*800-258-3826; www.supershuttle.com*), which services all three major airports, and New York Airport Service (*212-875-8200; www.myair-portservice.com*), which services JFK and LaGuardia, are two popular options.

WHAT IS THE BEST WAY TO NAVIGATE THE SUBWAY?

What may seem daunting at first glance is actually a very quick, inexpensive (and some think fun), round-the-clock way to move around the city. Generally, the subway is faster and easier to navigate than city buses. Each subway route is marked by either a number or a letter and is color-coded according to the line on which it runs. The names of subway stops correspond to the nearest street or landmark. For example, the 2 train stops at Penn Station (34th Street), as well as Times Square (42nd Street). Local trains make every stop along their routes, while express trains make only the major station stops (generally marked by a white dot on subway maps). Be sure to check—express trains might go past 50 blocks before stopping. Many stations have separate entrances for uptown and downtown trains, and some entrances are open 24 hours (marked by a green globe), while others have limited hours (and red globes). Likewise, train schedules can change, especially late at night and on weekends, so read posted signs carefully. On each train platform, overhead signs will indicate which trains stop on those tracks and during what hours, if any, the trains are express.

The Metropolitan Transportation Authority (*www.mta.info*) operates both the subway and buses; a MetroCard will work on both systems. You can buy one at subway station vending machines (they accept cash, credit and debit cards), from the station booth, at many hotels and at the NY Convention & Visitors Bureau (*www.nycvisit.com*). You can either load a card with money (from $4 to $80) and it will deduct $2.25 each time you ride a train or bus, or you can pay once for unlimited rides during a set number of days. With a pay-per-use card, up to four people can use the same card, and putting $20 on the card will actually credit you with 10 trips for the price of 9. If you'll be traveling often, an unlimited rides card is a smart choice. A one day Fun Pass costs $8.25, a 7-day pass costs $27, a 14-day pass costs $51.50 and a 30-day pass costs $89. You can't share a MetroCard that has unlimited rides on it with anyone else. Reduced fares are available for people 65 years or older and those with a disability. Children 44 inches and shorter can ride the subway (and bus) for free with an adult.

IS NEW YORK A WALKABLE CITY?

Manhattan is a walker's paradise—every block is densely packed with noteworthy sites and interesting people—and even the most geographically challenged will be able to navigate with ease. The island is 13.4 miles long by 2.3 miles at its widest point. While the older streets of Lower Manhattan can be a confusing tangle, most of the streets are on a simple grid, with streets running east-west and avenues running north-south. The other four boroughs don't have such simple layouts. To figure out how close a destination is, know that twenty city blocks equals one mile. When talking about locations, New Yorkers often refer to cross streets rather than exact addresses. So art lovers are more likely to say the **Museum of Modern Art** (MoMA) is on 53rd between Fifth and Sixth, rather than at its actual address, 11 W. 53rd Street.

WHAT IS THE BEST TIME TO VISIT NEW YORK?

Visitors fill New York City in pretty equal measure year-round, and while locals grouse about the winter (which can be very cold, though not usually too snowy) and summer (very humid), the weather is generally mild and the four seasons distinct. Autumn has the clearest skies and both it and spring are lovely. September and October have the most full-sun days, while July and August regularly have the highest temps (around 85 degrees) and the most humid weather. You'll find the streets a little quieter on summer weekends, when locals do their best to escape to the beaches and mountains.

YOUR QUESTIONS ANSWERED *continued*

HOW DO TAXIS WORK IN NEW YORK CITY?

Taxis are pretty abundant in Manhattan, particularly downtown (there are more than 13,000 of them operating throughout the city). If you're trying to hail a taxi (by moving to the curb and raising one arm—just like in the movies) and you don't see any, try walking to one of the busier avenues (north/south streets) for better luck. Use only licensed, yellow medallion taxis. Unregulated "gypsy" cabs and off-duty car service drivers may approach, but these vehicles may be uninsured and are unmetered— increasing the chance the driver might take your wallet for a ride. Look like a local by trying to hail only available taxis— you can tell it's unoccupied and on duty if the center lights on its roof are lit. If you're traveling with luggage or bulky packages, you can ask the driver to open the trunk. Once inside, simply tell the driver where you're going. Most drivers know the addresses of major sightseeing destinations, but if you're giving a lesser-known address, knowing the cross street is helpful. Some drivers may give you guff about driving to the outer boroughs, but legally, they're required to drive you anywhere within the city limits. Up to four people can ride in a taxi for the same price: $2.50 is the initial fee, plus 40 cents per every fifth of a mile or 40 cents per minute when the taxi is idling. Late-nights and rush hours may incur a small surcharge, and tipping (15-20 percent) is expected. Some taxis have an integrated machine on the back seat that allows you to pay by credit card, though if you plan to do that, its always best to check if it's possible before you get in. Taxi receipts have medallion numbers printed on them, so if you lose something, you can call New York City Taxi & Limousine Commission (*212-227-0700; www.nyc. gov/taxi*) to try and retrieve it.

WHAT ARE NEW YORK'S BOROUGHS?

New York City is made up of five boroughs: Manhattan (the smallest borough landwise and also the most dense; this is what most people have in mind when they think "New York City"), Brooklyn, Queens, the Bronx and Staten Island. Each borough is operated by a separate administrative division of the municipal government and has its own distinct character (Staten Island, accessible only by ferry or the Verrazano-Narrows Bridge from other points in the city, has a remote, suburban feel). Within each are dozens of neighborhoods boasting unique identities of their own, mostly because of their demographic makeup. For example, Williamsburg in Brooklyn is home to both artsy hipsters and one of the largest Orthodox Hasidic Jewish communities in the world—an only-in-New-York-style mix.

CHELSEA/HELL'S KITCHEN/GARMENT DISTRICT

The diverse neighborhood of Chelsea lies to the north of Greenwich Village on Manhattan's west side. Long known as a home to both art galleries and gay culture, the neighborhood is also loved by foodies who frequent the gourmet stalls and restaurants at Chelsea Market, and fitness-minded types who come to Chelsea Piers, a riverfront sports complex containing batting cages, volleyball courts and an ice rink. To the north, hugging the Hudson River, Hell's Kitchen once had a reputation as a crime-ridden, decaying part of the city. Gentrification means that these days, strollers line the sidewalks and brunch at one of the many bistros lining Ninth Avenue is the most common sight. Unfortunately, you won't find ateliers and couture shops in the Garment District, which sits in Midtown between the Javits Convention Center and the Empire State Building—just the warehouses used by garment manufacturers and offices of big and small names in the world of fashion.

WHAT TO SEE

CHELSEA MARKET

75 Ninth Ave., Chelsea, 212-243-6005; www.chelseamarket.com

This sprawling urban marketplace has the stuff to make foodies take notice and picky eaters cry uncle. Once home to the Oreo cookie factory (they also made Fig Newtons and Saltines), Chelsea Market encompasses an entire city block and houses gourmet-goods shops, drool-worthy restaurants and even a few TV studios (Food Network and Oxygen most notably). You better come hungry if you're going to scratch the surface of this gastronomical playland. Calm a nagging sweet tooth with luscious brownies at Fat Witch bakery (*212-419-4824; www.fatwitch.com*) or load up on carbs at Amy's Bread (*212-462-4338; www.amysbread.com*). Fill your pantry with olive oil and pastas at Buon Italia (*212-633-9090; www.buonitalia.com*) or dine on tuna pizza or rack of lamb at Iron Chef Masaharu Morimoto's eponymous restaurant (*212-989-8883; www. morimotonyc.com*). Once you're full, burn off some calories by shopping for housewares at Bowery Kitchen Supply (*212-376-4982; www.bowerykitchens. com*) or Moroccan sconces at Imports from Marrakesh (*212-675-9700; www. importsfrommarrakesh.com*).

Monday-Saturday 8 a.m.-8 p.m., Sunday 10 a.m.-8 p.m.

CHELSEA PIERS

Between 17th and 23rd streets at the Hudson River, Chelsea, 212-336-6666; www.chelseapiers.com

Long a mooring point for luxury liners (the *Titanic* was bound for Chelsea Piers when it struck that iceberg in April 1912), the Hudson River docks fell into a slow but steady decline as the jet-setting lifestyle sank nautical travel. Thanks to a $100 million renovation in the 1990s, Piers 59 through 62 were transformed into a 28-acre sports and entertainment complex boasting a 40-lane bowling alley, golf club (where swingers can tee off on 51-simulated championship courses), ice skating rinks, rock climbing wall, swimming pool, restaurants and a spa.

Hours vary by business.

WHAT ARE NEW YORK CITY'S CAN'T-MISS FIRST VISIT SIGHTS?

Central Park:
The most frequently visited urban park in the United States, Central Park is a tranquil oasis in the heart of Manhattan.

Empire State Building:
As New York's tallest—and most famous—skyscraper, it's no wonder many a movie moment has transpired atop this majestic marvel.

Rockefeller Center:
Many well-known tenants are housed in the center of this 19-building complex, including Radio City Music Hall, NBC studios and the famous Rockefeller Center Christmas tree.

Times Square:
Once a crime-riddled area, today's Times Square is a 24-hour tourist's haven, overflowing with shopping, dining and cultural activities.

DAVID ZWIRNER GALLERIES

525 W. 19th St. (between 10th Avenue and West Street), Chelsea, 212-727-2070; www.davidzwirner.com

David Zwirner Gallery has been in the business of beautiful things for more than 15 years. In just the past few years, it has become one of the largest and best known galleries in New York for pieces by emerging contemporary artists from here and abroad. Zwirner moved from his original locale in Soho to West 19th in Chelsea in 2002; then, in 2006 he expanded that space from 10,000 square feet to 30,000 square feet, stretching it down the block to accommodate up to three simultaneous exhibitions by artists like Tomma Abts, R. Crumb and Raymond Pettibon. With so much space, a visit here can seem more like a museum trip than a gallery stroll, though if you'd like to purchase something off the wall, we're sure Mr. Zwirner would oblige.
Tuesday-Saturday 10 a.m.-6 p.m.

GAGOSIAN GALLERIES

522 W. 21st St., Chelsea, 212-741-1717; 555 W. 24th St., Chelsea, 212-741-1111; www.gagosian.com

Larry Gagosian is considered among the world's biggest players in contemporary art, and because he's got eight galleries scattered around the globe—including two within blocks of each other in Chelsea (a third is located at 980 Madison Avenue, Upper East Side; others are in Beverly Hills, Rome and London)—we're not arguing otherwise. Thanks to rotating exhibitions of post-war American and European mixed media, sculpture, painting and photography, the Gagosian galleries are as much exhibition spaces as they are dealerships. The amount of star power on the walls—the 21st Street location recently exhibited Pablo Picasso, Andy Warhol, Hiroshi Sugimoto, Roy Lichtenstein and Marcel Duchamp in the same show—means these galleries can challenge many museum collections.
Tuesday-Saturday 10 a.m.-6 p.m. West 24th: Monday-Saturday 10 a.m.-6 p.m.

THE JOYCE THEATER

175 Eighth Ave., Chelsea, 212-691-9740; www.joyce.org

The Joyce has supplied a blank canvas in the form of a stage to more than 270 dance companies over its near-30-year existence. Local and international acts, modern and classical styles have all solidified this Chelsea venue as a major player in the avant-garde dance community. Well-established companies such

as Pilobolus, whose body-bending comedic antics leave audiences grinning for days, return year after year to sell-out crowds. Good seats are a given thanks to the intimate 472-seat design of this renovated old-school movie house. If that's still too big a crowd for you, try the theater's sister property, Joyce SoHo (155 Mercer St., Soho, 212-431-9233), which offers a tiny 74-seat performance space along with two rehearsal studios.
Check website for specific company dates.

MACY'S HERALD SQUARE
151 West 34th St., Garment District, 212-695-4400; www.macys.com

They don't call Macy's flagship the "World's Largest Store" without reason. With more than one million square feet of retail space, the shopping mecca might better be described as a small (and sometimes chaotic) city. Nine floors hold an expansive inventory of designer perfumes, handbags, clothing and housewares, plus eateries like Au Bon Pain and Starbucks for refueling. The behemoth also sponsors several holiday extravaganzas every year, most famously the Macy's Thanksgiving Day Parade, when crowds cram the streets to catch glimpses of celebrity-studded floats and balloons as they glide down Broadway and end up in front of the store.
Monday-Thursday 10 a.m.-9:30 p.m., Friday 9 a.m.-10 p.m., Saturday 9 a.m.-11 p.m., Sunday 11 a.m.-8:30 p.m.

MADISON SQUARE GARDEN
4 Penn Plaza, Eighth Avenue between 32nd and 33rd streets (next to Penn Station), Garment District; www.thegarden.com

The Garden is home to two basketball teams (the NBA's Knicks and the WNBA's Liberty) and New York's NHL club (the Rangers), plus a slew of touring music and entertainment acts on nongame days. The current Garden has been standing since 1968, but it's seen three other incarnations dating back to 1879: Two were at Madison Avenue at 26th Street (Madison Square) and a third–known for hosting boxing bouts during the sport's heyday (as depicted in the movie *Cinderella Man*)–was at 50th Street and Eighth Avenue, not far from Times Square. The Garden almost met the wrecking ball again in early 2008, but the plan was scrapped and a renovation of existing facilities was approved instead. The arena accommodates more than four million fans a year for its events, hosting celebrities on stage and in the stands. (A Knicks game alone is a who's who of Hollywood-types and rappers, most notable among them hyper-fan/filmmaker Spike Lee.) Note: Renovations will continue through 2012, but the arena will remain open and fully operational, leaving the Knicks' and Rangers' schedules unaffected.

POSTMASTERS
459 W. 19th St., Chelsea, 212-727-3323; www.postmastersart.com

New technology and new media are the stars of the show at Postmasters, and in the last 23 years this has been the go-to gallery to check out avantgarde rule-benders. So it's perfectly normal that their signature small, outré shows take place in a former garage in Chelsea. A recent 2009 show included In G.O.D. We Trust (the G.O.D. stands for Global Obama Domination) by Kenneth Tin-Kin Hung, featuring a digital video created with media images that hold political

satire using Obama in place of different cultural deities from Jesus Christ to Mohammad to Krishna to Buddha.
Tuesday-Saturday 11 a.m.-6 p.m.

UPRIGHT CITIZENS BRIGADE THEATER

307 W. 26th St. (at Eighth Avenue), Chelsea, 212-366-9176; www.ucbtheatre.com

Created by the comedy troupe of the same name (current members are Matt Besser, Amy Poehler, Ian Roberts and Matt Walsh), UCB made its way to New York from Chicago more than 10 years ago and is now a New York comedic mainstay. The theater showcases a mix of high-profile and up-and-coming talent, and tickets rarely go for more than $10 (Tina Fey, Conan O'Brien and others have performed for $8 or less). UCB often puts on three or four whip-smart improv shows per night, arranging more than 25 shows per week, a feat that's no laughing matter.
Daily. Check website for times and ticket prices.

CHINATOWN/LITTLE ITALY/NOLITA

Your senses will be on high alert when you head downtown and hit Chinatown. The visual and aural assault of crowds haggling for deals on knock-off designer handbags and tchotchkes in crammed retail stalls on Canal Street is only overshadowed by the aromas wafting from the fresh seafood shops. It's your taste buds that reap the real reward, thanks to what seems like an endless array of dim sum and noodle restaurants. If you prefer prosciutto to Peking duck, Little Italy is literally just steps away. It may be more tourist-trap than true Italian nowadays, except during the Feast of San Gennaro festival each September (*www.sangennaro.org*), when it's worth a squeeze through the crowds for a paper bag full of warm zeppoles (fried dough balls with powdered sugar). Nolita (just north of Little Italy, like its name suggests) mixes independent (and often tiny) bars and restaurants with one-of-a-kind boutiques.

CHINATOWN/LITTLE ITALY

Chinatown: Essex, Worth, Grand and East Broadway streets; www.explorechinatown.com. Little Italy: Houston to Canal streets and Lafayette Street to the Bowery; www.littleitalynyc.com

One moment you're picking through rare fruits and examining fresh seafood and the next, you're spooning gelato and sampling chicken parmesan. It's hard not to notice the curious juxtaposition of Chinatown and Little Italy—two neighborhoods that couldn't be more

---

WHAT IS THE NEWEST ATTRACTION IN NEW YORK CITY?

High Line:
Built upon an elevated railroad track which had been out of commission for nearly 20 years, this park offers New Yorkers an unexpected green space that runs from the Meatpacking District to Chelsea, and stretches one-and-a-half miles up the island's West Side, with another stretch completed in 2010.

different and that have somehow morphed into one. It's tempting to make food the focus of your excursion to these ethnic enclaves (for good reason), but there is so much more to these diverse neighborhoods. In Chinatown, stop at Chatham Square to pose by the Kim Lau Memorial Arch traditional Chinatown gate or head for Great World Inc. (*32 E. Broadway, 212-925-6606*), a video store that stocks thousands of martial arts titles. In Little Italy, get a pie at the city's oldest pizza joint (it's been around since 1905) at Lombardi's (*32 Spring St., 212-941-7994: www.lombardisoriginalpizza.com*) and be sure to pay a visit to St. Patrick's Old Cathedral (*263 Mulberry St., 212-226-8075; www.oldcathedral.org*), the original St. Pat's.

EAST VILLAGE/LOWER EAST SIDE

Long associated with the immigrants and working class who occupied the tenements here (especially Eastern European Jews), the Lower East Side's landscape changed in the 1990s to one with more art galleries, alt-rock venues, and hipster-haunt restaurants and bars than cheap apartments and kosher delis. The East Village was once considered a part of this low-income neighborhood, but the area east of the Bowery from Houston to 14th streets eventually developed a counter-culture vibe where artists and activists such as Andy Warhol, Keith Haring, Abbie Hoffman and The Velvet Underground made names for themselves. Gentrification—most notably by ever-expanding New York University—has led to a shift in the arts scene to the Williamsburg section of Brooklyn and other parts of the city.

WHAT TO SEE

ARLENE'S GROCERY

95 Stanton St. (between Orchard and Ludlow streets), Lower East Side, 212-995-1652; www.arlenesgrocery.net

It used to be a bodega, but since the mid-1990s Arlene's Grocery and the adjoining former butcher shop have been the go-to spots to catch rising stars on the music scene, not for buying cartons of milk. There are live performances of everything from country-western to hard rock, and if you're lucky you'll catch a band like the Strokes (before anyone's heard of them) for a measly $8 or $10 cover. The front Butcher Bar is always free—something the hipster crowd that keeps the place packed enjoys—and every Monday night you can join in rock 'n' roll karaoke (no cover).

Check website for performance calendar.

BOWERY BALLROOM

6 Delancey St. (at the Bowery), Lower East Side, 212-533-2111; www.boweryballroom.com

Bowery and Ballroom are two words paired together that longtime New Yorkers might have once considered an oxymoron. But this long down-and-out neighborhood has seen massive gentrification in the past decade and is now home to what many consider to be the best music venue in the city. You won't find anyone doing the waltz or the cha-cha here, but the sound is great, the bar is a happening spot in its own right and the space plays host to indie acts ranging from country-rock and folksy to the alternative Breeders. The cash-only box office is located at Mercury Lounge (*217 E. Houston St.*).

Check website for calendar of events.

WHICH ARE NEW YORK CITY'S TOP MUSEUMS?

American Museum of Natural History:
One of the largest natural history institutions in the world, this enormous Upper West Side museum is famous for its dinosaur exhibits.

Metropolitan Museum of Art:
More than two million works of art are housed in this Gothic-Revival building founded in 1870.

Solomon R. Guggenheim Museum:
Thousands flock to this contemporary and modern art museum for both its permanent collection (including works by Pablo Picasso and Henri Matisse) and to take in Frank Lloyd Wright's awesome creation.

Whitney Museum of American Art:
The museum frequently purchases works from up-and-comers to keep its ever-changing collection fresh.

LOWER EAST SIDE TENEMENT MUSEUM

103 Orchard St., Lower East Side, 212-431-0233; www.tenement.org

Looking to profit from the rising number of immigrants flooding New York in the mid-1800s, Lukas Glockner opened a cheap tenement at 97 Orchard Street to house them. Between 1863 and 1935, more than 7,000 tenants—primarily the poor and working class—occupied his sparse Lower East Side apartment building. It later fell into disrepair, but was refurbished and opened as a museum in 1988—the first of its kind. Visitors take guided tours to learn about the immigrant experience and the traditions they brought with them from all over the world.

Building tours: adults $20, students and seniors $15, children under 5 free. Daily 10 a.m.-6 p.m.

WEBSTER HALL

125 E. 11th St., East Village, 212-353-1600; www.websterhall.com

In 2008 the New York Preservation Society voted to name Webster Hall a landmark, and with good reason: The venue's been around since 1886, and many consider it the country's first nightclub. Frequented by everyone from Marcel DuChamp to Nine Inch Nails, it sure would be something if the walls of Webster Hall could talk. Its incarnations have included a bacchanal parlor, a recording studio and the Ritz nightclub in the 1980s, when it was considered one of the best places to see live music in New York City (Tina Turner, Eric Clapton and Prince have all played here). Nowadays, it's both a live music venue and a dance club. The club is open on Thursday, Friday and/or Saturday nights—beware, though, the crowd is heavy on college students who can dance.

Check website for calendar of events.

BOWLING GREEN

Broadway and Whitehall Street, Battery Park

This small, wedge-shaped plaza has at least two claims to historical fame. In 1626, it was the spot where Dutch governor Peter Minuit allegedly purchased Manhattan for $24 worth of goods, leading some to call this grassy parcel the birthplace of New York. It also happens to be New York City's first official park. Today, most visitors know it as the home of the 7,000 pound bronze sculpture *Charging Bull*. The bull represents financial optimism when stock prices are rising (contrasted with a bear market, when prices are falling). According to its sculptor, Arturo Di Modica, it also represents

HIGHLIGHT

WHAT ARE SOME EXAMPLES OF GREAT ARCHITECHTURE IN NEW YORK CITY?

CHRYSLER BUILDING
Designed to house the motorcar company's offices, architect William Van Alen added automotive accents such as metal hubcaps and radiator-cap gargoyles to the structure's façade.

FLATIRON BUILDING
One of the city's iconic buildings, this Beaux Arts beauty made of limestone and terra cotta measures an amazingly slim six-and-a-half feet wide at its apex.

GRAND CENTRAL TERMINAL
This architectural gem is both a bustling transportation center, and a lively retail and dining district.

THE PLAZA
The iconic hotel recently underwent a multi-million dollar renovation, while still keeping certain treasures in tact, like the chandelier-dripping lobby where afternoon tea is served.

ST. PATRICK'S CATHEDRAL
The largest gothic-style Catholic cathedral in the United States is well known for its stunning architecture, including altars designed by Tiffany & Co.

WOOLWORTH BUILDING
Coined the "cathedral of commerce," this Gothic-style headquarter's opening was celebrated by President Wilson, who pushed a button in the White House to illuminate each floor.

"the strength, power and hope of the American people for the future." He first installed the piece illegally next to the New York Stock Exchange as guerrilla art, and it was impounded by police. After a public outcry, it was placed—legally this time—at its current location.

FINANCIAL DISTRICT/BATTERY PARK CITY

There's more to the downtown Financial District than the New York Stock Exchange and a bunch of stiff suits. Even if it's a bear market, Wall Street's power inspires optimism, and if things are looking up, you can drop a pretty penny at South Street Seaport's touristy shops and restaurants. The area is also a somber stop for visitors who want a look at Ground Zero—and surrounding street vendors are at the ready, hawking everything from commemorative snow globes to t-shirts. A good place to escape them is adjacent Battery Park City, a planned community on the southern tip of Manhattan where you'll find sweeping views of New York Harbor and the Statue of Liberty.

WHAT TO SEE

CASTLE CLINTON NATIONAL MONUMENT

Battery Park at New York Harbor, 212-344-7220; www.nps.gov/cacl

This is where you hop the ferry to Ellis Island and the Statue of Liberty. Arguably one of New York's most storied sights, this monument, completed in 1811, began as a fort for protecting the island from British invasion during the War of 1812. The large circular structure was then converted into a theater where concerts and scientific demonstrations frequently got top billing. After 30 years as an entertainment venue, the building once again changed purposes, becoming an immigrant-landing depot until Ellis Island opened in the 1890s. A stint as an aquarium followed before the site was converted into a national monument where you can eat a picnic lunch, take a guided tour and get the ferry to Ellis Island and the Statue of Liberty.

Daily 8:30 a.m.-5 p.m.

ELLIS ISLAND

212-561-4588; www.ellisisland.org

More than 40 percent of Americans can trace their ancestors' first steps on U.S. soil to the country's first federal immigration station, which opened in the shadow of the Statue of Liberty in 1892. Roughly 12 million immigrants seeking the American dream passed through here before the station closed in 1954. Now it's open to visitors as an interactive museum, where you can take a self-guided tour of the grounds and check out photographs, artifacts and search records to locate family members.

Daily 9 a.m.-5:15 p.m. Check website for seasonal changes in hours.

GROUND ZERO

Lower Manhattan, bound by the West Side Highway and Vesey, Liberty and Church streets, Financial District

Ten years after the attacks of September 11, 2001, the old World Trade Center site is alive with the sound of jackhammers and bulldozers as new buildings begin to take shape against lower Manhattan's skyline. The first completed building, the office complex at 7 World Trade Center, opened its doors in May 2006. But for the most part, the site is still shrouded by chain link fences and barricades. The National September 11 Memorial and Museum is scheduled for a 2011 opening, but in the meantime, there are a variety of ways to pay tribute and recognize the events of September 11th. Pedestrian bridges across

West Street, located on both Liberty and Vesey streets, provide a view of the site, as does the PATH train station and the World Financial Center in nearby Battery Park. The Tribute WTC Visitor Center (*120 Liberty St., 866-737-1184; www.tributewtc.org*) houses numerous artifacts and highlights the stories of those lost during the tragedy.

SOUTH STREET SEAPORT

Fulton and South streets, Pier 17, Financial District, 212-732-7678; www.southstreetseaport.com

Part mall, part historic landmark, Lower Manhattan's South Street Seaport has a little something for everyone. In the shopping center you'll find all the usual suspects (Abercrombie & Fitch, Bath and Body Works, Gap, Victoria's Secret) plus a TKTS discount ticket booth, in addition to restaurants like the Pan-Asian Pacific Grill and food-court fare including Subway sandwiches and pizza. It's the South Street Seaport Museum, however, that really captures the spirit of the former commercial and transportation hub. The museum boasts an extensive collection of luxury liner memorabilia and visitors can see a scale model of the *Titanic*. The site also features a recreated working paper press that makes cards and stationery to order, printed on 19th century treadle-powered equipment.

Monday-Saturday 10 a.m.-9 p.m., Sunday 11 a.m.-8 p.m. Restaurants and bars have extended hours.

STATEN ISLAND FERRY

1 Whitehall St., Battery Park, 718-815-2628; www.nyc.gov

Commutes aren't supposed to be romantic, but that's the best way to describe the 5.2-mile run between St. George Terminal in Staten Island and the Whitehall Terminal in lower Manhattan. Pragmatists would point out that the ferries provide Staten Islanders with free (that's right, free!) transportation to their Manhattan day jobs. Those with a little imagination know the 25-minute ride is a tourist treasure, too, far more a sightseeing pleasure cruise than a weary work trip. From the decks, passengers can take in picturesque views of the Statue of Liberty, Ellis Island and Manhattan's scraper-filled skyline.

Check website for schedule.

STATUE OF LIBERTY

Liberty Island, 212-363-3200; www.nps.gov/stli

Perhaps the most enduring symbol of America's promise of freedom and democracy, the Liberty Enlightening the World statue (its formal name) has served as a beacon welcoming immigrants and visitors for more than 120 years. A gift of friendship from the French, the monument was dedicated on October 28, 1886, and stands more than 305 feet from the ground to the top of the torch. Designer Frederic-Auguste Bartholdi placed several symbolic touches throughout the monument: The seven rays of Lady Liberty's crown represent the seven seas and continents of the world, and the tablet she holds in her left hand reads in Roman numerals "July 4, 1776." The lady was restored for her centennial on July 2, 1986. Visitors are allowed onto the Statue's observation deck and can also get an inside view through a glass ceiling with a new lighting and video system.

Admission: adults $12, seniors $10, children 4-12 $5, children 3 and under free. Hours are adjusted seasonally. Ferries run daily from 9 a.m.-5 p.m. from Castle Clinton in Battery Park. Visit www.statuecruises.com for more information.

WALL STREET

Between Broadway and South Street near the East River, Financial District

A flurry of crisp business suits and Blackberrys, Wall Street is a stretch of pavement that has become synonymous with the U.S. financial industry. The street begins at Broadway, where you'll find Trinity Church, and stretches east to the East River. Named for the blockade constructed by Dutch colonists to protect themselves from British attacks, today Wall Street is known far better as the home of financially and historically relevant sights, including the New York Stock Exchange and Federal Hall. The NYSE, also known as the "Big Board," is the largest exchange in the world based on the value of its securities. As the nation's first capitol, Federal Hall was the sight of George Washington's inauguration, the first congressional meeting and the signing of the Bill of Rights. Since 9/11, the Exchange is no longer open to the public. You can, however, tour the Federal Reserve Bank (*33 Liberty Street, 212-720-5000; www.newyorkfed.org*), where about a quarter of the world's gold is stored, by calling ahead for tickets at least one month in advance. You can also learn more about the history of Wall Street at the Museum of American Finance (*48 Wall Street, at Williams Street, 212-908-4110; www.moaf.org*), located in the former headquarters of the Bank of New York. Exhibits include a history of money, a timeline on the credit crisis and more. Next, pay a visit to Trinity Church (*Broadway at Wall Street, 212-602-0800; www.trinitywallstreet.org*) and its sister church, St. Paul's Chapel (*five blocks north on Broadway, 212-233-4164; www.stpaulschapel.org*), two of the most historic churches in the United States—George Washington worshipped at St. Paul's. The Trinity Courtyard is a lovely patch of green inside the financial district, where many bankers bring their lunches. Its famous graveyard contains the remains of Alexander Hamilton.

Federal Reserve: Admission: Free. Monday-Friday 9 a.m.-5 p.m. Tours are every hour on the half hour. Last tour is at 3:30 p.m. Museum of American Finance: Admission: adults $8, students and seniors $5, children 6 and under free. Tuesday-Saturday 10 a.m.-4 p.m. (until 6:00 p.m. Wednesday from July-October). Trinity Church: Admission: Free. Monday-Friday 7 a.m.-6 p.m., Saturday 8 a.m-4 p.m., Sunday 7 a.m.-4 p.m. Hours for the churchyard vary with the season. During daylight-savings time, the churchyard remains open until 5 p.m., weather permitting; otherwise, it closes at 4 p.m. during the week and at 3 p.m. on weekends. St. Paul's Chapel: Admission: Free. Monday-Friday 10 a.m.-6 p.m., Saturday 10 a.m.-4 p.m., Sunday 7 a.m.-3 p.m. Churchyard: Admission: Free. Monday-Saturday 10 a.m.-4 p.m. (until 5:30 during daylight savings), Sunday 7 a.m.-3:30 p.m.

GREENWICH VILLAGE/SOHO/WEST VILLAGE

Once the center of New York's bohemian scene, Greenwich Village is a little less counter-culture these days, but no less colorful. It's anchored at the southern tip of Fifth Avenue by Washington Square Park, where street performers intermingle with protestors and chess players. The giant arch at its center is one of New York City's most recognizable symbols. Soho is the neighborhood south of Houston Street, which can be summed up in one word: shopping. Designers such as Anna Sui and John Varvatos mix it up with the likes of the Apple Store and Bloomingdale's, and the crowds never cease. Things are a little more diverse between Sixth Avenue and the Hudson River in the West Village, where the cobblestone streets are lined with bars, bistros and boutiques. The neighborhood has long been famous as a home for artists and writers both real (Dylan Thomas, Charlie Parker) and fictional.

WHAT TO SEE

WOOLWORTH BUILDING
233 Broadway, Financial District

This Gothic-style skyscraper towering 792 feet above Manhattan's Financial District was built to house the now-defunct five-and-dime's headquarters. Funded completely with cash, the building was completed in 1913 and was the tallest in the world until the 927-feet tall 40 Wall Street came along in 1930. Its interior features a cruciform floor plan with vaulted ceilings, and boasts several humorous gargoyles depicting the building's key players, including Mr. Woolworth counting his dimes and architect Cass Gilbert holding a model of the building. Coined the "cathedral of commerce," its opening was celebrated by President Wilson, who pushed a button in the White House to illuminate each floor and the building's façade. Sold by the Woolworth Company in 1998, the building now houses the New York University School of Continuing and Professional Studies' Center for Global Affairs, in addition to other tenants.

ANGELIKA FILM CENTER & CAFÉ
18 W. Houston St., Soho, 212-995-2000; www.angelikafilmcenter.com

Check out the best in independent and foreign fare at Soho's six-screen Angelika Film Center. Its spacious café is a neighborhood favorite, where you don't need a ticket stub to get in and enjoy the gourmet pastries and coffee in addition to standard movie-musts like popcorn and Milk Duds. Just be prepared for the rumble—not from the onscreen action, but from the subway tracks running below the theater.

Check website for ticket information. Café open from beginning of the first show of the day to the beginning of the last.

CITY WINERY
155 Varick St. (between Spring and Vandam streets), Soho, 212-608-0555; www.citywinery.com

Big name musical guests, delicious food and a wine selection more than 500 bottles deep puts City Winery at the top of the charts for unique entertainment venues in Manhattan. The 21,000-square-foot space epitomizes industrial chic with exposed brick walls and splintery wood columns. The functioning winery is sequestered in a back room. Instead of waiters, City Winery has wine stewards to help select that perfect bottle of cabernet or pinot. Plates of imported salumi and fromage act as tasty accoutrements to the wine—and keep you from getting too tipsy. Then there's the music. A full stage and state-of-the-art sound system transform the soaring space into an intimate concert hall where acts like Steve Earle and Lisa Loeb make you feel less citified and more wine-country cool.

Check website for calendar of events.

STRAND BOOKSTORE
828 Broadway, Greenwich Village, 212-473-1452; www.strandbooks.com

Named after the famous London street, this independent bookstore was just one of 48 booksellers occupying New York's famous "Book Row" in the late 1920s. Today, the Strand is the only one left. The shop, which moved to its current location from Fourth Avenue in the 1950s, contains 18 miles of shelves stocked with new and used books, in addition to NYC's largest collection of rare books (such as the first

edition of *Alice's Adventures in Wonderland* by Lewis Carroll, which is on sale for $15,000). The expansive store also hosts author signings and events.
Monday-Saturday 9:30 a.m.-10:30 p.m., Sunday 11 a.m.-10:30 p.m.

VILLAGE VANGUARD
178 Seventh Ave. South, Greenwich Village, 212-255-4037; www.villagevanguard.com

John Coltrane and Wynton Marsalis recorded in the basement of the Village Vanguard, and "Live at the Vanguard" albums have become synonymous with "making it" among jazz artists. The space opened in 1935, first showcasing bohemian performers like Pete Seeger before switching strictly to jazz. Today, the walls of the Vanguard are adorned with a fading black-and-white mosaic of the greats who've performed here, and jazz connoisseurs gather around small cocktail tables to hear the new vanguard emerging in the wedge-shaped room renowned for its acoustics. Call ahead to make a reservation—just leave the relevant information on the answering machine, and you'll be set.
Daily 8 p.m.

WASHINGTON SQUARE PARK
West Fourth and MacDougal Streets, Greenwich Village; www.nycgovparks.org

This potter's field-turned-park was once home to the public gallows, but today the hanging around is much more leisurely. Located in the heart of Greenwich Village, this green space is not only a popular haunt for sunbathing students from adjacent New York University, but a haven for chess players and street performers. The park's most famous landmark, Washington Arch, an Arc de Triomphe replica, was built between 1890 and 1892 to replace a wooden arch that had been built to commemorate the centennial of George Washington's inauguration. In the 1960s, the park was a popular gathering spot for hippies and artists. Today, it's currently a perfect spot for a little New York City people-watching.
Daily 6 a.m.-1 a.m.

MIDTOWN/MIDTOWN EAST

Midtown Manhattan is just that—the middle of the island (from 34th to 59th streets), and with all this bit of prime real estate has going on, it may as well be the center of the universe. This is where you'll find the Empire State Building, Chrysler Building, Rockefeller Center and Madison Square Garden. The business district—from the 40s up and along the Avenue of the Americas, a.k.a. Sixth Avenue—is where some of the world's most influential advertising, financial and media companies have their headquarters. Midtown East, between the East River and Madison Avenue, is home to the United Nations and Grand Central Terminal.

WHAT TO SEE

BRYANT PARK
Between 40th and 42nd streets and Fifth and Sixth avenues, Midtown; www.bryantpark.org

The park's central location (just one block from Times Square), free entertainment all summer long and free wireless Internet access makes it very popular with office workers and tourists alike. Entertainment includes concerts and movies on Monday nights after dusk. Bring a blanket and picnic and come early—the lawn starts filling up quickly after 5 p.m. The park also includes four 'wichcraft kiosks, where you can sample some of chef Tom Colicchio's gourmet sandwiches, soups and salads, or simply grab a coffee, ice cream or hot chocolate. A favorite spot in the park is the Reading Room, an open-air library where you can sit and read books and magazines for free. The Pond is a free ice skating rink in winter.

Daily. January-March, 7 a.m.-7 p.m.; January, until 10 p.m. (while the pond is open); March, until 8 p.m. after Daylight Saving change; April, 7 a.m.-10 p.m.; May-September, 7 a.m.-11 p.m.; October, 7 a.m.-8 p.m.; November-December, 7 a.m.-10 p.m.

CARNEGIE HALL

881 Seventh Ave., Midtown, 212-247-7800;
www.carnegiehall.org

If someone asks you how to get to Carnegie Hall, you probably already know the answer: practice. The subject to one of the city's most tired jokes, this famous Midtown concert hall has played host to some of the most well-practiced classical, pop and jazz musicians of the last century, including Maria Callas, Sergei Rachmaninoff, Bob Dylan, Judy Garland, Frank Sinatra and Billie Holiday. Built by and named after wealthy businessman and philanthropist Andrew Carnegie, this six-story structure with an Italian Renaissance façade of terra cotta and brick boasts not one, but three performance spaces. The Hall faced demolition in 1960 before the city bought it for $5 million. Concert seasons run October through June. Tours are also available during that time.

Box office: September-June, Monday-Saturday 11 a.m.-6 p.m., Sunday noon-6 p.m.; July-August, Monday-Thursday 9 a.m.-6 p.m.

CHRYSLER BUILDING

405 Lexington Ave., Midtown

One of the most iconic examples of Art Deco architecture, the Chrysler Building rises more than 1,000 feet (77 stories) above Lexington Avenue and 42nd Street. Designed to house the motorcar company's offices, architect William Van Alen added automotive accents like metal hubcaps, car fenders and radia-tor-cap gargoyles to the structure's façade. Briefly the tallest skyscraper in the world, it was soon eclipsed by the taller Empire State Building. The Chrysler is no longer owned or occupied by the automaker; a 90-percent stake in the structure was purchased in 2008 by the Abu Dhabi Invest Council for $800 million. (Its largest tenants include the law firm Blank Rome LLP and YES Network, the cable television operation of the New York Yankees.) Though there are no guided tours of the edifice, the lobby is open to visitors who wish to gaze at the ceiling fresco dotted with depictions of buildings, airplanes and the Chrysler assembly line.

EMPIRE STATE BUILDING

350 Fifth Ave., Midtown, 212-736-3100; www.esbnyc.com

King Kong perched atop its lofty spire. Cary Grant and Deborah Kerr made the observation deck a quintessential spot for romantics in 1957's *An Affair to Remember.* As New York's tallest—and most famous—skyscraper, it's no wonder many a movie moment has transpired atop this majestic marvel. Constructed shortly after its Art Deco cousin the Chrysler Building, the Empire State Building stands 1,224 feet tall—that's 1,860 steps to the top if you were thinking about climbing it on foot—with a design inspired by the simple pencil. Observatories on the 86th and 102nd floors, open year-round, promise an unparalleled view of the Big Apple.

Admission: adults $20, seniors $18, children 6-12 $14, children 5 and under free. Observatory hours: Daily 8 a.m.-2 a.m.

FAO SCHWARZ
767 Fifth Ave., Midtown, 212-644-9400; www.fao.com

Kids big and small will have a blast at the 50,000-square-foot playland that serves as the flagship for the famous high-end toy giant. (Yes, you can dance on the huge floor piano like Tom Hanks did in the movie *Big*.) The oldest and swankiest toy store in the country moved to its current Fifth Avenue location in 1986, where three floors are stuffed to the rafters with plush stuffed animals, dolls, toy cars and books. Kids can even create their own playthings at toy factories dedicated to Hot Wheels, Madame Alexander Dolls and Barbie.

Monday-Thursday 10 a.m.-7 p.m., Friday-Saturday 10 a.m.-8 p.m., Sunday 11 a.m.-6 p.m.

GRAND CENTRAL TERMINAL
87 E. 42nd St., Midtown, 212-340-2583; www.grandcentralterminal.com

This Beaux Arts-style behemoth is more than just a place to hop a train. Originally constructed in 1871 at the behest of Cornelius Vanderbilt, then rebuilt between 1903 and 1913, Grand Central Terminal is an architectural gem, a bustling transportation center, and a lively retail and dining district. The station's expansive main concourse—with its celestial ceiling (keep your eyes peeled for backwards constellations) and acorn and oak-leaf decorations (symbols of the Vanderbilt family)—is by far the building's most iconic section. Whether you're waiting for a train or not, stop in for a drink at the Campbell Apartment, the private office of 1920's tycoon John W. Campbell, which has been restored and turned into a handsome lounge, or have a bite in one of the many restaurants, including American brasserie Métrazur (*212-687-4600; www.charliepalmer.com*), the landmark Oyster Bar and Restaurant (*212-490-6650; www.oysterbarny.com*) or Cipriani Dolci (*212-973-0999; www.cipriani.com*), an outpost of the famous New York restaurant dynasty that invented the Bellini (you can have one here) and which serves tasty beef carpaccio and hearty pastas.

MUSEUM OF MODERN ART (MOMA)
11 W. 53rd St., Midtown, 212-708-9400; www.moma.org

Modern art skeptics should think twice before discounting a visit to this pioneer institution. Since 1929, MoMA has harbored one of the most impressive contemporary art collections in the world. Thanks to a recent $425 million face-lift spearheaded by Yoshio Taniguchi, the museum's exhibition space has nearly doubled in size, allowing for large-scale installations as well as a devoted education and research facility. Famous works lurk around every bend in the museum. You may find yourself gazing at Monet's *Water Lilies* one moment and Van Gogh's *The Starry Night* the next. Opt for a personalized audio tour if you think you'll be lost on the contemporary aesthetic. If modern art still isn't your thing, come for the academic programs, film screenings—there are roughly 22,000 films in house—and the food. A meal at chef Gabriel Kreuther's onsite restaurant The Modern is a fine finish to an exceptionally avant-garde afternoon. *Admission: adults $20, seniors $16, students $12, children 16 and under free. Sunday-Monday, Wednesday-Thursday, Saturday 10:30 a.m.-5:30 p.m., Friday 10:30 a.m.-8 p.m.*

NEW YORK PUBLIC LIBRARY

Fifth Avenue at 42nd Street, Midtown, 917-390-0800; www.nypl.org

It took 500 workers two years to dismantle Fifth Avenue's Croton Reservoir (New York City's main water source), but once they were finished in 1902, the coast was clear for New York's first truly public library. This majestic Beaux Arts-style building (and the largest marble structure constructed in the U.S.) is also known as the Humanities and Social Sciences Library. Guarded by marble lions Patience and Fortitude, the library's initial collections were a conglomerate of materials from John Jacob Astor's and James Lenox's failing libraries. The library now has four major research libraries and 87 branches spread throughout the city. Most of the materials are free to use onsite and there are two free guided tours (Monday-Saturday at 11 a.m. and 2 p.m. and Sunday at 2 p.m.). The library also hosts a variety of lectures, author readings and wonderful special exhibitions; check the website for a calendar of events.

Monday, Thursday-Saturday 10 a.m.-6 p.m., Tuesday-Wednesday 10 a.m.-9 p.m., Sunday 1 p.m.-5 p.m. Admission: Free.

THE PLAZA

Fifth Avenue at Central Park South, Midtown, 212-759-3000; www.theplaza.com

This famous Beaux Arts hotel—built in 1907 for $12.5 million—is an iconic New York landmark that's played host to a number of movie production sets. The Plaza made its proper film debut in Alfred Hitchcock's *North by Northwest* and has appeared in *The Way We Were* and *The Great Gatsby*. It has also had its share of famous guests; perhaps most famous is the fictional Eloise from the beloved children's books by Kay Thompson. The iconic hotel, located at the picturesque corner of Central Park and Fifth Avenue, recently underwent a staggering $400 million renovation and now boasts 182 condos meant for permanent residence in addition to 282 guest rooms, which come complete with a white-gloved butler on each floor and a touch-screen panel for room customization. If a stay here isn't an option, don't fret: You can still have afternoon tea in the lovely lobby. The legendary Oak Room also remains.

RADIO CITY MUSIC HALL

1260 Avenue of the Americas, Midtown, 212-307-7171; www.radiocity.com

This venue drips with stardom, thanks to the many luminaries who have graced the Great Stage (among them the Dalai Lama, Bill Cosby and Frank Sinatra), not to mention those leggy bastions of Americana, the Radio City Rockettes. Some stars show up to perform, others to receive accolades at the Grammys, the Tonys or the MTV Video Music Awards, which have all been held here. The annual Radio City Christmas Spectacular starring the Rockettes sells out quickly every year for a reason—it's just plain holiday fun, so buy tickets far in advance if you're in town during Christmas. Check the website for performance information.

Tour tickets: adults $18.50, seniors $15, children 12 and under $10. Tours: Daily 11 a.m.-3 p.m. Box office: Monday-Saturday 11:30 a.m.-6 p.m.

ROCKEFELLER CENTER

From Fifth to Seventh Avenues, between 47th and 51st streets, Midtown, 212-632-3975; www.rockefellercenter.com

John D. Rockefeller leased this space in the heart of Midtown from Columbia University in 1928 hoping to create a new home for The Metropolitan Opera. Though his plans were derailed by the Great Depression, today Rockefeller Center is a bustling 19-building complex full of shops, restaurants and offices. Many well-known tenants are housed in the center, including Radio City Music Hall, NBC studios and the famous Rockefeller Center Christmas tree, for which an elaborate lighting ceremony is held and televised to kick off the holiday season each year. (Insider tip: The Top of the Rock observation decks at 30 Rockefeller Center on the 67th, 69th and 70th floors offer expansive views of Manhattan and are often less crowded than the Empire State Building observation deck.) Other popular activities include the NBC Studio Tour (peek backstage at *Saturday Night Live*, *Late Night with Jimmy Fallon* and more), *Today* show tapings and wintertime skating in the plaza's famous ice rink.

Concourse hours: Daily 7 a.m.-midnight. NBC Studio Tour: adults $19.25, children 6-12 and seniors $16.25. Monday-Thursday 8:30 a.m.-4:30 p.m. (departs every 30 minutes), Friday-Saturday 9:30 a.m.-5:30 p.m. (departs every 15 minutes), Sunday 9:30 a.m.-4:30 p.m. (departs every 15 minutes).

ST. PATRICK'S CATHEDRAL

14 E. 51st St., Midtown, 212-753-2261; www.saintpatrickscathedral.org

Opened in 1879, St. Patrick's Cathedral is the largest gothic-style Catholic cathedral in the United States and the seat of the Archbishop of New York. Though a popular tourist attraction (call 212-355-2749, extension 409, to set up a volunteer-guided tour, or just stop in to have a look by yourself), this ornate place of worship still hosts weekly masses. Located in Midtown and facing Rockefeller Center, the cathedral is well known for its stunning architecture—including its beautiful rose window, a pieta which is three times the size of Michelangelo's, and altars designed by Tiffany & Co.

Daily 6:30 a.m.-8:45 p.m.

UNITED NATIONS

First Avenue at 46th Street, Midtown East, 212-963-8687; www.un.org

The 18-acre headquarters of this peacekeeping organization isn't technically in New York, but situated atop international territory belonging to all member countries. The complex encompasses four buildings, one of which is the Secretariat, an iconic, 39-story structure with a green-glass-curtained exterior. Tours of the U.N. are available Monday through Friday and take visitors through various council chambers and the General Assembly Hall. *Tour tickets: adults $16, seniors and students $11, children 5-12 $9. Tour hours: Monday-Friday 9:45 a.m.-4:45 p.m. (Tours may be limited during debates of the General Assembly from mid-September to mid-October.)*

THEATER DISTRICT/TIMES SQUARE

Who hasn't watched—at least on television—the ball drop in Times Square on New Year's Eve? Once a seedy, crime-plagued pocket of peep-shows and adult movie theaters, Times Square is now more family friendly than down-and-out, catering to mobs of tourists visiting the G-rated retail flagships of Hershey, Toys 'R' Us and the like. The adjacent Theater District is where the lights of Broadway theater marquees illuminate what's affectionately known as the Great White Way.

WHAT TO SEE

B.B. KING BLUES CLUB & GRILL

237 W. 42nd St. (between Seventh and Eighth avenues), Times Square, 212-997-4144; www.bbkingblues.com

This supper club is probably your best bet to catch a blues legend coming through town—everyone from Taj Mahal to Buddy Guy plays here. Plenty of quirkier acts take the stage, too—from The Misfits, Ghostface Killah and KC and the Sunshine Band to a host of tribute bands playing homage to the likes of George Harrison, the Eagles and Bruce Springsteen. There's a Beatles tribute brunch on Saturday and a gospel brunch on Sunday, and a bit of a touristy vibe thanks to the gift shop and saxophone-shaped beer taps. Don't let that sway you from hitting one of the best spots in the city to catch a host of different kinds of music.

Check website for calendar of events.

IRIDIUM JAZZ CLUB

1650 Broadway, Theater District, 212-582-2121; www.iridiumjazzclub.com

Unlike many of New York's most beloved music venues, the Iridium's history only goes back fifteen years. But the history lesson at this subterranean Theater District supper club is on the stage. Greats from bygone eras including drummer Louis Hayes and Thelonious Monk, Jr. sometimes stop in to jam for an entire weekend. Ticket prices vary, and make sure to read the fine print as weekend shows often entail a food and drink minimum (usually $10 or $15 per person).

Check website for specific shows and times.

NEW AMSTERDAM THEATER

214 W. 42nd St., Times Square, 212-282-2900; www.newyorkcitytheatre.com

Smack in the heart of Times Square, this theater has a history as tumultuous as the city's, weathering the cultural and economic ups and downs of fickle New York. But the circle of life here saw an upturn when Disney took over and began to rehab the New Amsterdam in 1993 for its eventual launch of *The Lion King* in 1998 (the show ran until 2006). Now it's home to Disney's *Mary Poppins*. Balcony dwellers, mind the flying umbrellas.

Check website for show times.

ROSELAND BALLROOM

239 W. 52nd St. (between Broadway and Eighth Avenue), Times Square, 212-247-0200; www.roselandballroom.com

The Roseland has been around since 1919, and has pretty much seen it all. It started out a block away on East 51st Street as a dance club where big-band-era groups played. Quirkiness was a large part of its original appeal, too: Everything from marathon dancing and staged female prize fights were held here before more formal dancing took center stage. In 1956, Roseland Ballroom moved to its current location, a former ice skating rink. Today, the 3,500-person standing-room-only venue is mostly popular with indie rockers and as a site for special events—when the hall gets a custom makeover for the occasion, whether it's a Thai boxing match, a premiere party for shows like Entourage or a tattoo convention.

Check website for calendar of events.

BILLY ELLIOT

Imperial Theatre, 249 W. 45th St. (between Broadway and Eighth Avenue), 212-239-6200; www.billyelliotbroadway.com

It's hard to forget the endearing 2000 movie about a small-town, blue-collar boy with big dreams of being a ballet dancer and now the musical based on the movie is exploding, with ten 2009 Tony Award wins including Best New Musical. With director Stephen Daldry (The Reader), who also directed Jamie Bell in the movie; choreographer Peter Darling and a score from none other than Sir Elton John, you'll see why this musical is earning raves.

Admission: $41.50-$136.50. Tuesday 7 p.m., Wednesday 2 p.m., Thursday and Friday 8 p.m., Saturday 2 p.m. and 8 p.m., Sunday 2 p.m. and 7:30 p.m.

TIMES SQUARE

Broadway and Seventh Avenue, Times Square, 212-768-1560; www.timessquarenyc.org

More than one million people flock to the "crossroads of the world" each year to ring in the New Year by seeing the ball drop. But there's plenty to see and do in this bustling neighborhood the other 364 days of the year. Named in honor of *The New York Times* (the iconic newspaper's offices were once located at the intersection of Seventh Avenue, Broadway and 42nd Street), Times Square is full of non-stop activity, overflowing with shopping, dining, corporate offices (everyone from Morgan Stanley to MTV), television studios (*Good Morning America*) and, of course, theater. Restaurant Row (West 46th Street between Broadway and Ninth Avenue) provides eclectic options from Thai to tapas. Then it's just a short walk to one of the dozens of Broadway theaters for a production of *Mamma Mia!*, *The Lion King* or more serious fare, like the 2009 Tony Award-winning play, *Next to Normal*. (Get tickets at the TKTS booth.) Nothing beats a late-night stroll under the wash of Times Square's millions of twinkling lights. It may be 4 a.m., but you'll swear it's 4 p.m. Thanks to a zoning ordinance, businesses must display illuminated signs to move into the area— it's actually against the law not to add that flash.

WINTER GARDEN THEATER

1634 Broadway, Theater District, 212-239-6200; www.wintergarden-theater.com

Of all the theaters that line the Theater District, the Winter Garden is one of the most storied venues: It catapulted the likes of Barbra Streisand (*Funny Girl*) to stardom, and gathered stars like Bob Hope, Eve Arden and Josephine Baker on the same stage in a 1936 version of the Ziegfeld Follies. Starpower aside, the Winter Garden is perhaps most famous as the home to *Cats*, one of the longest running shows in Broadway history. It was performed here 7,485 times between 1982 and 2000 (Just think: That's 7,485 beltouts of "Memory.") *Mamma Mia!*, the feel-good musical based on the Swedish pop group ABBA's songs (also released as a movie in 2008), has been playing here since 2001, with no end to the crooning of "Dancing Queen" and "Fernando" in sight.

Monday, Wednesday-Saturday 8 p.m., Sunday 7 p.m. Matinees: Saturday-Sunday 2 p.m.

HIGHLIGHT

WHERE ARE DISCOUNT THEATER TICKETS SOLD IN NEW YORK CITY?

If you're looking for discount theater tickets—or if you didn't make up your mind to see a show until the bright lights of Times Square beckoned—then your first stop should be TKTS. People line up down the block at the Times Square fixture (*Duffy Square, 47th Street and Broadway, 212-221-0013; www.tdf. org*) to get reduced-price, day-of tickets—some for as cheap as 50 percent off the original price. You'll need to be flexible about what to see, and get in line at 5:30 p.m. if you want the shortest wait and the best selection (producers often send tickets over later in the day that they haven't sold). Besides selling more tickets, TKTS was created to get people talking about the theater. The fun of standing in line is the opportunity to chat with your fellow theater-goers about what you're going to see. Two other locations also sell matinee tickets the day before (these also usually have shorter lines).

Box office: Monday, Wednesday-Saturday 3-8 p.m., Tuesday 2-8 p.m., Sunday 3 p.m.-1 hour before last curtain. Matinees: Wednesday and Saturday 10 a.m.-2 p.m., Sunday 11 a.m.-3 p.m. There's a $4 ticket handling surcharge. Other locations: South Street Seaport, corner of Front and John streets; Brooklyn, 1 MetroTech Center.

TRIBECA/MEATPACKING DISTRICT

Tribeca—an acronym for Triangle Below Canal (Street)—is a downtown neighborhood where industrial warehouses have been converted into pricey loft apartments. The influential Tribeca Film Festival was co-founded by longtime resident Robert De Niro to spur the neighborhood's economy following the September 11 terrorist attacks at the nearby World Trade Center. Just to the north, the animal carcasses and butchers that once defined the Meatpacking District—which spans from the Hudson River to Hudson Street to the north—have made way in the last decade for pretty people who like to see and be seen at velvet-ropes clubs and restaurants.

WHAT TO SEE

HIGH LINE

From Gansevoort Street to 34th Street, between 10th and 11th avenues, Meatpacking District, 212-500-6035; www.thehighline.org

Even aging eyesores have potential in the Big Apple—especially if those eyesores include water views and open space. The recently unveiled High Line is Manhattan's newest, and highest, park. Utilizing the original elevated freight train tracks from the 1930s, designers and city planners have transformed the formerly neglected industrial strip into a verdant modern parkway with concrete paths, natural grasses and sleek wooden seating areas. The park stretches one-and-a-half miles up the island's West Side; when it's complete, you'll be able to stroll from Gansevoort Street to 30th Street without interruption, 30 feet above the usual fray of horns, crowds and traffic jams.

Daily 7 a.m.-10 p.m.

SPECIAL EVENTS

WHAT ARE THE TOP SHOWS ON BROADWAY?

There's no business like show business—and in New York, there is no show business quite like theater. From megawatt Broadway musicals to off-Broadway theater, you'll never lack for stage productions, thanks to a steady stream of actors, playwrights and dramatists who flock to the city to hit it big or starve trying. It wouldn't be a real trip to Manhattan without squeezing in a show, so make time to check out one of our favorites.

CHICAGO: THE MUSICAL

Ambassador Theater, 219 W. 49th St., Theater District, 212-239-6200; www.chicagothemusical.com
The Second City takes center stage in this raucous production set during the prohibition era. Based on a real 1924 murder trial, *Chicago* tells the tale of hoosegow hottie Velma Kelly and new girl on the (cell) block, Roxie Hart, following their jailhouse hijinks and kooky attempts to retain their ill-gotten fame. Full of "all that jazz" and hot dance numbers, this six-time Tony Award winner is even more of a hoot than the Richard Gere/Renée Zellweger film adaptation, and is perfect for first-time theatergoers.
Admission: $64-$131.50. Monday-Tuesday, Thursday-Friday 8 p.m., Saturday 2:30 p.m. and 8 p.m., Sunday 2:30 p.m. and 7 p.m.

FUERZA BRUTA: LOOK UP

Daryl Roth Theatre, 101 E. 15th St., Union Square, 212-375-1110; www.fuerzabrutanyc.com
Forget the heels, pack the comfy sneakers, and prepare to stand for a while (because there aren't any seats). But prepare to be dazzled as well. Fuerza bruta means "brute force" in Spanish, and the off-Broadway show doesn't really have a plot—it's more performance art in the vein of Cirque du Soleil or the Blue Man Group. The troupe's charismatic performers swim atop Mylar sheaths, swing from colorful tapestries and run atop long treadmills while boxes hurtle their way. Pounding beats, flashing Technicolor lights, even a barrage of rainfall are all a titillating treat for the senses.
Admission: $75. Wednesday-Friday 8 p.m., Saturday 7 p.m. and 10 p.m., Sunday 7 p.m.

MAMMA MIA!

Winter Garden Theatre, 1634 Broadway, Theater District, 212-239-6200, 800-432-7250; www.mamma-mia.com
One girl. Three possible fathers. A whole lot of ABBA. On the eve of 20 year-old Sophie's wedding, the young bride-to-be vows to have her father walk her down the aisle. The only problem? She doesn't know who he is. After discovering her mother's diary revealing three former flames, she invites the men to her wedding to discover the truth. Set to the music of the '70s Swedish quartet (including their biggest hits like "Dancing Queen" and "Take a Chance on Me"), you might be tempted to dance in the aisles, just like the show's

premiere audience did a decade ago.
Admission: $69.50-$127.50. Wednesday-Saturday 8 p.m., also at 2 p.m. on Wednesday, Saturday and Sunday, and 7 p.m. on Sunday.

NEXT TO NORMAL

Booth Theatre, 222 West 45th St., Theater District, 212-239-6200; www.nexttonormal.com
From the director of *Rent* comes this original musical which takes the audience on an emotional journey of how one family lives with the challenges that come from mental illness. Alice Ripley won the 2009 Tony award for Best Leading Actress in her role as Diana, a bipolar suburban housewife who struggles with her unpredictable moods and worse, taking pills that make her numb to life. Although the core of the musical is how mental illness affects those who suffer from it, as well as those they love, you'll leave feeling hopeful and happy to be alive, not an easy task given the heavy content. Adding to the emotional performance is a can't-get-it-out-of-your-head score by composer Tom Kitt and lyricist Brian Yorkey (they also won the 2009 Tony award for Best Score).
Admission: $36.50-$200. Monday 8 p.m., Tuesday 7 p.m., Thursday-Friday 8 p.m., Saturday 2 p.m. and 8 p.m., Sunday 3 p.m. and 7:30 p.m.

THE PHANTOM OF THE OPERA

The Majestic Theatre, 247 W. 44th St., Theater District, 212-239-6200, 800-432-7250; www.thephantomoftheopera.com
Perhaps it's the haunting melodies penned by famed composer Sir Andrew Lloyd Webber. Or maybe it's the intriguing story of a masked man, his soprano protégé and their unrequited love. It could also just be the slew of talented performers the production's bolstered throughout the years, such as powerhouses Sarah Brightman and Michael Crawford. Whatever the reason, this monumental musical is one of the most iconic and longest-running shows on Broadway.
Admission: $26.50-$201.50. Monday 8 p.m., Tuesday 7 p.m., Wednesday and Saturday 2 p.m. and 8 p.m., Thursday and Friday 8 p.m.

WICKED

Gershwin Theatre, 222 W. 51st St., Theater District, 212-586-6510; www.wickedthemusical.com
Long before Dorothy donned her ruby reds, a green gal named Elphaba and an ethereal beauty named Glinda met and became pals while studying at Oz's Shiz University. How one became the Wicked Witch of the West and the other Glinda the Good Witch is the tale at the heart of this popular Great White Way production. Based on the novel by Gregory Maguire (itself a take off from L. Frank Baum's endearing childhood fantasy), the show has garnered three Tony wins and will keep the family dreaming about somewhere over the rainbow all night long.
Admission: $65-$300. Tuesday 7 p.m., Wednesday and Saturday 2 p.m. and 8 p.m., Thursday and Friday 8 p.m., Sunday 3 p.m.

UNION SQUARE/FLATIRON DISTRICT/GRAMERCY PARK/ MURRAY HILL

Union Square is the entry to Greenwich Village and downtown, and is anchored by Union Square Park—a mammoth four-square block plaza that never stops bustling. The park is a popular meeting spot and home to the city's best-known farmers' market, a dog run and one of the city's largest subway stations. To the north, the Flatiron District is named for the Flatiron Building, a striking, triangular building at 23rd Street where Broadway and Fifth Avenue converge, and which was one of the world's earliest steel structures. Gramercy Park is a nearby residential neighborhood lauded for a residents-only private park. Murray Hill is a quiet, no-nonsense eastside neighborhood that lies between 29th and 42nd streets, known for its solidly middle-class inhabitants.

WHAT TO SEE

FLATIRON BUILDING
175 Fifth Ave. (between 22nd and 23rd streets), Flatiron District

It's been said that when this iron-shaped wonder was completed in 1902, it caused such irregular wind patterns that women's skirts would blow up as they walked down 23rd Street. Throngs of men crowded the street hoping to catch a glimpse of the show, but they were shooed away by police officers giving them what became known as the "23 Skidoo" (a derivative of skedaddle). The structure may not cause such a ruckus nowadays, but it is still considered a jewel of New York's skyline and one of the city's iconic buildings. Designed by famed Chicago architect Daniel Burnham, this Beaux Arts beauty made of limestone and terra cotta measures an amazingly slim six-and-a-half feet wide at its apex.

UNION SQUARE GREENMARKET
17th Street East and Broadway, Flatiron District; www.cenyc.org/greenmarket

Shop alongside the city's top chefs (who often build their menus based on what's available here) at this year-round farmer's market where everything is local and much of what you'll find is organic. In addition to the best seasonal produce, the market offers all kinds of goods, including hot cider, doughnuts, pretzels and homemade pies. Fill up a bag and then head to Union Square Park to relax and enjoy.
Monday, Wednesday, Friday and Saturday 8 a.m.-6 p.m.

UNION SQUARE PARK
14th Street at Broadway, Flatiron District; www.nycgovparks.org

This European-style piazza brims with all sorts of activity. You might see students from the New York Film Academy honing their craft, home cooks and chefs alike browsing the famous greenmarket, dogs breaking free from apartment life on the narrow dog run, folks protesting (the park has been a location for protests and rallies ever since labor activists gathered here in the 1920s), and kids enjoying the park's three playgrounds. In the days following September 11, the park also became a meeting place for the grieving city. Hotels, restaurants and retail giants line the area. The large public art installation on the south end is the Metronome, commissioned by the developers of One Union Square South. Puffs of white steam are released throughout the day and seemingly random numbers indicate when it's 7:04 a.m. and 36.9 seconds and that there are 16 hours, 55 minutes and

23.1 seconds remaining until midnight. It's easier to figure out what the park's statues are, including an equestrian one of George Washington. (You might wonder what a statue of Mohandas (Mahatma) Gandhi has in common with those of George Washington and Abraham Lincoln. This was added because of the park's history of social activism.)

UPPER EAST SIDE

Society types reside in stunning, sprawling pre-war apartments with Central Park views on the Upper East Side. That's why it's no accident that many of these residences are also just steps away from the high-end boutiques (Michael Kors, Chloé) and department stores (Bergdorf Goodman, Saks Fifth Avenue) along Madison and Fifth avenues. Lots of notable museums make their home here, too, including the Whitney Museum of American Art, the Guggenheim Museum and the Metropolitan Museum of Art. Gracie Mansion, the official residence of the Mayor of New York City, is located in the neighborhood.

WHAT TO SEE

CENTRAL PARK
From Central Park South to 110th Street, and from Fifth Avenue to Central Park West, Upper East Side; www.centralparknyc.org

The most frequently visited urban park in the United States, Central Park spans 843 acres in the heart of Manhattan, creating an oasis of towering trees, tranquil lakes and budding blooms in the midst of New York's concrete jungle. The sprawling green space, designed by famous landscape architects Frederick Law Olmsted and Calvert Vaux in the mid-1800s, is not just an ideal spot for sun-soaked picnics and throwing a Frisbee—it also has a plethora of cultural, architectural and athletic activities.

Daily 6 a.m.-1 a.m.

THE METROPOLITAN MUSEUM OF ART
1000 Fifth Ave., Upper East Side, 212-535-7710; www.metmuseum.org

Monet, da Vinci, Picasso, van Gogh and Degas—they're all part of the two-million-plus-piece collection at this enormous Gothic-Revival building. Founded in 1870, the museum moved into this building on the eastern edge of Central Park along what's known as Museum Mile. The works here span more than 5,000 years and include the most definitive collection of American art in the world. Arguably the finest Egyptian collection outside of Cairo is here, and the collections from Europe and Asia are equally impressive. Those art history classes you took will pay off when you recognize such works as van Gogh's *Cypresses*, Gauguin's *la Orana Maria* and Degas's *The Dancing Class*.

Suggested admission: adults $20, seniors $15, students $10, children under 12 and members free. Tuesday-Thursday, Sunday 9:30 a.m.-5:30 p.m., Friday-Saturday 9:30 a.m.-9 p.m.

SOLOMON R. GUGGENHEIM MUSEUM
1071 Fifth Ave., Upper East Side, 212-423-3500; www.guggenheim.org

Critics the world over weren't sure what to make of this coiling ivory-colored tower rising from Manhattan's Upper East Side when it was unveiled in 1959. One heralded it "the most beautiful building in America," while another dubbed it "an indigestible hot cross bun." Many argued that its grandiose design overshadowed the art housed within its walls, though its famed architect Frank Lloyd Wright insisted that it perfectly complimented the works, creating an "uninterrupted, beautiful symphony." The building's design seems to bother few nowadays, as thousands flock to this contemporary and modern art museum for both its permanent collection (including works by Pablo Picasso, Marc Chagall and Henri Matisse) and to take in Wright's awesome creation.

Admission: adults $18, students and seniors $15, children under 12 free. Sunday-Wednesday 10 a.m.-5:45 p.m., Friday 10 a.m.-5:45 p.m., Saturday 10 a.m.-7:45 p.m.

WHITNEY MUSEUM OF AMERICAN ART

945 Madison Ave., Upper East Side, 212-570-3600; www.whitney.org

In 1931, Gertrude Vanderbilt Whitney founded the Whitney Museum when she purchased a brownstone at 10 West Eighth Street and turned it into the Whitney Studio, an exhibition space and social center for young progressive arts. It began with 700 works of contemporary American art, most from Whitney's own collection. Today, at its current location, the museum houses one of the foremost collections of 20th-century American paintings, sculptures, multimedia installations, photographs and drawings from Edward Hopper, John Sloan, Max Weber and more. Well-known for its annual and biennial exhibits that highlight current artists, the museum frequently purchases works from up-and-comers to keep its collection fresh.

Admission: adults $18, seniors and students $12, New York City public school students and children under 12 free. Wednesday-Thursday, Saturday-Sunday 11 a.m.-6 p.m., Friday 1-9 p.m.

UPPER WEST SIDE/COLUMBUS CIRCLE

Cultural bastions including Lincoln Center and the American Museum of Natural History can be found on the Upper West Side, along with thousands of New Yorkers who love the neighborhood's proximity to their Midtown jobs and plethora of shops, restaurants and accessibility to Central Park. Come hungry: New York's legendary H&H Bagels and Zabar's gourmet deli are both here. Columbus Circle, at 59th Street and the southern opening to Central Park, was long-known as nothing more than a super-congested traffic circle before the Time Warner Center—a mixed-use building containing shops, upscale restaurants, a hotel and music halls—opened here in 2003.

WHAT TO SEE

AMERICAN MUSEUM OF NATURAL HISTORY

79th Street and Central Park West, Upper West Side, 212-769-5100; www.amnh.org

One of the largest natural history institutions in the world, this enormous Upper West Side museum is famous for its fossil halls, including two dinosaur halls that are home to more than one million specimens (about 600 are actually on display). Throughout the museum you'll also find life-like dioramas with taxidermied animals such as bears, elephants and jaguars in their natural habitats. A few of the stuffed elephants on display in the Hall of African Mammals came courtesy of famous folks like Theodore Roosevelt, who often sent the museum animals he bagged during safaris. The Rose Center for Earth and Space, which was completed in 2000, features a renovated planetarium and exhibit halls covering the 13-billion year history of the universe.

Admission: adults $16, children $9, seniors and students $12, children 1 and under free. Daily 10 a.m.-5:45 p.m.

THE CLOISTERS MUSEUM & GARDENS

99 Margaret Corbin Drive, Upper West Side, 212-923-3700; www.metmuseum.org

An extension of the Metropolitan Museum of Art, the Cloisters houses approximately 5,000 pieces of medieval European art dating back to 800 A.D. with emphasis on works from the 12th through 15th centuries. Originally located in the main branch of the Met, the collection outgrew its digs by 1927. Buoyed by the support of John D. Rockefeller (who not only purchased the extension's plot in Fort Tyron Park but also a portion of land directly across the Hudson River to keep the Cloister's view unsullied), the extension was dedicated in 1938. This castle-like edifice incorporates elements from five medieval French cloisters and is a piece of art itself. Inside, you'll find the Cloisters' best-known works: seven wool-and-silk woven tapestries depicting the Hunt of the Unicorn. Many additional tapestries, sculptures, manuscripts and stained glass windows are also on display. The Cloisters' gardens—based on horticultural information gleaned from medieval treatises, poetry and garden documents—are another popular stop.

Admission: adults $20, seniors $15, students $10, children under 12 free. November-February, Tuesday-Sunday 9:30 a.m.-4:45 p.m.; March-October, Tuesday-Sunday 9:30 a.m.-5:15 p.m.

COLUMBUS CIRCLE

Broadway and Central Park South, Columbus Circle

Once nothing more than a traffic nightmare—New York architecture critic Paul Goldberger described Columbus Circle as "a chaotic jumble of streets that can be crossed in about 50 different ways, all of them wrong"—the historic plaza is now a destination for shopping, top-notch dining and general lounging, with traffic thankfully not so much an issue any longer. In the heart of the circle stands a 77-foot granite column topped with a marble sculpture of explorer Christopher Columbus (a gift from the Italian-American community to commemorate the 400-year anniversary of his historic voyage) surrounded by a large fountain where locals and visitors relax. Standing behind this is the Time Warner Center, home to more than 50 shops, the Mandarin Oriental hotel, an enormous Whole Foods Market that locals love (and a great place to pick up a picnic before heading into the park), Jazz at Lincoln Center (where some of the best names perform on a regular basis), and CNN's New York studio. Trump International Hotel and Tower is also just next door.

DAVID H. KOCH THEATER

20 Lincoln Center, Upper West Side, 212-870-5570; www.nycballet.com

The New York City Ballet makes their home inside this theater at Lincoln Center when they're not summering at their other headquarters in Saratoga Springs. There is no doubt that the New York City Ballet is one of the world's premiere dance companies. Conceived by Lincoln Kirstein—an early acolyte of modern American film, dance, literature, architecture and all things cerebral—the company was created with the idea that New York was too great a city to import its talent from abroad. He landed the Russian-educated George Balanchine in

HIGHLIGHT

WHAT'S THE BEST WAY TO SEE CENTRAL PARK IN ONE DAY?

It would be tough to see everything this expansive 843-acre park has to offer in just one day (or even two). But with a little planning, you can take in many of the must-see sites in the country's most well-known park. Here's how:

10 A.M.

Start with a bike ride along the park's six-mile loop of paved pathway. **The Loeb Central Park Boathouse** (*72nd Street and Park Drive North, 212-517-2233; www.thecentralparkboathouse.com*) offers an array of cycle rentals, including tandems and cruisers. If a run is more your style, there's a popular one-and-a-half mile running track surrounding the Jacqueline Kennedy Onassis Reservoir. Or saddle up for a horseback ride along the park's 4.5-mile bridle path; rides start at the North Meadow Recreation Center (*midpark; enter at West 96th Street, 212-348-4867*). You can simply ride the painted wooden version on the park's carousel (*www.centralpark.com*) at 64th Street—a mere two bucks gets you a three-and-a-half-minute ride.

NOON

Sure, you could make do with a hot dog or braided pretzel from one of the park's many concession stands, but you can do better than that. After dropping off your bike, enjoy a serene lunch by the lake at the boathouse's restaurant (*midpark; around 72nd Street, 212-517-2233*), where you can watch rowboats, ducks and even an occasional gondola float by. Options run from quick-and-easy sandwiches at the Express Café to the decadent entrées at the Lakeside Dining area.

1:30 P.M.

The park may be a testament to Mother Nature's handiwork, but many of the awe-inspiring man-made wonders here are worth a look, too. Head southwest to take in the "heart" of Central Park—**Bethesda Terrace**, which overlooks the lake and Bethesda Fountain. The site is a popular filming location. Next, walk northeast to see one of the park's oldest landmarks—**Cleopatra's Needle**. A 71-foot-tall obelisk nestled behind the south side of the Metropolitan Museum of Art, the sculpture came from Egypt in 1881 and dates back to about 1500 B.C.

3 P.M.

Grab a cab just outside the park's bounds heading south along Fifth Avenue for a quick trip to **Central Park Zoo** (*www.centralparkzoo.com*) at 64th Street. The zoo—open 365 days a year—is organized by climate zones, so you can chill out with the polar bears, check out parrots in the rain forest exhibit and visit rare red pandas in their jungle habitat, all in one trip. Or spend some quiet time in Strawberry Fields, the stretch of park from 71st to 74th streets dedicated to John Lennon. In the center is the famous "Imagine" mosaic that was donated by the city of Naples, Italy.

5 P.M.

Have a bite at **Le Pain Quotidien** (*2 W. 69th Street, Mineral Springs Pavilion near Sheep Meadow, 646-233-3768; www.lepainquotidien.com*) near the Sheep Meadow. The indoor/outdoor spot serves delicious tartines and salads, plus offers beer and wine. You can also purchase picnic boxes and pick up dessert to enjoy during your next activity.

8 P.M.

During the summer, the **New York Public Theater** (*425 Lafayette St., 212-539-8500; www.publictheater.org*) hosts Shakespeare in the Park, performing the Bard's greatest hits like Hamlet and more recent productions like Hair—often with a Hollywood star or two. The Great Lawn also puts on concerts by the **New York Philharmonic** (*www.nyphil.org*) and **The Metropolitan Opera** (*www.metoperafamily.com*).

HIGHLIGHT

WHAT MAJOR EVENTS TAKE PLACE THROUGHOUT THE YEAR IN NEW YORK CITY?

Though there are bound to be festivals, concerts and community events planned on nearly every single day somewhere in the city, the following is a taste of notable events that draw national crowds each year.

FALL

The **New York Film Festival** and Halloween Parade in **Greenwich Village** (October); **New York City Marathon** (November); the **Macy's Thanksgiving Day Parade**, as well as the pre-parade balloon inflating the night before (November).

WINTER

The **Radio City Christmas Spectacular** (December); **Christmas Tree-Lighting Ceremony in Rockefeller Center** (late November/early December); **Times Square New Year's Eve Ball Drop** (December); **Chinese New Year Parade** (February).

SPRING

The **Tribeca Film Festival** (late April-May); **Cherry Blossom Festival** (May); **Bike New York** (May); **Lower East Side Festival of the Arts** (May).

SUMMER

The **Mermaid Parade** (June); **Gay & Lesbian Pride March** (June); **Nathan's Famous Fourth of July Hot Dog Eating Contest** (July); **Shakespeare in the Park** (June-August); the **Metropolitan Opera in the Park** (July/August); and **U.S. Tennis Open** (August/September).

1933, and together the two shaped the history of 20th century dance. Today, under the direction of Peter Martins, the company is responsible for training its own artists and creating original works, pushing modern ballet into the future. It still keeps one graceful, slippered foot in its past (*The Nutcracker* remains a Christmas tradition) as it performs around the city, the state and the world. *Check website for specific dates and locations of shows.*

LINCOLN CENTER FOR THE PERFORMING ARTS

70 Lincoln Center Plaza, Columbus Avenue and Broadway, Upper West Side, 212-875-5456; www.lincolncenter.org

Some of the Big Apple's most renowned performance groups, including the New York Philharmonic, the New York City Ballet and The Metropolitan Opera, make this Upper West Side cultural destination their home. Rising stars frequent the 16-acre complex, too, because it's also the site of the revered Juilliard School (alumni include Robin Williams, Kelsey Grammer and Patti LuPone) and the recently expanded Alice Tully Hall. The surrounding area, known as Lincoln Square, is a bustling restaurant and retail district. The nearby Time Warner Center contains a 1,200-seat theater designed specifically for jazz performances.

Hours vary by building and performance schedules.

RIVERSIDE PARK

59th Street to 158th Street along the Hudson River, Upper West Side, 212-408-0264; www.nycgovparks.org

Hugging the banks of the Hudson River, this nearly 330-acre park stretches more than four solid miles. Yet another Frederick Law Olmsted-designed recreational area, the park has basketball courts, baseball and soccer fields, playgrounds, dog runs, a skate park and even a public marina. You'll also find several monuments within the park's borders, including Grant's Tomb—the burial site of President Ulysses S. Grant and his wife Julia, which is the largest tomb in North America. Other highlights include a Joan of Arc statue and the Eleanor Roosevelt Monument.

ZABAR'S

2245 Broadway, Upper West Side, 212-787-2000; www.zabars.com

This Upper West Side gourmet grocer is practically a New York institution. As their slogan indicates, Zabar's really is New York. Started as a simple counter in 1934 by Louis and Lillian Zabar, the market now stretches nearly the length of an entire city block and sees more than 35,000 loyal customers every week. The grocer is known for both its extensive kitchen-gadget selection as well as its high-quality bagels, smoked fish counter, knishes, olives and cheeses; there is still always a member of the Zabar family in the store. If you're craving something sweet, Zabar's Café also serves native-to-New York desserts such as delicious black-and-white cookies and cheesecake.

Monday-Friday 8 a.m.-7:30 p.m., Saturday 8 a.m.-8 p.m., Sunday 9 a.m.-6 p.m.

BROOKLYN

With 2.6 million residents, Brooklyn is New York City's most populous borough and has a distinct culture all its own. Thanks to its proximity to downtown Manhattan, there is a vibrant arts and cultural scene—writers, painters, designers and restaurateurs migrate to Brooklyn for its less expensive rents and charming neighborhood-centric way of life. The borough is also home to some of the city's most recognized institutions, including the Brooklyn Academy of Music, Brooklyn Botanic Garden, Prospect Park and Coney Island.

WHAT TO SEE

BROOKLYN BRIDGE

Lower Manhattan/Downtown Brooklyn

One of four bridges spanning the East River (the others are the Williamsburg, Manhattan and Queensboro bridges), this 6,016-foot-long wonder connects the boroughs of Manhattan and Brooklyn, and was the longest suspension bridge in the world at the time of its completion in 1883. More than 150,000 people paid one cent to walk across the bridge on opening day (bringing a hog or sheep cost an additional two cents). Today, more than 126,000 vehicles cross the bridge each day, in addition to a steady stream of foot traffic from commuters and tourists looking to get a bit of exercise while enjoying the spectacular views of the river and the Statue of Liberty.

BROOKLYN HEIGHTS PROMENADE

Brooklyn-Queens Expressway, between Joralemon Street and Grace Court

If it's the perfect view you're after, you'll find it at this well-manicured pedestrian walkway above the hum of the Brooklyn-Queens Expressway. Overlooking lower Manhattan, the East River and the Brooklyn Bridge, the esplanade is a popular spot for joggers, Rollerbladers, sightseers, locals looking to relax and film crews coveting the picturesque skyline. (In case you're wondering, the traffic noise from below won't kill the mood.)

Daily 24 hours.

CONEY ISLAND

Surf Avenue between 37th Street and Ocean Parkway, South Brooklyn; www.coneyisland.com

Boardwalks, hot dogs and roller coasters: You'll find them all here. One of the most popular amusement areas of the early 20th century, the south Brooklyn neighborhood (which is actually a peninsula and not an island) feels stuck in a bit of a time warp, with its rickety boardwalks and old-school theme parks. The fate of these amusement parks—most notably the recently shuttered Astroland—has been up in the air for years, but for now some remain open, allowing a new generation to experience vintage rides such as the Cyclone, one of the oldest wooden roller coasters still in operation. Recent additions, including MCU Park (home of the minor-league Brooklyn Cyclones) have helped breathe new life into the stagnant neighborhood. But Coney Island is more than just fun in the sun. Indoor entertainment is also available in the form of the New York Aquarium and Coney Island Museum.

Open year-round.

PROSPECT PARK

95 Prospect Park West, Brooklyn, 718-965-8951; www.prospectpark.org

Central Park may be New York's most famous, but ask any Brooklynite about their favorite green space, and they'll be quick to sing the praises of this 585-acre park in the heart of their beloved borough. Designed by Central Park architects Frederick Law Olmsted and Calvert Vaux, Prospect Park features a 90-acre spread of grass aptly named the Long Meadow, plus Brooklyn's only forest and a zoo with nearly 400 animals. In the park's boathouse, you can visit the first urban Audubon Center for hands-on nature exhibits. The park is also

HIGHLIGHT

WHAT ARE THE BEST PLACES IN NEW YORK CITY FOR SPORTS FUN?

CHELSEA PIERS
This 28-acre sports and entertainment complex boasts a 40-lane bowling alley, golf club, ice skating rinks, rock climbing wall, swimming pool, restaurants and spa.

CENTRAL PARK
Each weekend, hords of joggers join the packs circling the park's closed-to-traffic roads. Besides being New York's favorite runner's destination, Central Park is also a great spot for trail riding (there are three bridle paths; tours are available through Riverdale Equestrian Center, www.riverdaleriding.com), inline skating, and playing baseball, basketball and countless other sports.

USTA
Billie Jean King National Tennis Center: The courts where champions are made each September at the U.S. Open are open daily to the public. Rates for court time at the National Tennis Center (*www.usta.com*) in Queens start as low as $20 per hour, and reservations can be made up to two days in advance. To put some polish on your game, sign up for a group or private lesson with one of the center's professional instructors.

NEW YANKEE STADIUM
Take a tour of the new home of the New York Yankees, where you'll see tributes to the team's top stars, including Lou Gehrig, Mickey Mantle, Joe DiMaggio and Babe Ruth. Fans can make a day (or night) of it by also adding lunch or dinner at one of the stadium's new dining venues.

home to an antique carousel and frequent concerts and performances.
Daily 5 a.m.-1 a.m.

THE BRONX
The Bronx is the northernmost of New York City's five boroughs and the only part attached to the North American mainland. It is most famous as the home of the New York Yankees (a.k.a., Bronx Bombers, who have a brand new stadium here just like the Mets) and the Bronx Zoo, the largest nature preserve in the United states, spanning 265 acres and containing more than 4,000 animals.

WHAT TO SEE

ARTHUR AVENUE

Arthur Avenue, Bronx; www.arthuravenue.com

Pay a visit to the real Little Italy of New York. Italians made the area of Belmont their home at the turn of the century, and many made their living by selling food items from pushcarts on Arthur Avenue. In 1940, Mayor Fiorello LaGuardia greenlighted construction of an indoor market where they could sell their goods. Seventy years later, the passion for artisanal foods and wines continues. Visit the European market (2344 Arthur Ave.) and you'll be overtaken by the smell of freshly baked breads, aromatic cheeses and house-cured meats. Beyond the market, there is also an abundance of restaurants, pizza parlors and pastry shops—some dating to the 1920s. At Roberto's (603 E. Crescent Ave., 718-733-9503; www.roberto089.com), everyone orders from the blackboard list of specials and waiters spoon heaps of fresh pasta on your plate. Calandra Cheese (2314 Arthur Ave., 718-367-7572) sells fresh mozzarella and other cheeses, while the bread sold at Terranova Bakery (691 E. 187th St., 718-733-6985) is a feast in itself.

BRONX ZOO

2300 Southern Blvd., Bronx, 718-220-5100; www.bronxzoo.com

The Bronx Zoo boasts 265-acres for more than 4,000 animals to roam, making it the largest urban wildlife conservation park in the country. Much of the zoo's land has been made into special habitats suited for its diverse variety of animals, including gorillas, lions, gibbons and grizzly bears. Take a 20-minute monorail ride along the Bronx River and take in the surroundings of the Wild Asia portion of the zoo with tigers, elephants and rhinos roaming nearby. An interactive children's zoo lets kids check out animal homes, try on simulated claws and paws, and get their picture taken with chickens. There are also several indoor exhibits to explore, including the Butterfly Garden, Monkey House and World of Birds.

Admission: adults $15, seniors $13, children 3-12 $11. April-October, Monday-Friday 10 a.m.-5 p.m., Saturday-Sunday 10 a.m.-5:30 p.m.; November-March, daily 10 a.m.-4:30 p.m.

NEW YANKEE STADIUM

161st Street and River Avenue, Bronx, 718-293-4300; www.yankees.com

After 85 years playing in historic Yankee Stadium, the Bronx Bombers opened their 2009 season in a new pasture, in the form of a $1.3 billion, 4,000-seat-smaller bowl shaped stadium. New Yankee Stadium is located next to the site of the old ballpark, so it offers the same easy access to public transit (via the B, D and 4 trains) and a field of identical dimensions to the old one, which was why it was probably so easy to win their 27th title in their new home. Though "The House that Ruth Built" (nicknamed for Babe Ruth's fan-drawing power) is missed by players and fans alike, the new stadium—perhaps "The House that A-Rod Built"—isn't having any trouble drawing crowds. If you're in town when the pinstripes are playing, try for tickets during the week, as the weekends can grow crowded. And if Boston is in town, be prepared to pay up for the privilege of watching one of the most heated rivalries in Major League Baseball.

THE NEW YORK BOTANICAL GARDEN

200th Street and Kazimiroff Blvd., Bronx, 718-817-8700; www.nybg.org

With more than one million plants, this is one of the largest and oldest (founded in 1891) botanical gardens in the country. It consists of 250 landscaped acres and 50 curated gardens. The property also contains the last 50 acres of the native forest that once covered New York City. The Enid A. Haupt Conservatory has 11 distinct plant environments with changing exhibits and permanent displays, including the Fern Forest, Palm Court and Rose Garden. There is a great emphasis on education, with programs on horticulture and science. For the kids, there is the Everett Children's Adventure Garden, a 12-acre space that offers a boulder maze and giant animal topiaries. The botanical garden is one of the best ways to get out of the city without leaving its borders.

Admission: adults $6, seniors and students $3, children 2-12 $1, children under 2 free. Free Wednesday, 10 a.m.-noon Saturday. March-mid-January, Tuesday-Sunday 10 a.m.-7 p.m.; mid-January-February, Tuesday-Sunday 10 a.m.-5 p.m.

HARLEM

Harlem is arguably the cultural epicenter of African-American arts and culture. The landmark Apollo Theater is credited with launching the careers of James Brown, Michael Jackson, Stevie Wonder and countless other singers and musicians, while Sylvia's Soul Food has long attracted a mix of locals and visiting celebs—especially politicians on the stump. The historic brownstones that line many of the neighborhood's residential streets have become some of the city's most coveted real estate in recent years.

APOLLO THEATER

253 W. 125th St., Harlem, 212-663-0499; www.apollotheater.org

The famous Apollo Theater first opened its doors in 1914. In 1934, Ralph Cooper, Sr. commenced his ever-popular Amateur Nite Hour, an extension of his already prominent radio show. That same year, Ella Fitzgerald and Benny Carter launched their careers by participating in Amateur Night. The rest is music history. Apollo Theater quickly became known for jump-starting the careers of many performing artists, including Stevie Wonder, Michael Jackson, Billie Holiday, James Brown and Lauryn Hill. Amateur Night still exposes fresh talent every Wednesday night. Tours are offered to groups of 20 people or more (smaller groups or individuals can join a tour if one is scheduled when you'd like to go).

Amateur night: Wednesday, 7:30 p.m. Prices vary.

QUEENS

Most visitors to New York City know Queens as the part of the city they fly into—it's where John F. Kennedy and LaGuardia airports are located. The borough is also one of the most diverse places in all of the United States—it's home to New York's Greektown (in Astoria), the city's second Chinatown (in Flushing) a "Little Guyana" (Richmond Hill) and a bevy of other ethnic pockets. The New York Mets play in brand-new Citi Field in Flushing Meadows, and right next door you can check out the unofficial symbol of Queens, the 12-story high Unisphere—a massive globe structure commissioned for the 1964-1965 World's Fair, which took place here.

HIGHLIGHT

WHAT IS THERE TO SEE AND DO IN BROOKLYN?

All you need is a MetroCard to hop a quick subway ride across the bridge to Brooklyn, which nearly 2.6 million people call home. This borough, located to the southeast of Manhattan, officially became part of New York City in 1898 and is home to many cultural attractions, entertainment options and historical draws. For an all-day trip that mixes the old with the ever-changing, pair a jaunt to Red Hook with an afternoon shopping in bustling, burgeoning Park Slope and strolling through Prospect Park. If it's a nice day, the best way to enter Brooklyn is on foot by crossing the Brooklyn Bridge, a National Historic Landmark since 1964. Start your two-mile walk in Manhattan at the Brooklyn Bridge-City Hall subway stop near City Hall Park, where you'll find the pedestrian overpass. Stop along the wood-planked walkway of the 6,016-foot bridge (the main span is 1,595 feet) to read plaques chronicling the construction of the steel structure—the longest suspension bridge in the world at the time it was built in 1883. Next, it's on to the Old World vibe of Red Hook. From the Brooklyn Bridge, make your way over to Red Hook by taxi, a train and bus combo, or water taxis

Walking through Red Hook, an industrial neighborhood that feels relatively removed from Manhattan, can feel like strolling through a slice of 1950s New York, with dilapidated trolley cars still on tracks of the Beard Street Pier and retro diners dotting the main drag. Today, it's a mishmash of bars and bake shops, artist studios and antiques stores, and the whole place has a hip-and-gritty atmosphere. Start with a walk down Van Brunt Street, the main drag, to get a feel for the area and do a bit of windowshopping. Stop for a bite at Hope & Anchor (*347 Van Brunt St., Brooklyn, 718-237-0276*), an appealing spot that kick-started the foodie focus in this neighborhood (try comfort dishes like flaky chicken pot pie and juicy burgers), before hopping onto one of the bright orange stools at retro sweet shop Baked (*359 Van Brunt St., Brooklyn, 718-222-0345; www.bakednyc.com*) and digging into old-school treats such as pillowy homemade marshmallows, sprinkle-topped cupcakes or Aunt Sassy's Pistachio Surprise—a thick slice of pistachio-infused white cake topped with vanilla honey buttercream frosting. Next, walk over to the offbeat Red Hook Bait & Tackle (*320 Van Brunt St., Brooklyn, 718-797-4892; www.redhookbaitandtackle. com*) to wash it all down with a beer or sample the impressive collection of local whiskeys and bourbons. Opened by four neighborhood friends, it's tucked into an actual old taxidermy-filled bait-and-tackle shop. For a real local treat, swing by Steve's Authentic (*204 Van Dyke St., Brooklyn, 718-858-5333; www.steves-authentic.com*), where Steve Tarpin has been handing out Swingles for more than 25 years. The frozen novelty is a wonderful sliver of frozen key lime pie (made with only freshly squeezed juice) that's dipped in chocolate. Antiques seekers should check out Atlantis (*351 Van Brunt St., Brooklyn, 718-858-8816; www.atlantisredhook.com*), where they can score treasures like hand-painted glassware from the 1970s, mid-century lamps, and kitschy, colorful 1960s dining sets. The Louis Valentino, Jr. Park and Pier (at Coffey and Ferris streets) affords some of the best land views of the Statue of Liberty, while Red Hook

Park (*155 Bay St.*) is given over on weekends from April to September to makeshift bazaars of pan-Latin food and music.

From quirky, laidback Red Hook, a short subway ride will land you in Park Slope for some of the best shopping and cultural attractions in Brooklyn. This neighborhood, known for its Victorian brownstones and boutique-packed streets, has undergone a seemingly never-ending, massive gentrification over the last 20 years or so. Fifth Avenue is the main drag for restaurants, including popular exports from Manhattan such as Blue Ribbon (*280 Fifth Ave., 718-840-0404; www.blueribbonrestaurants.com*), while Seventh Avenue is positively crammed with specialty shops and high-end stores where you can buy everything from heart-rate-sensing sports bras to handmade stationery and lamb's-wool throw blankets. Prospect Park (*718-965-8999; www.prospectpark.org*), a 585-acre, lush urban oasis that lies between the Park Slope and Prospect Heights neighborhoods, offers everything from waterfalls and bird-watching opportunities to a 400-animal zoo (*at Flatbush and Ocean avenues; 718-399-7339*), plus an antique carousel. Designed by Calvert Vaux and Frederick Law Olmsted (the same duo behind Central Park), this rolling green haven is also ideal for horseback riding (check out Kensington Stables, *51 Caton Place, 718-972-4588; www.kensingtonstables.com*), roller-blading, biking or just wandering the many trails. At the northern edge of the park, you'll find the Brooklyn Botanic Garden (*900 Washington Ave., 718-623-7200; www.bbg.org*), best known for the Cherry Blossom Festival that fills the verdant space with a riot of fragrant blooms each April. The 52-acre space, which includes beautiful formal Italian and Japanese gardens, is worth a visit any time of year. Finally, no trip to Brooklyn is complete without a stop at the Brooklyn Museum (*200 Eastern Parkway, 718-638-5000; www.brooklynmuseum.org*). Though delightfully less crowded than its Manhattan brethren, the museum is home to approximately one million art objects and is considered one of the premier art museums in the world. Highlights include one of the most important Egyptian collections in the world, the African galleries (one of the first of their kind in the U.S.), and a dizzying number of European classics by masters such as Claude Monet, Edgar Degas, Camille Pissarro, Paul Cézanne and Berthe Morisot. Whatever you do, don't leave the borough without stopping at any one of myriad pizza places for a requisite slice. You wouldn't really be going native without it.

How to get there: Take the MTA to the Brooklyn Bridge-City Hall subway stop by City Hall Park. To get to Red Hook from the base of the Brooklyn Bridge, you can either grab a taxi; take the F or G trains to Smith-9th Street, then hop on the B77 bus; or on weekends take the New York Water Taxi (www.nywatertaxi.com, $15-$25) from Pier 11 at South Street to the Red Hook Beard Street Pier. To get to Park Slope from Red Hook, take the F train from Smith-Ninth streets to Seventh Avenue.

ASTORIA

Just a few stops from Manhattan is where you'll find the prominent Queens neighborhood of Astoria. It is an eclectic community, largely populated by Greeks. However, with the bountiful parkland and culture that abounds here, it has attracted people from around the world, and is also popular with recent grads and artists, as the rental properties offer more for less. Astoria's main promenades include 30th Avenue, Steinway, Ditmars and Broadway. Along 30th Avenue and Broadway between 31st and Steinway streets, you'll find many of its classic Greek restaurants, markets and bakeries, which are known to be the best in Queens. On 24th Avenue, grab a seat at Bohemian Hall (*29-19 24th Ave., 718-274-4925; www.bohemianhall.com*), one of the city's oldest beer halls and gardens built in 1910. Steinway Street is best known for its shopping. Astoria Park (*19th St., www. nycgovparks.org*), which includes more than 65 acres of natural space, is located between the Hell Gate and Triborough Bridges, and has the largest public pool in New York City. The American Museum of the Moving Image (*34-12 36th St., 718-784-0077; www.movingimage.us*) is also nearby. Astoria was once the site of the Astoria Studios, which cultivated screen legends such as Rudolph Valentino and Gloria Swanson; renovated and reopened in the late 1970s, the studios are now known as the Kaufman Astoria Studios.

CITI FIELD

12301 Roosevelt Ave., Flushing, 718-507-8499; www.mets.com

The New York Mets started the 2009 season in their new home, and just like New Yankee Stadium, this one was built right next door to the old one (Shea Stadium). This is the Mets' third home (they played their first two seasons at the Polo Grounds in Manhattan), and by far their swankiest to date. Original plans were to make the venue part of the city's bid for the 2012 Summer Olympics, but when that fell through, they were scaled back. Still, this ballpark includes 12,000 square feet of integrated scoring and video boards throughout the stadium, expanded family and entertainment areas, and an interactive Mets museum. You can also expect wider seats, more legroom, fancier restaurants and more bathrooms. The main entrance is modeled after the rotunda at Brooklyn's old Ebbets Field and named for Major League Baseball's first African-American player, Jackie Robinson, who played there for the Brooklyn Dodgers. The entire project cost roughly $600 million, with the bulk of the tab picked up by the Mets organization, and the rest funded by New York City and state taxes as well as Citigroup, which purchased the naming rights to the park for $20 million a year for the next 20 years.

QUEENS JAZZ TRAIL

Queens; www.flushingtownhall.org

While jazz music has been claimed by the likes of New Orleans, Chicago, Harlem and others, many consider Queens to be the rightful "Home of Jazz." If you're a fan, tour the history of jazz that is ever present in this borough by visiting its cultural institutions, famous homes, local museums and archives. Make sure to include Flushing Town Hall (*137-35 Northern Blvd., Flushing, 718-463-7700; www.flushingtownhall.org*) the area's center for culture and the arts; The Louis Armstrong House Museum (*34-56 107th St., Corona, 718-478-8274; www.louisarmstronghouse.org*), which includes a tour of Armstrong's home and an assortment of audio clips; and Addisleigh Park (*St. Albans; www. addisleighpark.org*) where you'll be able to find the former Tudor-style residences of many of jazz's late greats.

STATEN ISLAND

Staten Island feels more like a suburb than one of the five boroughs with its wealth of (by New York City standards) sprawling homes with backyards and pools, as well as strip malls and chain restaurants. Separated from the other boroughs by New York Bay, Staten Island is the only part of the city not serviced by its subway system. One of the best tourist attractions in town is a round-trip ride between here and Manhattan on the free Staten Island Ferry, which offers breathtaking views of New York Harbor and the Statue of Liberty.

THE GREENBELT
700 Rockland Ave., Staten Island, 718-351-3450; www.sigreenbelt.org

This 2,800-acre nature preserve exists in the heart of Staten Island. The Greenbelt is made up of wetlands, forestry and miles of rolling meadows. Spend an afternoon hiking the numerous trails and discovering the natural land that spreads over this city island. Trek up Moses Mountain for a view of the sprawling woodlands and the Atlantic Ocean beyond. Within The Greenbelt are several traditional parks that offer many outdoor recreation opportunities, such as bird watching, archery and baseball. These parks include LaTourette, Willowbrook and High Rock. At Willowbrook, there is a traditional carousel with 51 hand-carved animals. There is also the 260-acre William T. Davis Wildlife Refuge with an observation deck and woodland trails, home to the first Audubon Center in New York City. For more information, stop by the Greenbelt Nature Center before hitting the trails.

Admission: free. Nature Center: April-October, Tuesday-Sunday 10 a.m.- 5 p.m.; November-March, Wednesday-Sunday 11 a.m.-5 p.m. Preserve: Daily.

STATEN ISLAND MUSEUM
75 Stuyvesant Place, Staten Island, 718-727-1135; www.statenislandmuseum.org

If you're planning to take a cruise on the Staten Island Ferry, schedule time to check out the Staten Island Museum, located just two blocks from the ferry terminal. This museum was founded in 1881 and was established to recognize the arts, natural sciences and history of Staten Island. Its current collections contain pieces that date back to 12,000 years, with more than two million artifacts from pre-history to present day, including the region's most inclusive representation of New York's early Native Americans. Recent temporary exhibits have included one on the history of the ferry.

Admission: adults $2, seniors and students $1, children under 12 free. Monday-Friday 12 p.m.-5 p.m., Saturday 10 a.m.-5 p.m., Sunday 12 p.m.-5 p.m.

STATEN ISLAND ZOO
614 Broadway, Staten Island, 718-442-3100; www.statenislandzoo.org

Opened in 1936, the Staten Island Zoo was organized and is now operated by the Staten Island Zoological Society. Achieving the Society's mission: "To disseminate a knowledge of zoology and an appreciation of animal life," the museum offers frequent educational programs and activities. Popular events include "Breakfast with the Beasts," and "Dinos and More," which includes prehistoric fossils and 3-D models. The zoo has a large and internationally recognized collection of native and exotic reptiles and numerous species of rattlesnakes (one of the largest collections in the United States), amphibians, marine reef fish, mammals and birds. The Staten Island Zoo is also famous for "Staten Island Chuck," the city's famous groundhog that predicts the fate of the winter each Groundhog Day. The event is an entertaining spectacle if you'll be in town on February 2nd.

Admission: adults $8, seniors $6, children 3-14 $5, children under 3 free. Free on Wednesday after 2 p.m. Daily 10 a.m.-4:45 p.m.

WHERE TO STAY

EAST VILLAGE/LOWER EAST SIDE
★★★THE BOWERY HOTEL
335 Bowery, East Village, 212-505-9100; www.theboweryhotel.com

This boutique spot in the Bowery—an area once home to legendary punk bar CBGB and long known for being more gritty than pretty—embodies the area's continuing gentrification. A short walk from Nolita, the East Village, the Lower East Side and Soho, the latest venture for hoteliers Eric Goode and Sean MacPherson (Waverly Inn, Maritime Hotel), has a dimly lit lobby with leather- and velvet-upholstered furniture that feels old and cozy, minus any mustiness. The lounge, with its velvet banquettes, dark wood walls and fireplace, draws a cocktail-seeking crowd, as do the outdoor patio and small back bar known for its absinthe-based concoctions. Guest suites have wood-slatted floors, marble bathrooms and floor-to-ceiling paned factory windows that overlook the neighboring tenements just to remind you that despite the HD television, and iPod stereo system and docking station, this isn't the Upper West Side. The location may be too rough around the edges for some, but the beautiful lounges, rustic restaurant and free copies of the New York Post will make you feel right at home.

135 rooms. Restaurant, bar. Business center. Pets accepted. $351 and up

★★★THE COOPER SQUARE HOTEL
25 Cooper Square, East Village, 212-475-5700; www.thecoopersquarehotel.com

The Cooper Square Hotel feels like staying in a friend's attractive modern home—that is, if they happened to live in the East Village. With no formal reception desk, check in happens in the library over a glass of wine or champagne. With walls of windows, the library is drenched in natural light and offers a view of the large patio that overlooks Fifth Street. The modern guest rooms feature clean lines and subdued colors. Beds have Sferra linens and pillow-top mattresses, while bathrooms feature tiled walls, Red Flower candles with a scent made just for the hotel, and three different types of bathrobes. You can purchase said candles in the mini-bar, as well as custom-made jewelry by New York artist Tina Thor and makeup by Loraine. You'll notice that there isn't any artwork in the rooms or in the hotel. The idea here is that the many windows allow New York City to become the art. There are thousands of books—more than 4,000 line bookshelves throughout the hotel. It's hard to miss, but be sure to take note of the Art Wall (on the south-facing wall of the hotel), a commissioned piece celebrating the emerging artists of the East Village. The hotel also

HIGHLIGHT

WHAT'S A GOOD BEACH OUTSIDE OF NEW YORK CITY?

Another escape accessible via subway, Rockaway Beach is located at the end of the A subway line. Rockaway Peninsula, known to locals simply as "the Rockaways," is a slim strip of land that's part of the borough of Queens. It abuts New York Harbor (and the Atlantic Ocean) on one side and Jamaica Bay lagoon on the other. Since the 19th century, New Yorkers who aren't the Hamptons- or Jersey Shore-types have been treating Rockaway Beach as a summer resort, and though year-round communities have since sprung up in the area, the sandy shores remain fair game for more than 4 million people who come here each summer seeking fun in the sun. Rockaway Beach, also nicknamed the Irish Riviera (more than a quarter of the residents here are of Irish descent), provides more than enough seaside entertainment. It's the city's longest and most diverse beach, so expect everything from family barbecues to pockets of nude sunbathers to fishermen perched on the many rocky outcrops. Numerous handball courts, beach volleyball nets and hiking trails are available, while the lengthy boardwalk just begs for a sun-kissed stroll or the simple pleasure of a melting ice cream cone. Look for Whalemena, a whale sculpture that used to reside at the Central Park Zoo, at the beach's 95th Street entrance for a great photo-op.

How to get there: Take the MTA to the Rockaway Park Beach 116th Street stop, at the end of the A subway line.

hosts a music series showcasing musicians in the 21st floor penthouse, which features a 360-degree view and a screening room with stadium seating.
145 rooms. Restaurant, bar. Pets accepted. $251-350.

★★★HOTEL ON RIVINGTON
107 Rivington St., Lower East Side, 212-475-2600;
www.hotelonrivington.com

The super-modern steel-and-glass Hotel On Rivington offers 21 stories of hip and luxurious guest rooms. All have floor-to-ceiling windows for sweeping Manhattan views, and most include balconies. Sensuous details range from velvet sofas and chairs in the living spaces, bathrooms constructed with glitzy Bisazza tiles and glass-enclosed showers with skyline views, to Swedish Tempur-Pedic mattresses and Frette linens. The hotel sits in the heart of the gentrifying Lower East Side, where there's no shortage of trendy boutiques, hip restaurants and popular local watering holes, including the 1,500-square-foot onsite restaurant and lounge, Levant East at Thor, which features the artwork of Keith Richard's daughter, Alexandra Richards.
110 rooms. Restaurant, bar. Fitness center. Business center. Pets accepted. $351 and up

FINANCIAL DISTRICT/BATTERY PARK CITY

★★★MILLENIUM HILTON

55 Church St., Financial District, 212-693-2001;
www.hilton.com

This Financial District hotel is a good choice for business travelers who need proximity to Wall Street as well as vacationers who want to be near popular spots such as Battery Park, Greenwich Village, Tribeca and Soho. The ho-hum guestrooms in the 55-story skyscraper aren't anything special in terms of décor, but they do have 42-inch flat-screen televisions, high-speed Internet access, personalized voicemail and Hilton's "Serenity Bed" with plush down pillows. Request a room with views of the Statue of Liberty or East River, with its iconic bridges. Fitness facilities are top-notch and include a heated indoor pool.

569 rooms. Restaurant, bar. Fitness center. Pool. Business center. Pets accepted. $351 and up

★★★NEW YORK MARRIOTT DOWNTOWN

85 West St., Financial District, 212-385-4900; www.marriott.com

This Financial District hotel has great access to Wall Street, and the South Street Seaport. Guest rooms in the 38-floor building were renovated in 2008, and include 32-inch flat-screen TVs, marble bathrooms, and beds with 300-thread-count linens and down comforters. Be sure to request the hotel's best perk, if it's available: a room with a view of New York Harbor and the Statue of Liberty.

497 rooms. Restaurant, bar. Fitness center. $351 and up

★★★★THE RITZ-CARLTON NEW YORK, BATTERY PARK

2 West St., Battery Park, 212-344-0800; www.ritzcarlton.com

Top-notch views of the Statue of Liberty, Ellis Island, New York Harbor and the downtown skyline make the Ritz's quieter downtown, waterfront location on the southwestern tip of Manhattan a great excuse to avoid the chaotic Midtown hotel scene. Harborside rooms are equipped with telescopes, and all the rooms have the typically plush Ritz-style amenities. Bulgari toiletries are in the marble bathrooms, and feather-beds come with 400-thread-count Frette linens, feather duvets and goose-down pillows. If that's not enough to lull you to sleep, a deep-tissue or hot-stone massage at the spa should do the trick.

298 rooms. Restaurant, bar. Fitness center. Spa. Business center. Pets accepted. $351 and up

GREENWICH VILLAGE/SOHO/WEST VILLAGE

★★★60 THOMPSON

60 Thompson St., Soho, 877-431-0400; www.60thompson.com

Beautiful is the operative term here. Opened in 2001, this boutique hotel's clientele and staff are just as attractive and stylish as the trendy rooms designed by Thomas O'Brien and Aero Studios. Sferra linens cover the dark-wood beds, products by Fresh stock the marble bathrooms and gourmet Dean & DeLuca goods fill the mini-bars. To top it all off, literally, the A60 rooftop lounge—with great downtown views that include water-tower topped lofts and the distant Empire State Building—is open only to members and hotel guests. More exclusive still is the "Thompson Loft"—a two-story penthouse with a marble fireplace and its own private rooftop terrace. Privacy in New York—now that's a beautiful thing.

100 rooms. Restaurant, bar. Fitness center. $351 and up

HIGHLIGHT

WHAT ARE NEW YORK CITY'S MOST LUXURIOUS HOTELS?

MANDARIN ORIENTAL, NEW YORK

If you crave luxury but prefer your surroundings on the sleek side rather than stuffy, this modern tower rising over Central Park delivers top-notch service with Asian flair. This super chic addition to the luxury hotel landscape in New York has jaw-dropping views, super-luxe amenities and a convenient location in Columbus Circle.

THE PENINSULA NEW YORK

A new Shanghai-style rooftop bar and gorgeously revamped spa up the luxury factor at this New York standby. But it's the personalized service (you might find yourself wondering how everyone from the doorman to the waiter at breakfast knows you by name) that makes a stay here special.

THE RITZ-CARLTON NEW YORK, CENTRAL PARK

Probably one of the best Ritz-Carlton hotels anywhere, this Uptown classic whispers luxury, with its exclusive, formal butler service available to cater to whatever you need, whenever you need it. Rooms are bathed in buttery tones and luxe touches such as cashmere throws.

THE ST. REGIS NEW YORK

For over-the-top pampering and white glove service, this Fifth Avenue hotel is the one to choose. The opulent landmark building has gilded cornices and Italian marble, a legendary bar and a thoroughly modern restaurant from Alain Ducasse.

TRUMP INTERNATIONAL HOTEL & TOWER

Rooms have Trump-style basics: marble bathrooms, European-style kitchens with china, crystal glassware and Christofle serving trays, and amazing park and city views through the floor-to-ceiling windows.

★★★CROSBY STREET HOTEL

79 Crosby St., Soho, 212-226-6400; www.firmdale.com

The Stateside outpost of U.K.-based Tim and Kit Kemp's Firmdale hotel group boasts the same eclectic English country-meets-modernist design as its London sisters (think layers of fabrics, textures and colors). Located on a cobblestone street in Soho, Crosby Street feels more residential than most hotels. Crosby Bar is a colorful spot for breakfast, lunch or dinner, while the adjacent sculpture garden is a great spot for a drink. The cozy Drawing Room's honor bar holds tea, snacks and buckets of wine on ice. Guest rooms are uniquely decorated, but include luxurious beds loaded with Frette linens and plush pillows that are almost too pretty to mess up. Bathrooms feature white marble, Miller Harris for Crosby Street amenities and towel warmers. The Meadow Suite includes its own private terrace and garden. On Sunday nights, enjoy the Film Club, which takes place in the state-of-the-art theater with leather seats and a high-definition screen.

86 rooms. Restaurant, bar. Fitness center. $351 and up

★★★THE MERCER

147 Mercer St., Soho, 212-966-6060;
www.mercerhotel.com

Housed in a landmark Romanesque revival building, this is a see-and-be-seen hotel that's all about modern luxury. All rooms have sleek Christian Liaigre interiors that artfully mix soothing neutral colors, hardwood floors and rich materials like leather upholstery and 400-count Egyptian-cotton linens. Bathrooms are just as inviting, with oversized marble tubs big enough for two and bath products from Swedish company FACE. Too tired to unpack? No problem—the staff can take care of that. Need a private trainer or an in-room massage? They've got that (and plenty of other person-alized services) available, too. If all that weren't enough, Jean-Georges Vongerichten's American-Provençal restaurant, The Mercer Kitchen, is onsite.

75 rooms. Restaurant, bar. $351 and up

★★★SOHO GRAND HOTEL

310 West Broadway, Soho, 212-965-3000;
www.sohogrand.com

Still one of just a handful of hotels in Soho, this property was the first to open in the neighborhood in more than a century when it came on the scene in 1996, and it has been a hipster mainstay ever since. The lobby's glass-bottle-paved staircase, cast-iron accents and concrete pillars were designed by William Sofield to mimic the neighborhood's characteristic warehouse lofts. Rooms are downtown-chic, with walls of massive windows, neutral color schemes, leather touches, iPod docks and even a pet goldfish upon request. You can bring along your cat or dog, too—the hotel is owned by pet-products company Hartz Mountain Industries, and offers everything from room service for your pet to on-call veterinarians and even a special pet-limo service. The hotel's Grand Bar & Lounge (a.k.a. "Soho's Living Room") is a good place to start exploring New York nightlife—it has long been popular with both New York's celeb set (Uma Thurman, Kevin Spacey and Heidi Klum) and out-of-towners. The adjoining Yard, open May through September, is a great place to get margaritas and light summer fare under the city sky.

363 rooms. Restaurant, bar. Fitness center. Business center. $351 and up

RECOMMENDED

THE JANE HOTEL

113 Jane St., West Village, 212-924-6700; www.thejanenyc.com

This historic hotel offers what may be the most unique accommodations in New York City. Originally built for sailors, the building also served as a theater in the '80s and '90s. Today, the bohemian hotel has been completely refurbished (save for the antique floors and marble staircases, which are original), but is still set up as it was in the past as ship's cabins (bit of history: the survivors of the *Titanic* stayed here). The 50-square-foot standard cabin features a single bed with a flat-screen TV attached to the wall, a DVD player, iPod dock, complimentary wireless Internet access, and storage built in to the beds and the walls. The bunk bed cabin is suitable for two people and features two TVs (at the end of each bed). These cabins share the communal bathrooms at the end of the hallways, each with two shower stalls and C.O. Bigelow amenities. If you're looking for luxury, this is by no means the hotel for you. But if you're in the mood for some adventure, you'll be more than comfortable here. Cabins are tiny, but if you're just looking for a place to bunk for a few hours, they'll meet your needs. Opt for the Captain's Cabin for more space (250 square feet) and a private, roomy bathroom. These rooms feature full, queen or king-sized beds and have views of the Hudson river (some also have terraces). Either way, guests can enjoy French/Moroccan cuisine at the charming Café Gitane and the Rhino bar, a dark and cozy space filled with artwork, textiles and a glass tile ceiling. The adjacent ballroom is filled with ornate vintage décor, with art and textiles reflecting a Moroccan feel, an antique fireplace, a stuffed ram and an out-of-place disco ball. If you're looking for something off-the-beaten path, The Jane may just fit the bill.

200 rooms. Restaurant, bar. $61-150

JUST OPENED

TRUMP SOHO

246 Spring St., Soho, 212-924-6700; www.thejanenyc.com

The latest from the Trump collection is a welcome addition to the downtown hotel scene with a dramatic, two-story lobby outfitted in bronze and leather and with soaring columns of brown and metallic blue Venetian plaster. To the left is the restaurant Quattro Gastronomia, and straight ahead is a second-floor library with a fireplace, wine rack and cherry-blossom wallpaper. Guest rooms have furnishings by Fendi Casa, custom-made Italian bedding by Bellino, thick wool carpeting, and in one-bedroom suites, a sliding hearth with built-in shelving that separates the sleeping quarters from the living space. Bathrooms have soaking tubs, rainshowers and Turkish Marmara stone on the walls. Bar d'Eau is an indoor and outdoor bar that overflows onto the Pool Deck, which features a blue Italian mosaic-lined pool with a cascading waterfall, private cabanas and a Bocce court. The 11,000-square-foot Spa at Trump includes two separate luxury hammams for men and women, offering traditional services of heat, scrub and relaxation.

391 rooms. Restaurant, bar. Fitness center. Spa. Pool. $351 and up

MIDTOWN/MIDTOWN EAST

★★★ACE HOTEL
20 W. 29th St., Midtown, 212-679-2222; www.acehotel.com

The Ace Hotel is every urban artist's dream hotel. The large and cozy lobby is overflowing with a variety of people working on laptops at the long communal tables, while local DJs play late into the night. Located off the lobby is the Portland, Oregon-based fair trade Stumptown Coffee Roasters—it's worth a visit here just for a cup (expect a line). Follow the mural of graffiti stickers from local artist Michael Anderson leading up a marble staircase to the guest rooms, where you'll find a variety of room sizes, many of which feature custom artwork from local artists and may include guitars, turntables equipped with new and used vinyl and full-sized Smeg refrigerators. All rooms feature custom and vintage furniture, plaid wool blankets, bathroom amenities from Rudy's Barbershop and mini-bars stocked with treats from local businesses. Stop in at The Breslin Bar & Dining Room to cozy up in the dark pub-like space. The English menu focuses on meats such as handmade sausages, charcuterie and seasonal products from farmers. If you're on the go, duck into the No. 7 Sub Shop to pick up a gourmet sandwich.

260 rooms. Restaurant, bar. Business center. Fitness center. Pets accepted. $251-350

★★★THE ALEX HOTEL
205 E. 45th St., Midtown East, 212-867-5100; www.thealexhotel.com

This 33-story hotel near the Chrysler Building whisks you away from New York's constant bustle to a serene oasis where David Rockwell's minimalist décor proves instantly soothing. Clutter-free guest rooms are awash in a palette of whites, creams and earth tones, while limestone bathrooms have Frette towels and products by Frédéric Fekkai. If you have to stay in the city for more than a quick visit—or just hate to say goodbye—extended-stay suites make your time here comfortable with luxury Poggenpohl-fitted kitchens sporting everything from Sub-Zero refrigerators to Miele dishwashers.

203 rooms. Restaurant, bar. Fitness center. Business center. Pets accepted. $351 and up

★★★BRYANT PARK HOTEL

40 W. 40th St., Midtown, 212-869-0100; www.bryantparkhotel.com

For years, this hotel has attracted a who's-who list of designers, media bigwigs and celebs during New York's Fall and Spring Fashion Weeks, thanks to its proximity to the tents erected to host the runway shows across the street. The shows have moved to Lincoln Center, but no matter: many of the same fashionistas frequent this boutique property all year round. They enjoy the amenities in the mod rooms (leather chairs, Tibetan rugs and Travertine marble bathrooms), such as high-definition flat-screen televisions, BOSE Wave music systems, and Obus Forme sound therapy machines that lull them to sleep with gentle waterfall sounds and wake them with chirping birds. There's also a loft meeting space that's popular for sample sales, a 70-seat theater-style screening room and "entertainment planner" (really just a clever title for the concierge) at guests' disposal. Japanese restaurant Koi and the large underground Cellar Bar are always packed with the young and fashionable. Book one of the 10 rooms that face the park—these come with terraces to enjoy the lovely views and all the activity that is always going on in Bryant Park.

129 rooms. Restaurant, bar. Fitness center. $351 and up

★★★THE CARLTON ON MADISON AVENUE

88 Madison Ave., Midtown, 212-532-4100; www.carltonhotelny.com

It wasn't long ago that this now-stunning 1904 Beaux Arts building was a run down property that seemed destined for decay. But a $60 million, five-year renovation project headed by architect David Rockwell breathed brand-new life into the hotel. Today, the three-story lobby and lounge areas are bathed in opulent golds and creams, and the sound of the cascading waterfall here serves as a soothing background soundtrack. Rooms are all about what's plush and new, with Frette bedding, free wireless, and iHome systems. Preserving the hotel's original décor was important, too: An ornate 28-foot Tiffany stained-glass dome, discovered during renovations under such thick layers of dirt and tobacco tar that it was thought to be painted black, has been restored.

317 rooms. Restaurant, bar. Fitness center. Business center. Pets accepted. $351 and up

★★★CHAMBERS HOTEL

15 W. 56th St., Midtown, 212-974-5656; www.chambershotel.com

From the large front door made from woven walnut wood to the more than 500 pieces of artwork by everyone from John Waters to Do-Ho Suh, the Chambers Hotel feels like a chic downtown gallery that's plopped down into the middle of New York's Midtown retail hub. In addition to the paintings that line the walls of the guest rooms, hallways and other public spaces, the hotel uses warm shades of brown throughout, and the rooms have a loft-like feel with large windows, sleek furniture and mini-bars stocked with Dean and Deluca goods. Massage therapists, babysitters and even personal shoppers from Henri Bendel are a phone call away.

77 rooms. Restaurant, bar. Pets accepted. $351 and up

★★★DREAM HOTEL NEW YORK

210 W. 55th St., Midtown, 212-247-2000, 866-437-3266; www.dreamny.com

Vikram Chatwal, the brains behind Time Hotel, turned the former Majestic

Hotel into this slumber-themed property in 2004. You'll feel like you've walked into a trippy dream the moment you hit the lobby, where a two-story aquarium and gold Catherine the Great statue are part of the eclectic design mix. The restaurant here is an outpost of the Serafina chain of northern Italian spots known all over town for their specialty pizzas. An Ayurvedic spa was designed by Deepak Chopra to allow guests to massage and meditate their way to peacefulness before turning in for the night in the minimalist rooms, outfitted with feather beds and 300 thread-count Egyptian sheets, and awash in blue lights that create a twilight feel. If a nightcap is more your style, take the elevator up to the Ava Lounge, which offers a seasonal rooftop garden that sits high above the city with views of Times Square and Columbus Circle.

220 rooms. Restaurant, bar. Fitness center. Spa. Pets accepted. $351 and up

★★★DYLAN HOTEL
52 E. 41st St., Midtown, 212-338-0500; www.dylanhotel.com

This 16-story 1903 Beaux Arts structure was once home to the Chemist's Club of New York, which explains the insignia over the stone entryway. The microscopes and test tubes are long gone, but designer Jeffrey Beers experiments with amber lightboxes suspended from the lobby ceiling and, in a nod to its origins, the hotel provides beakers in place of bathroom cups. Rooms are open and airy spaces, with 11-foot ceilings and large windows, and are accented with a mix of muted shades, jewel-toned materials and American walnut furniture; bathrooms are outfitted with Carrara marble. If you're feeling experimental, check yourself into the Alchemy Suite, which was once a Gothic chamber created to replicate a medieval alchemist's lab. It still has the original stained-glass windows and vaulted ceilings.

107 rooms. Restaurant, bar. Fitness center. Business center. $351 and up

★★★★★FOUR SEASONS HOTEL NEW YORK
57 E. 57th St., Midtown East, 212-758-5700; www.fourseasons.com

Well-heeled travelers kick off their shoes in the 52-story Midtown outpost of this luxe hotel chain, appropriately located steps from shopping-mecca Fifth Avenue. Designed by I.M. Pei, its jaw-dropper is the 33-foot-high backlit onyx ceiling in the lobby (which led Jacqueline Kennedy Onassis to nickname it "The Cathedral"). Sweeping views of Central Park and other parts of the city are part of the allure of the guest rooms, which range in size from 500 to 800 square feet—larger than many New York City apartments—with roomy seating areas (some have furnished terraces, too). Other treats include big marble bathrooms with soaking tubs, and silk drapes that you can control bedside to open or close on those views. Plenty of celebrities have stayed here because they can't get enough of the Four Seasons' signature top-notch service, luxurious spa and fine dining establishments, including L'Atelier de Joël Robuchon.

368 rooms. Restaurant, bar. Fitness center. Spa. Business center. Pets accepted. $351 and up

★★★HOTEL ELYSÉE
60 E. 54th St., Midtown, 212-753-1066; www.elyseehotel.com

Built in 1926 and named after one of the best French restaurants of that time, the Hotel Elysée combines the charm of an intimate bed and breakfast with the service and style of an upscale boutique hotel. The lobby is elegantly decked out with marble floors and mahogany walls, while the guest rooms are styled in French country décor. Stop by the Club Room for complimentary wine and hors d'oeuvres on weekday evenings and pick up free daily guest passes to the local branch of New York Sports Club at the front desk. Be sure to check out the famous Monkey Bar, littered with statues, pictures and paintings of its namesake animal. It was once a haunt for celebrities such as Ava Gardner, Marlon Brando and 15-year hotel resident Tennessee Williams, who lived here until his death in 1983.

100 rooms. Complimentary breakfast. Restaurant. Business center. $351 and up

★★★HÔTEL PLAZA ATHÉNÉE

37 E. 64th St., Midtown East, 212-734-9100; www.plaza-athenee.com

The Hôtel Plaza Athénée sits on a strip of prime real estate in Manhattan: a tranquil, tree-lined street just a few blocks from Central Park. The lobby is awash in marble and crystal, but also has a modern feel. Rooms were recently remodeled and feature European furnishings and rich silks, Sferra linens and plasma televisions with more than 300 channels. Suites have hardwood floors in the living areas and some have glass-enclosed atrium terraces. The 2,453-square-foot Penthouse Duplex suite on the 16th and 17th floors includes two bedrooms, a decorative fireplace, formal dining for six and a private terrace running half the hotel's length. If that's your style, you'll probably also love that Barneys New York and the other high-end shops along Fifth Avenue are just steps away.

142 rooms. Restaurant, bar. Fitness center. Business center. Pets accepted. $351 and up

★★★JUMEIRAH ESSEX HOUSE

160 Central Park South, Midtown, 212-247-0300; www.jumeirahessexhouse.com

Opened in 1931, this landmark hotel sits on Central Park and recently underwent a two-year, $90 million refurbishment. Rooms come with custom-designed furniture and other special touches including amber-colored glass sinks, red leather-framed mirrors and wall-to-wall cabinetry for extra storage space. Not everything is a throwback to the mid-20th century, however. Modern touches include touchscreen controls for lighting and music, flat-screen TVs and lighted footpaths to the bathrooms. If you're in need of a little restoration of your own, the in-house spa features a steam bath, sauna and a host of treatments such as massages and facials.

509 rooms. Restaurant, bar. Fitness center. Spa. Pets accepted. $351 and up

★★★LE PARKER MERIDIEN

119 W. 56th St., Midtown, 212-245-5000; www.parkermeridien.com

Business-minded types will appreciate the ergonomic touches at this Midtown hotel: built-in 6-foot-long workstations with adjustable Herman Miller Aeron chairs, 32-inch TVs set back in swiveling consoles and roll-away storage compartments for luggage. Junior suites add luxury in the form of two-person, cedar-lined baths and showers. There's a weight room, and both basketball and racquetball courts, but it's the rooftop pool that's a longtime-favorite of locals and tourists alike. Same goes for Norma's, one of three onsite restaurants, which caters to a mix of natives and visitors with popular breakfast items including the "Zillion Dollar Lobster Frittata" and "Artychoked Benedict." The hotel is also famous for its excellent burger joint.

731 rooms. Restaurant. Fitness center. Pool. Business center. Pets accepted. $351 and up

★★★LIBRARY HOTEL

299 Madison Ave., Midtown, 212-983-4500; www.libraryhotel.com

Bookworms will get a kick out of this concept hotel, located steps from the New York Public and Pierpont Morgan Libraries on what's known as "Library Way." Rooms are identified by one of 10 Dewey Decimal System categories, and 6,000-plus books are shelved throughout the hotel. Whether you're mad for math or hungry for literature, you can choose a room based on more than 60 themes. The rooms are pleasantly unstuffy, thanks to a décor that's heavy on creams, whites and other light colors. Social readers should check out the mahogany-paneled Writers' Den, which has a cozy fireplace and greenhouse.

60 rooms. Complimentary breakfast. Restaurant, bar. $251-350

★★★THE LONDON NYC

151 W. 54th St., Midtown, 212-307-5000; www.thelondonnyc.com

Anglophiles will love this Midtown luxury hotel which offers the finest elements of British sophistication and understatement. The 500-square-foot London Suites, with bed chamber and separate parlor, were conceptualized by British interior architect David Collins, and are decorated with parquet flooring, custom-woven banquettes and embossed-leather desks, plus tech pleasures such as iHome players and Mitel touchscreen phones. If the biggest and best is what you're after, book the 2,500-square-foot penthouse, which is spread out on two floors with 180-degree views that include Central Park and the George Washington Bridge. It also offers a dining room that seats eight and access to the Chef's Table in Gordon Ramsay's restaurant. Calls across the pond are on the house eight hours a day.

561 rooms. Restaurant, bar. Fitness center. Business center. $351 and up

★★★MILLENNIUM U.N. PLAZA HOTEL

1 United Nations Plaza, Midtown East, 212-758-1234; www.millenniumhotels.com

Diplomats, business travelers and a few guests from the *Rachael Ray* show (this is the show's official hotel) all find something to like about this Midtown East hotel located next to the United Nations. Plenty of meeting and banquet space is available, including a fitness center, a pool and even indoor tennis courts. The rooms are sparsely decorated and have a calm, neutral pallete, allowing sweeping views of the U.N. and the rest of the city to take center stage instead. Unbothered by looming skyscraper neighbors (guest rooms start on the 28th floor), the hotel has some of the best panoramic views of the city, making the rooms feel more like private penthouses than part of a hotel. The only con here: The property is pretty far east, so you'll have to walk several avenues over to catch the subway at Grand Central Station.

427 rooms. Restaurant, bar. Fitness center. Pool. Business center. Pets accepted. Tennis. $251-350

★★★THE NEW YORK PALACE

455 Madison Ave., Midtown East, 212-888-7000; www.newyorkpalace.com

The moment you step through the Madison Avenue gates of the Villard

Mansion and walk down the grand staircase, this hotel's motto, "Old World Elegance—New World Opulence," clicks into place. First built as a luxury apartment building in 1882, the structure was transformed into a hotel in 1980. The spacious and sumptuously appointed rooms throughout the 55-story tower include marble bathrooms, comfortable seating, work desks and large cozy beds. If you're looking to splurge, Triplex Suites are up to 5,000 square feet and boast Art Deco décor and unforgettable views from their 18-foot windows and private rooftop terraces.

899 rooms. Restaurant, bar. Fitness center. Spa. Business center. Pets accepted. $351 and up

★★★OMNI BERKSHIRE PLACE

21 E. 52nd St., Midtown, 212-753-5800; www.omnihotels.com

Pillow-top mattresses and feather pillows in all the rooms should make it easy to get a good night's sleep amid the never-ending frenzy outside this Midtown luxury hotel. Rooms range in size from a 271-square-foot deluxe—with options for one king-size or two double beds—up to the 1,000-square-foot Rodgers & Hammerstein Suite, lavishly appointed with a wraparound terrace, fireplace and spa tub. There's also a sundeck and a fitness center on the 17th floor.

396 rooms. Restaurant, bar. Fitness center. Business center. Pets accepted. $351 and up

★★★★★THE PENINSULA NEW YORK

700 Fifth Ave., Midtown East, 212-956-2888; www.newyork.peninsula.com

Rising 23 stories above some of the best shopping in New York, the Peninsula's Midtown location in the middle of Fifth Avenue is a shopaholic's dream. The Beaux Arts building was completed in 1905 and has luxurious, bright guest-rooms with large windows and simple, contemporary furnishings that give nods to the chain's Asian roots with details like lacquered dressers and armoires. Tech-types get their due, too: Bedside controls mean you don't have to move to manage your music, temperature and lighting settings, and flat-screen TVs and speaker phones are within reach of the bathtubs. The hotel's library-like Gotham Lounge serves afternoon tea, which includes a selection of finger sandwiches such as smoked salmon and egg salad. For a spicier cocktail, head to the rooftop lounge Salon de Ning where 1930's Shanghai meets Midtown Manhattan in an exotic blend of pillow-strewn chaises, potent potables and Asian-influenced appetizers. The Peninsula Spa by ESPA continues the Far East theme with rich bamboo floors and orchid arrangements aplenty. Don't forget your swimsuit; the glass-enclosed rooftop pool is ideal for an evening dip amidst the city skyline.

239 rooms. Restaurant, bar. Fitness center. Pool. Spa. Business center. $351 and up

★★★★THE PIERRE, A TAJ HOTEL

2 E. 61st St., Midtown East, 212-838-8000; www.tajhotels.com

This New York classic reopened in 2009 after a $100 million renovation to the guest rooms and public spaces. The first floor now accommodates a new restaurant (Le Caprice, the first U.S. location of the U.K. favorite) and a lounge (Two E, which serves classic cocktails and delicious snacks). Today, the 1930s Georgian-style building is a mix of old and new. The gorgeous hand-painted murals are still there (even in the fitness center), but they now share space with Indian artwork, some of which hails from the Taj flagship in Mumbai. Guest rooms have been updated to include larger bathrooms (with separate tub and shower) but retain the same elegant, traditional décor longtime guests have come to expect. Rooms are dressed in a soothing palette of ivory and taupe with touches of coral and soft blue, and feature dark wood furnishings and plush beds with tufted headboards and rich fabrics. A variety of large suites have kitchens, and dining rooms, and some have large terraces with views of Central Park. However, one important thing remains the same: Brides still dream of being married inside the ornate Grand Ballroom with its hand-painted silver and gold ceiling and enough space to seat 1,500 guests.

189 rooms. Restaurant, bar. Fitness center. Business center. $351 and up

★★★★★THE RITZ-CARLTON NEW YORK, CENTRAL PARK
50 Central Park South, Midtown, 212-308-9100; www.ritzcarlton.com

The Ritz is all about, well, being ritzy. This link in the exclusive hotel chain is no exception, epitomizing New York glamour and sophistication at every turn. Guests barely lift a finger from the time they arrive in the wood-paneled lobby and are escorted to rooms with 400 thread-count French sateen linens, feather duvets and a selection of seven pillow types. Oversized marble bathrooms have deep soaking tubs, Etro toiletries and a choice of terry-waffle or sateen-cotton bathrobes. Visitors in the park-view rooms get telescopes for bird (or people) watching, and when they tire of that, it's a toss-up between having a jet-lag therapy, facial or other treatment at the second-floor La Prairie spa or taking one of the hotel's on-call limos for a leisurely drive around the park, before indulging in a deliciously seasonal meal at BLT Market.

259 rooms. Restaurant, bar. Fitness center. Spa. Business center. Pets accepted. $351 and up

★★★ROYALTON HOTEL
44 W. 44th St., Midtown, 212-869-4400; www.royaltonhotel.com

Many consider the Royalton to be the original boutique hotel. It's the one that set the standard for hipness with its famously spare Philippe Starck design and a fashion-magazine crowd that frequented the lobby bar in the '90s. A recent renovation upped the sophistication level in a quiet, clubby way. The dark lobby, with a mix of icy glass, varnished wood, steel and brass, is softened by a giant fireplace, warm leather-covered walls and furniture upholstered in suede and hide. The large guest rooms have also been updated, and use soft colors like light blues, grays and whites as a backdrop for the built-in banquettes that run from one end of the room to the other. Flowing curtains, down comforters and Philippe Starck-designed bathrooms with five-foot circular tubs and steel sinks continue the cozy-meets-mod aesthetic. Back downstairs, restaurateur John McDonald (Lure Fishbar, Lever House), has overhauled Bar 44 and the intimate 100-seat Brasserie 44 with honey-teak walls, rope arches and white-glass globe lighting.

168 rooms. Restaurant, bar. Fitness center. Business center. Pets accepted. $351 and up

★★★★★THE ST. REGIS NEW YORK
2 E. 55th St., Midtown East, 212-753-4500; www.starwoodhotels.com

No New York hotel may be better suited for shoppers than the St. Regis, with its prime location near Saks Fifth Avenue, Henri Bendel, and with the famed De Beers boutique right in the lobby. The opulent 1904 Beaux Arts landmark building (restored in a $100 million undertaking in 2006) is an impressive throwback to old-school New York elegance. The lobby is dripping with gilded cornices and Italian marble, and if that isn't glitzy enough, a large glittering chandelier hangs over the reception desk from the soaring Trompe l'oeil ceiling, which resembles a bright-blue sky. A visit to the legendary King Cole Bar—with its famous 1906 Art Nouveau oil mural by Maxfield Parrish—is definitely in order. Ask for a Red Snapper (people call it a Bloody Mary everywhere else, but don't try that here—the bar claims to be its birthplace) and then head to Adour, chef Alain Ducasse's onsite restaurant and wine bar. Guest rooms have a lavish appeal with silk wall coverings and antique furniture. Beds come dressed in soft Egyptian-cotton sheets and feather-down comforters, and the Remède bath amenities are pure indulgence for the skin. If you have any last-minute needs before falling asleep, each floor has its own 24-hour butler.

229 rooms. Restaurant, bar. Fitness center. Spa. Business center. $351 and up

★★★SOFITEL NEW YORK
45 W. 44th St., Midtown, 212-354-8844; www.sofitel.com

You'll be greeted with a polite "bonjour" at this 30-story French export, a curved, modern limestone-and-glass building in the heart of Midtown. Paris- and New York-influenced Art Deco motifs are mixed throughout the hotel, including in photographs of the two cities in each room. Guest suites are compact and comfortable, with beautiful maple headboards affixed to the walls above the beds and marble baths. Top-floor rooms have private terraces and dazzling city views to boot. Enjoy French cuisine at Gaby restaurant and bar.

398 rooms. Restaurant, bar. Fitness center. Business center. Pets accepted. $351 and up

★★★THE WALDORF ASTORIA
301 Park Ave., Midtown East, 212-355-3000; www.waldorfnewyork.com

Opened in 1893 by millionaire William Waldorf Astor, this grande dame of New York hotels moved to its present location in 1931 from one a little further south on Fifth Avenue, and it still retains some of the original hotel's Art Deco interior. The lobby has the decadent feel of a ballroom with its sweeping marble staircases, and glamour seeps from every crevice of the hotel, which sits on a full city block. As you would suspect from such a historic hotel, every room located in the Waldorf Astoria and Waldorf Towers (which has a separate lobby, concierge, long-term leases and roomier suites) is adorned with thick draperies and ornately carved furniture, though some rooms are quite small. The hotel's Bull and Bear Steakhouse & Bar and cocktail terrace overlooking the Park Avenue lobby are always busy. A new Guerlain Spa offers complimentary valet parking and relaxing foot baths upon arrival.

1,416 rooms. Restaurant, bar. Fitness center. Spa. Business center. Pets accepted. $351 and up

RECOMMENDED

ALGONQUIN HOTEL
59 W. 44th St., Midtown, 212-840-6800; www.algonquinhotel.com

Since 1902 the Algonquin has been popular with theatrical and literary glitterati, most notably members of the legendary Round Table luncheons: This exclusive group of creative types-including Dorothy Parker, Edna Ferber and

Harpo Marx-met at the hotel almost daily during the decade following World War II to exchange ideas and barbs (financing for *The New Yorker* magazine was secured here). Today, it's still loaded with character, from the antique furniture to its most popular current resident, Matilda—the latest in a long line of felines that have called the hotel home since a wayward cat first wandered in and ended up staying in the 1930s. Rooms have recently been remodeled and include comfortable pillow-top beds, duvets and modern amenities like flat-screen TVs. For a special treat, make a reservation for dinner and a cabaret show at the famous Oak Room Supper Club, the hotel's dark-wood paneled restaurant where crooners such as Harry Connick, Jr. and Diana Krall got their starts.

174 rooms. Restaurant, bar. Fitness center. Business center. Pets accepted. $251-350

HOTEL ROGER WILLIAMS

131 Madison Ave., Midtown, 212-448-7000; www.hotelrogerwilliams.com

The name is a bit lackluster, but we can assure you that there's nothing drab about this recently renovated 16-story hotel named for Rhode Island's founder. The modern rooms range from the simple, single-bed superior rooms and Japanese-inspired doubles where furnishings include shoji screens, to garden terrace rooms that have landscaped patios and great city views. All have special touches, whether it's a colorful quilt on the bed or a bright-blue armchair and orange bench in the corner. The unique Help Yourself Breakfast Pantry is a casual, buffet-style service where you can choose from New York specialties such as croissants from Balthazar, bagels from H&H or just a complimentary newspaper in the morning. The Mezzanine Dining Room is a little more formal, with a menu that changes as the day progresses.

193 rooms. Complimentary breakfast. Restaurant, bar. Fitness center. Business center. $251-350

THEATER DISTRICT/TIMES SQUARE

★★★RENAISSANCE NEW YORK TIMES SQUARE HOTEL

714 Seventh Ave., Theater District, 212-765-7676; www.marriott.com

An extensive makeover by famed designer Jordan Mozer transformed this Marriott-owned hotel from cookie-cutter to au courant. The lobby is modern without being steely, thanks to blue and red leather chairs and funky orb-shaped ceiling fixtures. Rooms have stylish, dark hard-wood furniture and blue and gold accents, plus modern necessities such as technology panels where you can plug in all your electronics—iPod, cell phone, laptop—in one place. Bathrooms have robes and Aveda products. The restaurant Two Times Square on the second floor has sweet views of Times Square. (For just-as-cool views of the square, ask for an upper-floor room overlooking Seventh Avenue.)

305 rooms. Restaurant, bar. Fitness center. Pets accepted. $251-350

★★★W NEW YORK TIMES SQUARE

1567 Broadway, Midtown, 212-930-7400; www.starwoodhotels.com

Located in Times Square, this hotel is just as colorful as its surroundings. The ultra-contemporary lobby, located on the seventh floor, has tile floors and leather benches, and it houses the hip Living Room bar. Recently renovated guest rooms were given splashes of color. The Wonderful Room has a floor to ceiling headboard, while the Fantastic Suite is done up in electric blue and features a metallic plane with flat-screen television separating the bedroom and living areas. It goes without saying that the views from the rooms can't be beat: Watch the action unfold below on Times Square as you relax on your pillow-top bed and goose-down pillow. Though this W doesn't have a Bliss Spa, it does have the homegrown spa's signature products sink-side. Once you're rested, head down to the Blue Fin restaurant before heading out into the square, just outside the lobby doors.

507 rooms. Restaurant, bar. Fitness center. Business center. Pets accepted. $351 and up

★★★THE WESTIN NEW YORK AT TIMES SQUARE

270 W. 43rd St., Theater District, 212-201-2700; www.westinny.com

This 45-story hotel near Times Square is an oasis in a sea of nonstop action. Regular rooms are kitted out with the hotel's trademarked Heavenly Bed & Bath, and have views of Times Square and the Hudson River. The "Spa-Inspired" guest rooms take relaxation to the next level with aroma air diffusers, a Kinjoy Shiatsu massage chair that can be adjusted to "zero gravity" position and a variety of soothing CDs for your listening pleasure. Book a $2,000-a-night "Renewal suite" and your own personal "host" (in other words, butler) caters to your every wish so you can focus on rejuvenation. There may not be much more you'll need beyond the fresh white roses, orchids and lotus flowers supplied throughout the suite, a bamboo-floored exercise space which includes a spinning cycle and other exercise equipment, and spa bathroom with a Kohler Chromatherapy whirlpool bath, plus cashmere robes and slippers.

863 rooms. Restaurant, bar. Fitness center. Spa. Business center. $251-350

TRIBECA/MEATPACKING DISTRICT

★★★THE GREENWICH HOTEL

377 Greenwich St., Tribeca, 212-941-8900; www.thegreenwichhotel.com

If individuality is your thing, The Greenwich Hotel should be your auberge of choice. Each of the 88 guest rooms is unique, adorned with global influences such as Parisian antiques, Moroccan tilework, Tibetan rugs and repurposed Japanese lumber. The brainchild of actor/director Robert De Niro, this boutique property is yet another resplendent addition to the ever-expanding Tribeca neighborhood. The 2,000-square-foot Greenwich Suite is a worthy splurge with 30-foot skylit windows, two master bedrooms and a wood-burning stone fireplace. Don't forgo a trip to the sublevel Shibui Spa; it may be your one opportunity to relax under a 250-year-old Japanese wooden farmhouse and lantern-lit swimming pool. Be sure to check out the artwork in the lobby, drawing room and hallways as they are all by the late Robert De Niro Senior. For a good gauge of the neighborhood, snag a sidewalk table at Locanda Verde and watch the locals sashay by.

88 rooms. Restaurant, bar. Fitness center. Pool. Spa. Pets accepted. $351 and up

★★★HOTEL GANSEVOORT

18 Ninth Ave., Meatpacking District, 212-206-6700; www.hotelgansevoort.com

This hotel is just as stylish as its trendsetting neighbors in the Meatpacking District, a neighborhood home to high-end-but-downtown-chic retailers such as Scoop and Stella McCartney. Room palettes consist of neutrals with blue-purple splashes. Everything, including headboards, armoires and walls, is awash in leather and fabrics, while 9-foot ceilings add airiness. The hotel is famous for its rooftop destination Plunge, a restaurant, bar and lounge with wraparound views of the city and a 45-foot-long outdoor, heated pool that's surrounded by glass panels and open year-round.

180 rooms. Restaurant, bar. Fitness center. Pool. Spa. Business center. Pets accepted. $351 and up

★★★THE STANDARD

848 Washington St., Meatpacking District, 212-645-4646; www.standardhotels.com/new-york-city

Possibly one of the last new hotels to open before 2009's recession put a stop to new building construction in New York, the Standard, sister to L.A.'s sleek and modern boutique hotel, made its way east last year to New York's Meatpacking District. The hotel resides in two newly constructed Modernist towers that literally straddle one of New York's greatest new attractions, the High Line elevated parkway. The same sleek, spare and stylish design seen in André Balazs's other properties can be seen here, with rooms featuring minimalist furnishings, luxury linens and spacious baths, and cutting edge tech toys such as oversized high-def TVs and iPod-friendly sound systems. The fully stocked gym is open 24 hours, and the onsite restaurant, the Standard Grill, serves bistro favorites late into the night.

337 rooms. Restaurant, bar. Fitness center. $251-350

★★★TRIBECA GRAND HOTEL

2 Avenue of the Americas, Tribeca, 212-519-6600; www.tribecagrand.com

This edgy-but-elegant hotel is a goldmine for those looking to party like rock stars, or just appear like they do. The soaring triangular atrium off the lobby is where an international roster of DJs spin in the sofa-filled Church Lounge, and the lower level has a 100-seat theater for private movie screenings. Rooms are smallish, but have phones and TVs in the bathrooms, gourmet mini-bars, and, if you request one, a live goldfish to keep you company. Some suites look out over the lounge, which can feel like opening the door into a round-the-clock party, but that's fine by most of the people who stay here. If you're into gadgets, book an iStudio, tricked out with Apple's latest goods, including G5 computers with film-, photo- and sound-editing software.

203 rooms. Restaurant, bar. Fitness center. Business center. Pets accepted. $351 and up

UNION SQUARE/FLATIRON DISTRICT/GRAMERCY PARK/ MURRAY HILL

★★★GRAMERCY PARK HOTEL

2 Lexington Ave., Gramercy Park, 212-920-3300; www.gramercyparkhotel.com

Despite being a favorite haunt of the likes of Humphrey Bogart and Babe Ruth, who frequented the bar here, the Gramercy has been known as a low-key (and at times tired) spot since its opening in 1925. When hotelier Ian Schrager gave the place a major overhaul before reopening it in 2006, he managed to make improvements without turning it into yet another cookie-cutter Mid-Century modern property. The lobby now boasts impressive smoked-wood beams, a 10-foot-high fireplace and a Moroccan checkered-tiled floor. Rooms are decorated in rich reds, royal blues and other jewel tones instead of de rigueur minimalist neutrals, velvets, leathers and tapestries adorn Julian Schnabel-designed furniture. Maialino is a Roman-style trattoria from Danny Meyer. The

Rose Bar is lined with paintings by Andy Warhol, Jean-Michel Basquiat and Schnabel himself. But the prettiest perk is something even lifelong New Yorkers never see: keys to the exclusive and elegantly landscaped Gramercy Park, an honor normally reserved for residents of the 39 buildings that surround the oldest private park in the country.

185 rooms. Restaurant, bar. Fitness center. Business center. $351 and up

★★★W NEW YORK-UNION SQUARE

201 Park Ave. South, Union Square, 212-253-9119; www.starwoodhotels.com/whotels

This Union Square outpost of the contemporary hotel chain does a nice job blending an uptown atmosphere with some downtown coolness. Set on the open square with a leafy park in its center, this W (there are four others around Manhattan) located in the 1911 Beaux Arts Guardian Life building has the same clean modern lines and comfortable beds that guests swear by, and twice-daily maid service, as the other locales. There's also an in-hotel lounge and a branch of Todd English's Italian/Mediterranean restaurant Olives, but with the East Village, Tribeca and Soho so close, you're better off heading out on an adventure than staying in.

270 rooms. Restaurant, bar. Fitness center. Pets accepted. $351 and up

UPPER EAST SIDE

★★★★THE CARLYLE, A ROSEWOOD HOTEL

35 E. 76th St., Upper East Side, 212-744-1600; www.thecarlyle.com

Everyone from heads of state to celebrities including Tom Cruise and Katie Holmes favor this classic hotel when they're in New York City, but the attentive and discreet staff is famous for treating all guests like visiting A-listers. Opened in 1930, the classic Art Deco hotel (named for British essayist Thomas Carlyle) is all about understated, old-fashioned elegance. Uniformed elevator operators guide you to floors where rooms and suites are mixed with 60 residential apartments (lucky live-ins get the same perks as hotel guests). The rooms were originally designed by Dorothy Draper and later updated by Mark Hampton, Thierry Despont, Alexandra Champalimaud and other well-known designers. The furnishings range in style from classic British to modern, and some of the larger suites include powder rooms, foyers with full wet bars and even grand pianos. Luxurious touches include custom-made Limoges ashtrays, oversized umbrellas at the ready, and a significant nod to modern technology with plasma televisions, DVD players and iPod docking stations. Step back in time outside your room by hitting the classic Café Carlyle, where acts include Ute Lemper and, occasionally, a clarinet-playing Woody Allen.

188 rooms. Restaurant, bar. Fitness center. Spa. Business center. Pets accepted. $351 and up

★★★★THE LOWELL

28 E. 63rd St., Upper East Side, 212-838-1400; www.lowellhotel.com

Located in a landmark 1920s building on the Upper East Side, the Lowell captures the essence of an elegant country house with a blend of English prints, floral fabrics and Chinese porcelains that surprisingly works. Many suites boast wood-burning fireplaces, a rarity in Manhattan. All rooms are individually decorated, and the Lowell's specialty suites are a unique treat. The Hollywood Suite reflects the 1930s silver-screen era with photos of glamorous ingenues.

The English influences extend to the Pembroke Room, where Anglophiles can throw their pinkies up at tea time (breakfast and brunch is also served). But for something uniquely American, check out the clubby Post House, a well-respected New York steakhouse that serves terrific chops.

72 rooms. Restaurant, bar. Fitness center. Business center. Pets accepted. $351 and up

★★★THE MARK

25 E. 77th St., Upper East Side, 212-744-4300; www.themarkhotel.com

Located on the Upper East Side near Central Park and all of New York City's best museums, this 1927 landmark building is now the glam Mark Hotel. Designed by French designer Jacques Grange, public spaces feature dramatic black and white striped floors and artwork commissioned by Pierre Passebon, the owner of Galerie du Passage in Paris. Staff here are dressed in crisp and elegant uniforms from London's Turnbull and Asser. Guest rooms are comforting, with neutral tones of white, beige, brown and splashes of color found in the artwork. Custom-made beds feature luxurious Quagliotti linens and horsehair headboards. Unique technology fills the rooms, with Bang & Olufsen flat-screen TVs and audio systems with iPod/MP3 docks, and a Crestron control panel, that operates everything in the room. Subzero refrigerators and freezers are built into the granite mini-bar, where you can fix a cocktail. Bathrooms are just as elegant, with heated towel racks, flat-screen televisions built into the mirrors, and stylish mint green vanities. Suites are more like lavish apartments, with large living rooms, kitchens and dining areas. Get pampered at the Fekkai Salon, which offers a full salon menu including manicures, pedicures and makeup applications. The Mark Restaurant by famed chef Jean-Georges Vongerichten serves up new American cuisine with a French/Asian influence and a raw bar. Mark's Bar draws in guests and neighborhood dwellers alike with its stylish and fun design, with hot pink carpeting, a lit-up pink bar and cow-print couches and chairs.

150 rooms. Restaurant, bar. Business center. Fitness center. Pets accepted. $351 and up

★★★★THE PLAZA

768 Fifth Ave., Upper East Side, 212-759-3000; www.theplaza.com

With a standard for luxury that dates back more than a century, it is no surprise that the renovated Plaza hotel reopened its doors in 2008 to universal pomp and pageantry. After three years and $450 million, The Plaza now bridges Old World enchantment and contemporary technology. Guest rooms are thoughtfully detailed in Beaux Arts-inspired décor with spacious closets, custom Italian Mascioni linens and bathrooms flaunting 24-karat gold-plated Sherle Wagner faucets, handcrafted solid marble vanities, inlaid mosaic tiles and Miller Harris bath products. If that's not enough pampering for you, make your way to the Caudalié Vinothérapie Spa, the first of its kind in the United States, where face and body treatments can—and should—be followed up by a visit to the French Paradox Wine Lounge. The 8,300-square-foot fitness center includes an Olympic-sized lap pool and basketball court. Stop by the storied Palm Court for sumptuous afternoon tea, or enjoy a cocktail at the Rose Club or the Champagne Bar. Todd English's European-style food hall features a wine bar, seafood grill, pizza station and more.

282 rooms. Restaurant, bar. Fitness center. Business center. Spa. Pets accepted. $351 and up

★★★THE SURREY

20 E. 76th St., Upper East Side, 212-288-3700; www.thesurreyhotel.com

The elegant pre-war Surrey has a brand-new look and feel. Recently reopened after a complete renovation, the stylish hotel includes a sophisticated gray and white color palette, eye-catching artwork (like the giant painting of Kate Moss near the elevators) and a wall of candles in the lobby. The hotel's eatery Café Boulud is buzzing every day of the week—guests receive priority seating and can order room service from the restaurant. The cozy bar off the lobby has a living room feel and is a great spot for a drink and a quick meal. Snacks and drinks are also available on the open-to-guests-only outdoor garden. Guest rooms here are spacious, especially by New York standards, and include plush custom beds, window seats, mini-bars stocked with local treats, and white marble bathrooms with Pratesi robes. The spa is small, but has lovely treatment rooms that include showers and everything you need to freshen up after a treatment. The Presidential suite is a stunner, with a large living area, plenty of windows, a baby grand piano, a full kitchen and two luxurious bathrooms.

190 rooms. Restaurant, bar. Fitness center. Spa. $350 and up

UPPER WEST SIDE/COLUMBUS CIRCLE

★★★6 COLUMBUS

6 Columbus Circle, Columbus Circle, 212-204-3000; www.sixcolumbus.com

There's an überchic aesthetic at this mod hotel, which replaced a dive that sat here long before it. The lobby's slender leather couch, white shag rug and powder-blue saucer chairs read *I Dream of Jeannie*, and that '60s feel carries through to the blue-toned, Steven Sclaroff-designed rooms, decked out with teak walls, Saarinen-style side chairs and tables, and classic Guy Bourdin prints on the wall. The continental crowd doesn't seem to mind unloading their Euros for maki from onsite Blue Ribbon Sushi, or shelling out $5,000 a night for the privilege of staying in a two-story loft space with a terrace overlooking Central Park and Columbus Circle.

88 rooms. Restaurant, bar. $351 and up

★★★★★MANDARIN ORIENTAL, NEW YORK

80 Columbus Circle, Columbus Circle, 212-805-8800; www.mandarinoriental.com

With all that the Mandarin Oriental offers, it's possible you may never want to leave. First, there are the views: The hotel, which occupies the 35th to 54th floors of the Time Warner Center, boasts impressive floor-to-ceiling windows that look out onto Columbus Circle, midtown Manhattan, the Hudson River and Central Park. Then there are the shops and restaurants: They include the buttoned-up shirtmaker Thomas Pink and famed $450-per-person sushi restaurant Masa. Finally, there's the décor: Standard rooms are dressed in black, red, gray or cream colors with Asian cherrywood furniture and fresh orchids, while superior rooms have lavish Spanish marble bathrooms with Italian granite vanities. The best amenity may be the view; each room serves up a panorama of either Central Park or the Hudson River. For the supreme pampering experience, reserve the 2,640-square-foot Presidential suite on the 53rd floor, which includes a living and dining area, gourmet kitchen and study, all outfitted with oriental rugs, upholstered silk walls and other Asian artifacts. Dine at the Mandarin's wonderful Asiate restaurant, take a dip in the 75-foot lap pool (rumored to be the largest in Manhattan), or order room service and a movie—and put the high-tech entertainment system that's standard in every room to good use.

248 rooms. Restaurant, bar. Fitness center. Pool. Spa. Business center. Pets accepted. $351 and up

★★★★★TRUMP INTERNATIONAL HOTEL & TOWER

1 Central Park West, Columbus Circle, 212-299-1000; www.trumpintl.com

As with most things Trump, this 52-story building at the crossroads of Broadway, Columbus Circle and Central Park is anything but understated. Designed by architects Philip Johnson and Costas Kondylis, only a portion of Trump's black-glass tower—fronted by an unmistakable, massive silver globe sculpture—is taken up by the hotel's just renovated 167 rooms. The premises are also home to the lauded French-fusion restaurant Jean Georges and the luxurious 6,000-square-foot Trump spa. Rooms have Trump-style basics: marble bathrooms, European-style kitchens with china, crystal glassware and Christofle serving trays, and amazing park and city views through the floor-to-ceiling windows. Leave it to the Donald to add an extra-special touch by assigning each of the hotel guests their own personal attaché to assist with everything from personalized stationary to a custom-stocked fridge.

167 rooms. Restaurant. Fitness center. Pool. Spa. Business center. Pets accepted. $351 and up

RECOMMENDED

HOTEL BEACON

2130 Broadway, Upper West Side, 212-787-1100; www.beaconhotel.com

This Upper West Side hotel was converted from a residential building, and many of its rooms are still leased as long-term apartments. All of the Beacon's spacious rooms are simply furnished and decorated in a floral motif, and one- and two-bedroom suites come with one king or two double beds in each room as well as a pull-out couch, making this a good option for larger families who want to be near neighborhood institutions like the American Museum of Natural History and Lincoln Center. Fully equipped kitchenettes in all the rooms include microwaves and coffeemakers. Otherwise, the hotel restaurant is open 24-hours.

260rooms. Restaurant. Business center. $151-250

WHERE TO EAT

CHELSEA/HELL'S KITCHEN/GARMENT DISTRICT

★★★★DEL POSTO

85 Tenth Ave., Chelsea, 212-497-8090; www.delposto.com

If you're looking for checkered tablecloths and the quaint fare of typical red-sauce joints, keep moving. The ambitious, sprawling Del Posto reflects the bold, larger-than-life persona of its famous owner-partner, Mario Batali. At 24,000 square feet, with soaring columns and enough mahogany to give environmentalists palpitations, this high-end Italian restaurant dwarfs its competition in size and style, but still pays attention to tiny details like purse stools for the ladies. Sliced jalapeño peppers in the spaghetti with Dungeness crab will have you reaching for water to cool your lips. That's the kind of bold touch one expects from Batali, as is serving whole fish dramatically and expertly portioned tableside by attentive servers. Dinner here is expensive, but one taste of dishes such as orecchiette with lamb sausage and the remarkably flaky torta Carotina—sliced and served tableside with cool, creamy gelato—will quickly quell your doubts about whether the meal was worth every penny.

Italian. Lunch (Monday-Friday), dinner. Reservations recommended. $36-85

★★★SCARPETTA

355 W. 14th St., Chelsea, 212-691-0555; www.scarpettanyc.com

It's all about the pasta at this unassuming Italian spot on the edge of the Meatpacking District. Located within a rehabbed Greek revival townhouse, the restaurant is modern, yet cozy with dim lighting and exposed brick walls. Executive chef Scott Conant has created a menu that offers impressive dishes, such as fennel-crusted lamb loin with mint and pecorino, and imported turbot over white asparagus in a mustard-riesling emulsion. But it's the simple spaghetti with tomato and basil that will have your tastebuds buzzing. The pasta is cooked al dente and piled high on the plate, coated with a fresh, sweet tomato sauce and just the right balance of basil. Forgo dessert for the cheese plate; the ricotta di bufala with truffle honey satisfies any after-dinner sweet tooth.

Italian. Dinner. Outdoor seating. Reservations recommended. Bar. $36-85

RECOMMENDED

THE RED CAT

227 Tenth Ave., Chelsea, 212-242-1122; www.theredcat.com

Folksy but also art-house cool, the Red Cat is the kind of unpretentious restaurant that leaves you wondering why there simply aren't more places like it. With its art-adorned barn walls, warm red banquettes and hanging iron lanterns, this neighborhood Mediterranean-American charmer is frequented by horn-rimmed-glasses-wearing professionals who sit solo at the bar, tearing into the thick double-cut pork chop and sipping a glass of peppery pinot noir. The vegetables are so fresh and thoughtfully prepared—rapini comes sautéed in garlic and chili flakes—that you'll wonder whether there really is a farm out back from which the chef is plucking his ingredients.

Contemporary American. Lunch (Tuesday-Saturday), dinner. $16-35

EAST VILLAGE/LOWER EAST SIDE

★★★WD-50

50 Clinton St., Lower East Side, 212-477-2900; www.wd-50.com

Dining at WD-50 is part feast and part science experiment, thanks to heralded chef Wylie Dufresne's cutting-edge techniques. Here, even mayonnaise goes from plain-Jane to wow as Dufresne fries it and serves it in a neat row of white pellets alongside calf's tongue. The restaurant also serves squab with carob and cream soda, a combination that you likely won't find anywhere else. Even the carb-averse can dive into a plate of noodles, which are actually made of ground shrimp. The food here intrigues, but more important, it's delicious. Pack your sense of adventure and be prepared to spend—the 12-course tasting menu costs $215 with wine pairings.

Contemporary American. Dinner. Closed Monday-Tuesday. Reservations recommended. $36-85

RECOMMENDED

DBGB KITCHEN & BAR

299 Bowery, East Village, 212-933-5300; www.danielnyc.com

It seems that anything Daniel Boulud touches turns to culinary gold, and DBGB Kitchen & Bar is proving no exception. Boulud's newest downtown venture is a more casual approach to French brasserie fare with sausage leading the charge. There are more than a dozen links to choose from including standouts such as the Berliner, German currywurst alongside turnip confit, and the Tunisienne, lamb and mint merguez with harissa, lemon-braised spinach and chickpeas. But the menu highlights extend beyond encased meat. The lemon and rosemary roasted chicken is moist and flavorful, and the Frenchie burger is a fun play on a traditional burger with pork belly, arugula and morbier cheese on a peppered brioche bun. Floor-to-ceiling open shelves stocked with glassware, copper pots and dry goods tastefully salute the restaurant's Bowery location, which long stood as New York's industrial restaurant supply district. In case you forget you're dining in a Boulud restaurant, the chef's favorite culinary quotes line the mirrors around the bar.

French, German. Lunch, dinner. Bar. $16-35

THE MERMAID INN

96 Second Ave., East Village, 212-674-5870; 568 Amsterdam Ave., Upper West Side,
212-799-7400; www.themermaidnyc.com

This seafood eatery boasts a well-stocked raw bar and is decked out with framed maritime maps and fish prints, plus dishes of goldfish pretzels on the bar. An herb roasted chicken (East Village location) and a grilled strip steak (Upper West Side location) infiltrate the otherwise exclusively seafood menu, and the short-but-well-chosen wine list complements the ocean fare. A lobster sandwich bears chunks of celery and comes heaped on a buttery brioche roll with a side of Old Bay-seasoned fries, and complimentary chocolate pudding served in a demitasse cup rounds out the night. The dark wooden tables are placed liberally throughout the dining room, back garden and front patio, so it never gets too noisy.

Seafood. Dinner, Saturday-Sunday brunch (Upper West Side location). Outdoor seating. $36-85

MOMOFUKU SSÄM BAR

207 Second Ave., East Village, 212-254-3500; www.momofuku.com

Star chef David Chang dabbles in pork the way great artists work in clay or watercolor. His steamed pork belly buns (also available at nearby Momofuku Noodle Bar), regional country ham selections and crispy pig's head torchon make Chang New York's reigning prince of pork. The jewel in his crown is bo ssäm—a hefty roasted Boston pork butt that takes six to eight hours to prepare. (Ordering this dish in advance for a party of at least six is the only way to get a reservation.) It's served with Chang's interpretation of traditional accoutrements: kimchi, oysters, Korean rice and bibb lettuce. Communal tables keep the mood here light and fun, and the hipster staff is blissfully helpful. If you're craving more of a challenge, try getting a table at sister property Ko; the ultra-strict reservation policy may be frustrating, but if you get in, it doesn't take long to see what all the fuss is about. You can also try your luck at getting a reservation (you have to do it online and have a least four people in your party) at the noodle bar for the popular fried chicken dinner. This is the only other

HIGHLIGHT

WHAT ARE THE BEST CELEBRITY CHEF RESTAURANTS IN NEW YORK CITY?

CRAFT
Tom Colicchio of TV's *Top Chef* obviously knows food, and it shows at his hyper-seasonal restaurant where diners build their own meals.

BABBO
Mario Batali is the bad boy of the restaurant world. It's at Babbo where he lets his rebel personality shine with dishes like the melt-in-your-mouth beef cheek ravioli with rich squab liver and black truffles.

DANIEL
Chef Daniel Boulud is fastidious about details—like the clarity of his veal stock, the flower petals suspended in ice cubes in some of the cocktails and the complimentary warm madeleines at meal's end.

JEAN GEORGES
The novelty may have worn off, but Jean Georges is still as good as it was when it opened back in 1997. Today, the chef has countless other restaurants, but you can always count on a consistently wonderful experience at his flagship.

L'ATELIER DE JOËL ROBUCHON
This is lauded chef Joël Robuchon's fourth outpost of L'Atelier worldwide, and he further establishes his talented flair for flavor with an ambitious small-plate French menu.

meal for which they take reservations. Otherwise, you just have to show up at any of David Chang's places and pray you get a seat. Má Pêche in midtown is the chef's latest restaurant.
Asian. Lunch, dinner. $16-35

OTTO ENOTECA PIZZERIA
1 Fifth Ave., East Village, 212-995-9559; www.ottopizzeria.com
Mario Batali's bustling pizza joint near Washington Square Park is one of the few spots in the city where a large group can dine really well and not break the bank. Thin pizzas (like the memorable pane frattau, made with tomato and pecorino romano and topped with a velvety sunny side up egg) are crisped on a griddle, while $9 pastas (spaghetti alla carbonara, rigatoni with escarole

and Italian sausage) are hearty and satisfying. The housemade gelato that's out of this world, especially the fruity and unexpected olive-oil flavor. The staff is highly knowledgeable about wine—no small feat, as there are more than 700 Italian bottles on the menu.

Italian. Lunch, dinner. $16-35

PRUNE
54 E. First St., East Village, 212-677-6221; www.prunerestaurant.com

A place that serves 10 different kinds of Bloody Marys (including the Caesar, served with Boodles gin, clam juice and a pickled egg) obviously knows a thing or two about brunch. That's why you'll wait north of 90 minutes on weekend mornings for a seat in the snug-though-charming dining room. If you tough it out, your prize is delicious fare such as housemade lamb sausage with oysters and grilled pheasant bread, or the Dutch style pancake cooked in the oven with blueberries and served with sour cream and powdered sugar. Lunch and dinner offerings are equally innovative and consistently sensational, and service is pleasantly cheery.

Contemporary American. Lunch (Monday-Friday), dinner, Saturday-Sunday brunch. $16-35

GREENWICH VILLAGE/SOHO/WEST VILLAGE
★★★BABBO
110 Waverly Place, Greenwich Village, 212-777-0303; www.babbonyc.com

Mario Batali is the rock 'n' roll bad boy of the restaurant world. He's got a notorious temper, a ragtag wardrobe and a cameo in a Bloodsugars' music video to his credit along with all those fabulous restaurants. It's at Babbo where he lets his rebel personality shine; a close friend of R.E.M.'s Michael Stipe, Batali understandably skips Old Blue Eyes and plays whatever he wants over the dining room sound system at this traditional-with-a-twist Italian restaurant. So rock out while tucking into Batali's creative dishes such as "mint love letters"—delicate pasta pockets of spicy lamb sausage with just a hint of mint to cool your palette—and melt-in-your-mouth beef cheek ravioli with rich squab liver and black truffles. A $125 "traditional" tasting menu with wine is a song compared to similar menus at other restaurants—and you can bet those places won't likely have that rustic, rock combo.

Italian. Dinner. Reservations recommended. $36-85

★★★BALTHAZAR
80 Spring St., Soho, 212-965-1414; www.balthazarny.com

This warm, noisy French bistro—a hot spot of the '90s and now a reliable standby—is a transporting experience, from the sunshine-yellow walls to the European crowd devouring steak au poivre, duck confit and other "I-must-be-in-Paris" staples. The brunch is among the best in town; the smartest calls are the pillowy brioche French toast and baskets of baked goods—but don't eat that entire croissant or you might not fit between the snugly packed tables when you get up to leave. The late-night menu keeps Balthazar bustling until after midnight seven days a week. No time for a full meal? Stop at the adjacent bakery for one of the city's best baguettes or a crisp, buttery chocolate chip cookie before hitting the Soho shopping circuit.

French. Breakfast, lunch (Monday-Friday), dinner, Saturday-Sunday brunch. $36-85

HIGHLIGHT

WHICH PLACES HAVE THE BEST PIZZA IN NEW YORK CITY?

CO

230 Ninth Ave., Chelsea, 212-243-1105; www.co-pane.com

What started as a half-baked test-case from a mobile pizza truck at the Union Square Greenmarket has evolved into one of the hottest pie shrines in Manhattan. Jim Lahey of Sullivan St. Bakery fame serves up thin-crusted Neapolitan pizzas with toppings such as shaved black truffles, veal meatballs and béchamel. The menu says it best: "Our pies are not always round." But their free-form shape and often charred crust only augment the complimentary blend of ingredients, which may include fennel and sausage, sprinkled with red onions and chilis, or the bird's nest, a generous mix of raschera, tome de savoie, shaved asparagus, quail eggs and parmesan. The 54-seat space is both modern and casual, and rarely has a seat to spare. So come early, or prepare to wait for your little slice of heaven.

Pizza. Lunch (Tuesday-Sunday), dinner. Reservations recommended. $36-85

FRANNY'S

295 Flatbush Ave., Park Slope, Brooklyn, 718-230-0221; www.frannysbrooklyn.com

With recycled paper menus, organic ingredients, renewable energy and biode-gradable to-go containers, Franny's is as environmentally-friendly as they come. The fact that the Italian fare coming from the kitchen actually tastes good is a bonus. The menu is small and centers around thinner-than-thin Neapolitan pizzas, though there are a number of farm-fresh appetizers and a few pasta dishes. Order one of the pies that incorporates the buffalo mozzarella. More adventurous sorts can try the pizza with clams, chilies and parsley. Located in Brooklyn's chic Park Slope, there is no lack of good restaurants to try. But how many of them can say they convert kitchen grease to biodiesel fuel?

Pizza. Lunch, dinner. $36-85

KESTE' PIZZA AND VINO

271 Bleecker St., West Village, 212-243-1500; www.kestepizzeria.com

Roberto Caporuscio knows good pizza. After spending years as an Italian cheese salesman, Caporuscio made it his mission to bring authentic Neapolitan pizza to Manhattan. The menu is packed with nearly 20 varieties of pizza—a good thing since Caporuscio refuses to add or omit ingredients from any of his pies. Purists should stick to the margherita, which offers just the right ratio of sauce to cheese. Otherwise, try the pizza del papa with butternut squash cream, smoked mozzarella and artichoke or the pizza del re with prosciutto di parma and truffle spread.

Pizza. Lunch, dinner. $16-35

★★★BLUE HILL

75 Washington Place, West Village, 212-539-1776; www.bluehillnyc.com

Chef Dan Barber is one of New York's masters of farm-to-table cuisine, using ingredients sustainably grown at the Stone Barns Center for Food and Agriculture, a farm and educational center 30 miles away in the Hudson Valley. (A country-chic dining experience is available at the farm, too.) Much of the produce, from the pickled ramps in the martinis to the shiitake mushrooms in the warm asparagus soup, is grown on the farm. Other ingredients such as guinea hen, goat cheese and veal are from local purveyors, and you can taste their freshness. The below-street-level dining room is calm, warm and elegant.

Contemporary American. Dinner. $36-85

★★★BRAEBURN

117 Perry St., West Village, 212-255-0696; www.braeburnrestaurant.com

Eating at Braeburn is like wrapping yourself up in a cashmere blanket: warm, comforting and exquisite. Diners hug small handcrafted mesquite tabletops while digging into dishes such as crab ravioli and butter poached lobster with sweet corn, bacon and bittersweet onion sauce. Daily specials include butter-milk fried chicken and braised St. Louis ribs. Chef Brian Bistrong, who honed his skills at Bouley and The Harrison, among other restaurants, before finally opening up his own restaurant with Braeburn, simply knows how to elevate comfort food. It's worth surrounding yourself with his perfect dishes every time.

Contemporary American. Dinner, Saturday-Sunday brunch. $36-85

★★★CRU

24 Fifth Ave., West Village, 212-529-1700; www.cru-nyc.com

The elegantly restrained décor at this Village restaurant oozes wealth in that subtly showy kind of way, and service is warm and proper. The ever-changing menu demands attention with its global influences and creative combinations. East Coast cod packs a Latin punch with chorizo crust and piquillo-blood orange compote, while chilled foie gras over white chocolate and basil elevates the concept of sweet and savory to a new level. The extensive wine list—it's the size of a phone book and has two volumes, one for whites and one for reds—will make you gasp. Cru boasts an astounding 150,000 bottles from the private collection of its owner, Roy Welland, and sways toward French wines from Burgundy.

Contemporary European. Dinner. Closed Sunday-Monday. $36-85

★★★★GOTHAM BAR AND GRILL

12 E. 12th Street, West Village, 212-620-4020; www.gothambarandgrill.com

Gotham Bar and Grill opened in 1984 and proves that, just like skinny jeans, some holdovers from the '80s just get trendier with age. Acclaimed chef Alfred Portale is a perfectionist who pioneered architecturally-inspired food presenta-tion. His edible compositions—the roasted Maine lobster is presented with lobster claws wrapped around the tail which sit atop spaghetti squash along with potato purée and toasted brussels sprout halves—are the stuff of true epicurean delight. Bright and airy with stylish, silk-draped lighting and not a hint of vanity, this landmark feels like a comfortable pair of jeans, albeit one with a high-end designer label.

Contemporary American. Lunch (Monday-Friday), dinner. $36-85

★★★SAVOY

70 Prince St., Soho, 212-219-8570; www.savoynyc.com

Located on two floors of a Soho townhouse, Savoy embodies the art of organic, seasonal cuisine. In fact, chef Peter Hoffman can be seen loading up his bike with the freshest finds from the Union Square farmers market early in the morning to prepare the day's menu. The beauty of Savoy is that produce is allowed to shine on its own with little adornment. Asparagus might be simply grilled and topped with sea salt and shaved parmesan, and entrées typically have no more than five main ingredients. Savoy can be this side of precious (check out the honey from Hoffman's rooftop hives), but the freshness and high quality of the food can't be beat. The fireplace makes this charming setting a must in winter, while heavy wooden beams overhead and warm walls surrounding the small dining room give Savoy a country-in-the-city feel.

Contemporary American. Lunch (Monday-Saturday), dinner. $36-85

★★★STRIP HOUSE

13 E. 12th St., Greenwich Village, 212-328-0000; www.striphouse.com

From the neon sign out front to the loungy interior with burgundy banquettes, red velvet walls and pictures of semi-nude burlesque girls on the walls, this is a far cry from traditional steakhouses. Many a business deal is made over plump shrimp cocktail and thick bone-in strip steak or dry aged ribeye. Don't skimp on the sides; the truffled creamed spinach tops the list, but the mashed potatoes are a close second. It's no surprise at this machismo palace that the portions are huge, and the theme carries through to dessert where a single slice of chocolate cake is enough to feed a family of five.

Steak. Lunch, dinner. $36-85

RECOMMENDED

BLUE RIBBON BRASSERIE

97 Perry St., Soho, 212-274-0404; 280 Fifth Ave., Park Slope, Brooklyn, 718-840-0404; www.blueribbonrestaurants.com

Blue Ribbon is everything a good brasserie should be—woody and warm, with a menu that leans heavily on upgraded comfort classics such as strip steak and fried chicken but expertly folds in worldly touches like paella. The candlelit eatery (the crown jewel of the local empire that includes Blue Ribbon Sushi and Blue Ribbon Bakery) excels with its always-fresh raw bar and juicy bomb of a burger. Tip for the chef-obsessed: With a kitchen that serves until 4 a.m. (at the Soho location), Blue Ribbon has long been a favorite late-night hangout for chefs after they finish shifts at nearby restaurants.

Contemporary American. Dinner. $36-85

CORNER BISTRO

331 W. Fourth St., West Village, 212-242-9502

Nothing about this former speakeasy is fancy—the kitchen is the size of a closet, the bar is dark, and food comes on either paper or plastic plates—but everything is memorable. The small pub menu is posted on the wall, but skip it and just order the bar's namesake, the legendary Bistro Burger (eight ounces of broiled beef topped with bacon, cheese, onions, lettuce and tomato) and a side

HIGHLIGHT

WHICH FOODS ARE QUINTESSENTIALLY NEW YORK?

Some foods are as synonymous with the city as yellow cabs and the Empire State Building. From bagels to thin-crust pizza, there are some foods that say New York like nothing else.

BAGELS

Many New Yorkers bemoan the demise of the bagel, which they say is supposed to be dense and chewy not airy and fluffy. Nothing ignites more debate, but **H+H Bagels** (*2239 Broadway, at 80th Street, 212-595-8000, 800-692-2435; www.hhbagels.com*) is often cited as the best New York bagel (though detractors maintain they're too sweet). If you're looking for bagel sandwiches—or even cream cheese—you can forget it; H+H sells bagels and bagels only. For all the fixings, try **Ess-a-Bagel** (*359 First Ave., at 21st Street, 212-260-2252; www.ess-a-bagel.com*) or **Murray's Bagels** (*500 Avenue of the Americas, at 13th Street, 212-462-2830; www.murraysbagels.com*).

PIZZA BY THE SLICE

Pizza in New York must be thin and foldable, oozing with cheese and light on the sauce. The pizza cognoscenti all have their own opinions, but the most popular place for a slice (especially late night) is at a Ray's. You'll find them all around the city, each with a slightly different name, "**Ray's Original**," "**Ray's Famous Original**," "**Famous Ray's Pizza**." None of them are actually related but they all offer the same New-York style pizza that, at least after a few drinks, appeals to slice hounds all over the city.

HOT DOGS

You can buy one from any street cart, but there are two places for classic dogs: **Gray's Papaya** (*2090 Broadway, 212-799-0243*) and **Papaya King** (*179 E. 86th St., between Third and Lexington avenues, 212-369-0648; www.papayaking.com*). Both serve the same crispy-on-the-outside grilled hot dogs and frothy papaya drinks that may just be the city's best cheap eats.

BLACK AND WHITE COOKIES

These cakelike cookies with half-moons of black and vanilla icing are a New York staple. You can buy them in practically every deli or bakery in the city, but the people at **Glaser's Bake Shop** (*1670 First Ave., between 87th and 88th streets, 212-289-2562; www.glasersbakeshop.com*) have been making them since 1902.

PASTRAMI ON RYE

For this classic New York deli sandwich, pastrami is sliced and served warm on rye bread. Some claim the best is found at **Katz's Deli** (*205 E. Houston St., 212-254-2246; www.katzdeli.com*). Others claim **Second Avenue Deli** (*162 E. 33rd St., 212-689-9000; www.2ndavedeli.com*) is the best Jewish (and kosher) deli for pastrami, as well as brisket, matzah ball soup, hot dogs and everything else.

KNISHES

You can find them at delis all over the city but for the real-deal Yiddish snack that consists of mashed potatoes, ground beef and other fillings covered in fried or baked dough, head to **Zabar's** (*2245 Broadway, at 80th Street, 212-787-2000; www.zabars.com*), the famous Upper West Side market that's as New York as you can get.

FROZEN YOGURT:

New Yorkers' love of fro-yo goes back way before Pinkberry and all those other natural yogurt franchises. It's actually not even yogurt, but the most popular alternative for ice cream in New York was and is **Tasti D Lite** (*www.tastidlite. com*). The best part: This made-from-milk treat is only 80 calories per serving, which makes ordering up a large serving an easy indulgence.

of fries. You'll still have money left to plug the jukebox and get a mug or two of $2.50 drafts. But get here early—the line for one of the precious few tables gets long and frustrating, particularly on weekend nights.

American. Lunch, dinner. $15 and under

HOME RESTAURANT

20 Cornelia St., West Village, 212-243-9579; www.homerestaurantnyc.com

Like many New York City apartments, Home Restaurant is tiny. The understated wood dining room is small. The tables are small (some diners think too small). Even the menu is small, with only a handful of dishes offered. But what Home lacks in size, it makes up in flavor. Every dish is made from local farmfresh, sustainable products. Even the wines come from regional vineyards in the Hudson Valley, Finger Lakes and North Fork of Long Island. The mac and cheese, with or without chorizo, is gooey and delightful, while the coriandercrusted double cut pork chop caters to a more sophisticated appetite. Don't leave Home without trying the butterscotch pudding. There's an adorable outdoor garden, too, if you can find an open table.

Contemporary American. Lunch (Monday-Friday), dinner. $36-85

INO

21 Bedford Street, West Village, 212-989-5769; www.cafeino.com

Ten years ago, the concept of Italian-style grilled sandwiches was groundbreaking (and inspired copies everywhere). Today, this panini pioneer is still as good as ever. The tiny (25-seat) restaurant has everything you could ask for: wonderful wines and cheeses, and hot and crispy panini in combinations such as Italian sausage with butternut squash mustard, rucola and fontina, and wonderfully satisfying breakfast options, including an Italian BLT (pancetta, tomato, arugula and lemon mayo) and truffled egg toast. Best of all, Ino serves until 2 a.m., making it the perfect spot for a casual breakfast, lunch or late-night snack.

Italian. Lunch, dinner, late-night. $16-35

PEARL OYSTER BAR

18 Cornelia St., West Village, 212-691-8211; www.pearloysterbar.com

This New England clamshack by way of the West Village has many outstanding seafood options, from briny raw oysters and clam chowder with smoky bacon to whole-grilled fish and bouillabaisse. Really, there's only one item you need to think about: the lobster roll. The one here will bring you to your knees. A toasted, buttery hot dog bun cradles chunks of sweet lobster and shares the plate with a nest of shoestring fries. It's a perfect mix of sweet, salty, crunchy and creamy. The secret's long been out on the food here, so expect a wait despite a long-overdue expansion a few years back.

American, seafood. Lunch (Monday-Friday), dinner. Closed Sunday. $16-35

RAOUL'S

180 Prince St., Soho, 212-966-3518; www.raouls.com

Cramped quarters and a rushed waitstaff are part of the charm of this downtown bistro mainstay. Opened in the 1970s by the Alsatian Raoul brothers, the restaurant has grown from a struggling neighborhood eatery to a bustling Manhattan hotspot for scene-seeking locals and tourists in the know. Tightly packed tables provide a bustling atmosphere, especially in the main dining room. (For a quieter dining experience, request a table in the covered garden behind the kitchen or in the upstairs loftspace.) Signature dishes include the artichoke vinaigrette soaked in Raoul's famous dressing and extra peppery steak au poivre with French fries. Portions are generous, but it's worth leaving a bit on your plate in order to save room for the profiteroles.

French. Lunch, dinner. $16-35

JUST OPENED
QUATTRO GASTRONOMIA
Trump Soho, 246 Spring St., Soho, 212-842-4500; www.trumpsoho.com

It's sort of a family affair at Quattro Gastronomia. The Trump family, of course, runs the hotel in which the restaurant is located. And the kitchen is overseen by Chef Fabrizio Carro, who ran the popular Quattro Gastronomia Italiana in Miami with his twin brother, and now brings the family's Northern Italian dishes to New York. Many of the dishes are reminiscent of growing up in Alessandria in the Piemonte region, such as the tangy vitello tonnato (thiny sliced veal with tuna sauce and capers) and rich gnocchi with toma cheese sauce. Other dishes include osso buco and braised beef ravioli, with many ingredients hailing from Italy. The dazzling emerald-green bi-level space with black granite and leather seating somehow works for groups, business dinners and romantic dates alike, and while you may spot celebrtties here, the warm and friendly staff treats everyone like, well, one big family.

Italian. Breakfast, lunch, dinner. Bar. Reservations recommended. $36-85

MIDTOWN/MIDTOWN EAST/MIDTOWN WEST
★★★'21' CLUB
21 W. 52nd St., Midtown West, 212-582-7200; www.21club.com

This classic institution, a former speakeasy with a hidden wine vault, is a place where suited men sip tumblers of Scotch with the guys in the downstairs Bar Room while digging into medium-rare steaks and inflating stories about business and broads. Is this the '50s, or 50-plus years later? That's precisely the beauty of '21' Club, where time seems to have stopped and a who's who of celebrities and power brokers (George Clooney, Bill Gates) eating burgers and Caesar salads provides more noteworthy decoration than the hanging model airplanes downstairs, or the murals and chandeliers in the upstairs dining rooms.

American. Lunch (Tuesday-Friday), dinner. Closed Sunday. $86 and up

★★★★ADOUR ALAIN DUCASSE
The St. Regis New York, 2 E. 55th St., Midtown, 212-710-2277; www.adour-stregis.com

Legendary chef Alain Ducasse's Adour is a dramatic leap from the French master's previous endeavor, Alain Ducasse at the Essex House. Where the Essex House scared away diners with a French elegance rarely seen stateside, Ducasse's Adour is meant to be a subdued yet elegant wine bar. Draped in warm burgundy and gold with a corridor outfitted in leather and walls lined with well-stocked wine coolers and grape vines, the space is a perfectly warm setting for the expertly prepared and sophisticated French comfort food. Adour's dishes range from simple and straight-from-the-farm to quietly stunning and intricate. Start off with delicate foie gras or ricotta gnocchi and follow it with an expertly prepared duck breast or the braised

HIGHLIGHT

WHICH RESTAURANTS SERVE THE BEST BURGERS IN NEW YORK CITY?

BURGER JOINT

Le Parker Meridien, Midtown, 118 W. 57th St., 212-245-5000; www.parkermeridien.com
If you can find this tiny wood-paneled hole-in-the-wall (it lurks behind a shroud of drapes off Le Parker Meridien's lobby), you're in for a comfort treat. Burgers come topped with lettuce, tomatoes, onions, pickles, mustard, ketchup and mayo, and brown-bagged fries are hot and salty. The best part is that this juicy patty will run you only $7, which beats the $25 burger on the room service menu.

FIVE NAPKIN BURGER

630 Ninth Ave., Theater District, 212-757-2277; www.5napkinburger.com
Though there are seven burgers to choose from, the Original 5 Napkin Burger is the only real choice for burger aficionados—10 ounces of ground chuck beef, comte cheese, warm caramelized onions and a dollop of rosemary aioli on a white bread bun.

JG MELON

1291 Third Ave., Upper East Side, 212-650-1310
Around since 1972, this old-style pub still packs them in, thanks in large part to the meaty hamburgers it churns out daily. The buns are on the small side and toppings are slim to none (unless you consider a few pickles and onions well-dressed), but the burgers are charred to perfection and juicy. Don't waste the calories on the mediocre cottage fries, and remember to hit the ATM before you indulge. JG Melon only takes cash.

THE LITTLE OWL

90 Bedford St., 212-741-4695; www.thelittleowlnyc.com
The bacon cheeseburger at the Little Owl, with its mix of brisket and short ribs, maple-smoked bacon, Gus's brined pickles and slightly sweet homemade bun, is worth every single delicious calorie—or whatever wait you experience to get into this wonderful restaurant.

MINETTA TAVERN

113 MacDougal St., West Village, 212-475-3850; www.minettatavernny.com
The Black Angus burger—all $26 worth—blends dry aged New York strip, skirt steak and brisket into an eight-ounce patty that cooks on a griddle covered in grapeseed oil, while clarified butter is drizzled on top to form a charred crust. Toss in a homemade brioche bun, a stack of caramelized onions and some skinny fries and you've found nirvana.

SHAKE SHACK

Madison Square Park, Madison Avenue and E. 23rd St., Lower East Side, 212-889-6600; www.shakeshack.com
This tiny Madison Square Park burger stand may have "sold out" by opening outlets on the Upper West Side and Citi Field, but the freshly ground blend of sirloin and brisket patties still get people to wait in line for hours. A griddled potato bun and special shack sauce are the only accoutrements you'll need (in addition to a hand-spun chocolate shake, of course).

ZAITZEFF

72 Nassau St., Financial District; 18 Avenue B, Lower East Side, 212-571-7272; www.zaitzeffnyc.com
This Financial District mainstay keeps it simple, sort of—sirloin or Kobe beef, quarter- or half-pounder, Portuguese muffin or sourdough roll, cheese or no cheese. The secret here, apart from the fact that fast and fresh lunch options in the neighborhood are minimal, is the juiciness of the meat and the speed of the service. The hand-cut sweet potato fries aren't bad either.

wild striped bass. Adour's wine list is among the city's best, and the desserts, created by pastry chef Sandro Micheli, rank accordingly—they include a luxuriously rich dark chocolate sorbet and pear with roasted pecans.

Contemporary French. Dinner. $36-85

★★★ANTHOS

36 W. 52nd St., Midtown, 212-582-6900; www.anthosnyc.com

Expense-account businessmen now have a new place to lunch, and a new cuisine to lunch on. Chef-of-the-moment Michael Psilakis's Anthos carries the modernized Greek food that he is known for to a sophisticated upscale, if sterile, space in Midtown. The atmosphere is simple with white walls, pale pink and chocolate brown accents and images of cherry blossoms throughout (anthos is Greek for "blossom"). The menu rings far more complex. Olive oil-poached chicken with eggplant and rapini and arctic char with cracked bulgur, roasted grapes and moschofilero fondue are highlights. Psilakis also plays into the burger trend with a juicy lamb burger, accompanied by feta, spicy pepper purée and French fries. The small bar up front serves intricate and potent cocktails—and ouzo, of course—which makes returning to the office after lunch a challenge.

Greek. Lunch (Monday-Friday), dinner. Closed Sunday. Reservations recommended. $36-85

★★★AQUAVIT

65 E. 55th St., Midtown East, 212-307-7311; www.aquavit.org

The Scandinavian cuisine at this famous Midtown eatery is a far cry from the café at IKEA. The super-modern dining room is bright and minimal with angular booths, and the bar has stylish egg-shaped chairs reflecting a sharp Scandinavian aesthetic. The menu emphasizes traditional seafood and game, but with a sophisticated twist (foie gras ganache with quail egg, pickled tomato and mustard; duck atop parsley spätzle, radicchio and root vegetables). The onsite Aquavit Café features a more casual menu of Scandinavian staples including six different kinds of herring, beef Rydberg and, yes, Swedish meatballs. Then there are the dozen-plus housemade aquavits; we recommend both the horseradish and the mango, lime and chili pepper-combo flavors. A great way to try it all: The Sunday smorgasbord ($48 including a Danish Mary) is stocked with herring and hot potatoes, Swedish cheese, gravlax with mustard sauce and, of course, Swedish meatballs.

Scandinavian. Lunch (Monday-Friday), dinner, Sunday brunch. $36-85

★★★AUREOLE

135 W 42nd St., Midtown, 212-319-1660; www.aureolerestaurant.com

Owned by Charlie Palmer, Aureole specializes in the kind of stylish yet comfortable fine-dining experience completely devoid of pretension—here, it really is about the food and not a celebrity chef. Aureole now inhabits the famous Bank of America building under the kitchen leadership of executive chef Christopher Lee. Diners receive star treatment from courteous staff doling out hearty dishes such as veal tenderloin and sweetbreads, Australian rack of lamb or crispy black sea bass with French white asparagus. If you crave lighter fare, sit in the bar room where you will see more casual options such as the Aureole grilled burger or the diver sea scallop sandwich. A wine list heavy on European and California labels also includes the restaurant's own sparkling wine, Aureole Cuvée—no doubt a popular choice for the marrying kind of guests that you frequently see here on bended knee, popping the question before dessert.

Contemporary American. Lunch (Monday-Saturday), dinner. Bar. Reservations recommended. $36-85

★★★BLT MARKET

The Ritz-Carlton New York, Central Park, 1430 Sixth Ave., Midtown West, 212-521-6125; www.bltmarket.com

Laurent Tourondel's BLT (Bistro Laurent Tourondel) Market in the Ritz-Carlton hotel is a valentine to all things local and seasonal and another star in Tourondel's constellation of restaurants. Diners feast on peak-season ingredients, like spring's pea and ricotta ravioli with spicy sausage, mint and pea shoots. The soft shell crab comes from Maryland, while Jamison Farm provides the lamb, and nearly all of the vegetables come from farms nearby. No matter where it hails from, the food is delicious.

Contemporary American. Breakfast, dinner. Closed Sunday-Monday. Reservations recommended. $36-85

★★★BLT STEAK

106 E. 57th St., Midtown, 212-752-7470; www.bltsteak.com

It's a choose-your-own-adventure at this Midtown steak emporium. First, pick the cut: hanger, filet, New York strip, ribeye, porterhouse, double sirloin. Next, the sauce: béarnaise, peppercorn, red wine, mustard, blue cheese, horseradish, barbecue. Finally, the sides: oversized onion rings, creamed spinach, hash browns, stuffed mushroom caps, potato gratin to name a few. Fish and chicken options are available for those not in a beef mood, and there are enough sides to be a meal unto themselves. The backlit bar is a nice spot to sip a drink while waiting for a table, and the main dining room is pleasantly light and airy, a welcome change from the standard steak joint.

Steak. Lunch, dinner. $36-85

★★★CONVIVIO

45 Tudor City Place, Midtown East, 212-599-5045; www.convivionyc.com

If the aging socialites of NYC can get facelifts to increase their appeal, why can't a restaurant? That's exactly what restaurateur Chris Cannon and chef Michael White asked themselves before trading stuffy-and-serious L'Impero for a more casual, food-focused endeavor in the same locale. The result: A bright new star in Tudor City—about as far east as you can be in Manhattan without swimming in the East River—where the pasta sings and the price is palatable. The $62 four-course prix fixe dinner includes winners such as stracciatella (creamy cheese curd, tangy tomato and basil), maccheroni alla carbonara (pillowy pasta laced with pancetta, egg and pecorino) and scottadito di agnello (perfectly-grilled lamb chops over escarole in a sizzling salsa verde). As one of the few decent eateries neighboring the United Nations, it gets its share of foreign diplomats on expense accounts. But Convivio isn't stuffy in the least; rather it is a pleasant and welcoming spot, with a lovely tree-shaded courtyard out front for alfreso dining, and a warm and comfortable dining room with a friendly staff. The $28 two-course business lunch, which includes starters such

HIGHLIGHT

WHAT ARE THE CITY'S UNDERGROUND SUPPER CLUBS?

The first rule of underground supper clubs is that no one talks about underground supper clubs. Got it? Sometimes called "secret restaurants" or "speakeasies," underground supper clubs have been taking place around the city, where professional chefs looking for a creative outlet churn out restaurant-quality fare for groups of about 12 to 25 people in apartments all over town.

Cooks get to pursue their culinary dreams while avoiding city health department restrictions and high overhead costs associated with opening and operating an actual restaurant. Foodies dig the thrill of a stealth adventure in a secret location, usually for about 40 bucks. Getting in on the secret is easy: Consult the websites below for a list of upcoming events, then e-mail for reservations. Because most supper clubs are held in private apartments and intended to be intimate, you boost your chances of snagging a spot by responding as soon as something's posted and keeping the size of your group small (one to four people). The point of supper clubs is to meet new people, not just chat with those you came with. No need to bring beverages—cocktails and wine are included in the price.

The Whisk & Ladle (*www.thewhiskandladle.com*) is the most popular of these clubs, hosting a cocktail hour and five-course dinner with matched wines for $60 one weekend of every month in a former factory loft in Williamsburg, Brooklyn. Rotating works of local artists adorn the loft walls and musicians or DJs provide entertainment while you sip wine and enjoy dishes like beet and gorgonzola risotto prepared by a trio of twenty-somethings who met on Craigslist looking for like-minded cooks. The waiting list for this bimonthly experience is long, so make your reservation request stand out. A simple "Reservation for two, please," won't cut it with this creative crew, which is looking for the same in its guests.

Named after TV food personality Ted Allen and actress Amy Sedaris, **Ted & Amy**'s (*www.karamasi.com/supperclub*) supper club in Fort Greene, Brooklyn, was started by foodie friends Adam Quirk and Kara Masi (only Kara runs it now). Dinners for 8 to 12 are held once or twice a month in Kara's apartment and cost $30 to $35 a head. The fare is seasonal—seared scallops with summer corn from a local farm in summertime, and pumpkin ravioli and spiced pork tenderloin when the temperatures drop—and guests can hang out in the kitchen while dinner is prepared.

Even die-hard carnivores will enjoy chef Matteo Silverman's vegetables-only **Four Course Vegan** (*www.4coursevegan.com*) supper club. Held Saturdays at his off-the-beaten-path Williamsburg loft, dinners for 14 people feature imaginative dishes such as Thai eggplant roll with oyster mushrooms and tamarind chile sauce and spinach dumplings with fennel relish and chanterelle cream. You'll finish the $40 dinner with sweets like dark chocolate mousse studded with black raspberries. Sign up for the online mailing list so you can respond quickly to upcoming dinners as they're announced, typically a week or two in advance.

as a rich and creamy chicken liver crostini and Michael White's heavenly pastas, is also one of the best deals in town.

Southern Italian. Lunch (Monday-Friday), dinner. $36-85

★★★THE FOUR SEASONS RESTAURANT
99 E. 52nd St., Midtown, 212-754-9494; www.fourseasonsrestaurant.com

A sports jacket isn't the only thing you need when dining here. An expense account comes in handy as well, with a menu that charges $46 for Maryland crab cakes and $55 for an aged sirloin steak. Chances are you can find an equally good meal for less elsewhere in Manhattan, but you'll be hard pressed to find a better dining room in which to enjoy it. Both the Grill Room and Pool Room are considered prized destinations among New York's dining elite. The Grill Room hosted JFK's 45th birthday party and boasts walnut-paneled walls and soaring two-story windows. It doesn't get more New York than the Four Seasons Restaurant. On the opposite end of the restaurant, the Pool Room is anchored by Mies van der Rohe's legendary white marble pool and surrounded by trees that change with the seasons. Widely spaced tables and exemplary service make either room a good choice for a private affair.

Contemporary American. Lunch (Monday-Friday), dinner. Closed Sunday. $86 and up

★★★★GILT
The New York Palace Hotel, 455 Madison Ave., Midtown East, 212-891-8100; www.giltnewyork.com

Located in the Villard Mansion within the New York Palace Hotel, Gilt has been rejuvenated with new chef Justin Bogle and a constantly changing menu that spotlights seasonal flavors (lamb tartare with rhubarb, buckwheat and sorrel, and tandoori-spiced black cod with roasted eggplant, mustard greens and toasted coconut) in three-, five- and seven-course tasting menus. An impressive wine list features 1,400 bottles, including 50 selections under $50. Tippling not your thing? Gilt has assembled an extensive list of nearly 40 teas (like the rare, aged High Mountain oolong tea from Taiwan) chosen with seasonality in mind. The wood-paneled, library-like 52-seat dining room in this historic mansion is straight out of a Brontë novel, while the contrasting slick bar with futuristic décor suggests a modern club setting, perfect if you're looking for a more casual à la carte dining option. Or slip outside to the Palace Gate, a new seasonal seating area that serves up bar menu favorites amidst the melee of Midtown.

Contemporary American. Dinner. Bar (daily). Reservations recommended. Closed Sunday-Monday. $86 and up

★★★★GORDON RAMSAY AT THE LONDON
The London NYC, 151 W. 54th St., Midtown West, 212-468-8888; www.gordonramsay.com

The somewhat hushed, polished dining room decorated in a muted palette contrasts starkly with the salty, fiery chef and namesake of this celebrated 45-seat Manhattan restaurant in the London NYC hotel. You won't see TV cameras or hear Gordon Ramsay shouting at a skittish staff like he does on the reality TV shows *Hell's Kitchen* and *Kitchen Nightmares*. But you might utter an expletive in amazement at the innovative and expertly prepared cuisine here, including caramelized duck breast, roasted foie gras and ginger poached lobster. A three-tiered "Bon Bon trolley" weighed down with confections—think peanut brittle, salted caramels and handmade chocolates—provides a playful and sweet finale.

Contemporary European. Dinner. Closed Sunday-Monday. Reservations recommended. $86 and up

★★★★L'ATELIER DE JOËL ROBUCHON

Four Seasons Hotel New York, 57 E. 57th St., Midtown East, 212-829-3844; www.joel-robuchon.com

This is lauded chef Joël Robuchon's fourth outpost of L'Atelier worldwide, and he further establishes his talented flair for flavor with an ambitious small-plate French menu by way of Asia. "L'Atelier," which means "workshop" in French, offers a dizzying array of small-tasting portions on the regular menu, making your choices—from frog's legs croquettes to crispy langoustines—a bit overwhelming; but that's like saying a lottery jackpot is too big. The restaurant offers a mixture of table and counter seating similar to that of a sushi restaurant; if you're more inclined to keep tabs on the open kitchen rather than your dining companion, opt for a spot at the v-shaped bar.

French. Dinner. Reservations recommended. Bar. $86 and up

★★★★LA GRENOUILLE

3 E. 52nd St., Midtown East, 212-752-1495; www.la-grenouille.com

Decked out with more flowers than a royal wedding, this lovely and luxurious French restaurant is the kind of place where you'll want to dress up and carry a French phrase book so you can converse with the waiter. La Grenouille—which means "frog" in French, though this is actually a prince of a place—is where the most glittery and powerful personalities (Truman Capote in years past, Martha Stewart today) have dined since 1962, enjoying the polished service that is the pinnacle of attentiveness. Just as the cashmere twin set and diamond studs worn by the socialite at the next table will never go out of style, neither will the French classics on the menu here, from frog's legs to Dover sole. Notoriously pricey, La Grenouille has added an affordable $59 theater menu (from 5-6 p.m. and after 9:30 p.m.) plus a $29 three-course lunch menu upstairs, making it—at last!—on upscale dining option even for those on a budget.

French. Lunch (Tuesday-Friday), dinner. Closed Sunday. Jacket required. Bar. $86 and up

★★★★★LE BERNARDIN

155 W. 51st St., Midtown West, 212-554-1515; www.le-bernardin.com

It's hard to keep food in your mouth when your jaw keeps dropping in awe. And awestruck you'll be at chef Eric Ripert's skilled transformation of everything that swims into his pristine dishes. A sure thing since it opened in 1986, Le Bernardin has really hit its stride under perfectionist Ripert. Since he succeeded chef Gilbert Le Coze in 1995, Ripert has continued Le Bernardin's tradition of serving luxurious French seafood with a modern and international flavor (yuzu in the fluke marinade, and salmon served with a jalapeño emulsion). Ripert has divided the menu into playfully named sections: "Almost Raw" (oysters, kampachi), "Barely Touched" (poached white tuna, warm lobster carpaccio) and "Lightly Cooked" (pan-roasted monkfish, poached halibut). A handful of meat dishes available upon request—like seared Kobe beef and pan-roasted squab—will make carnivores sit up and take notice, too. With its butterscotch leather chairs and beige fabric-covered walls, Le Bernardin feels a bit like a corporate dining room, but enormous sprays of seasonal, twiggy flowers soften the décor. The prix fixe dinner menu is $110; the tasting menu with wine is $225.

French. Lunch (Monday-Friday), dinner. Closed Sunday. Reservations recommended. $86 and up

★★★★LE CIRQUE

151 E. 58th St., Midtown, 212-644-0202; www.lecirque.com

This venerable New York City mainstay of haute cuisine reincarnated itself in 2006 when it moved from its old digs at the New York Palace Hotel to the Bloomberg Tower in Midtown. Toss in a new chef, Craig Hopson, and a revitalized menu and you've got a winning combination. Plump foie gras ravioli is a standout appetizer, while lamb served with flaky eggplant in filo, goat cheese and a red pepper purée seals the deal for the entrées. Le Cirque's impresario-owner, Sirio Maccioni, presides over his creation each night, looking over a more subdued dining room compared to the outlandish previous space—there's no longer a baroque-carnival feel, but more of an Upper East Side party atmosphere, albeit encased in a gold tent. The new futuristic glass and steel space is more suited to Midtown's business crowd and the sometimes-cold Le Cirque service. But a towering napoleon dessert can make up for any missteps you may encounter from your waiter.

Contemporary French, Italian. Lunch (Monday-Friday), dinner. Closed Sunday. Reservations recommended. Jacket required. $36-85

★★★★MAREA

240 Central Park South, Midtown East, 212-582-5100; www.marea-nyc.com

Chef Michael White is seemingly everywhere these days (he and partner Chris Cannon are behind successful restaurants Alto and Convivio). At the upscale, seafood-focused Marea, they took a big gamble, opening up the unapologetically fine-dining spot (with prices to match) during the economic downturn. It seems they have another hit on their hands. Located right at the base of Central Park, this modern eatery aims to do for seafood what Chef White has done for pasta—in short, elevate it to new heights. Where he seemingly does this best is in many of the fresh, whole fish options priced by the pound and simply adorned with olive oil and salt. Regardless of whether you go with the pasta, seafood or the well-edited selection of land animals, don't miss the first course of sea urchin spread on crispy toast with lardo or pork fat to enhance the already over-the-top dish. While the dining room is elegant with sea shells dipped in silver, plan your visit to begin with a drink at the gorgeous, back-lit European honey onyx-backed bar and start with a plate of the signature crudo.

Italian, seafood. Lunch (Monday-Friday), dinner. Bar. $85 and up

★★★★THE MODERN

Museum of Modern Art, 9 W. 53rd St., Midtown, 212-333-1220; www.themodernnyc.com

The Modern, an elegant sun-lit Midtown addition to restaurateur Danny Meyer's dense portfolio (which includes Blue Smoke, Gramercy Tavern and Union Square Café) is really two restaurants in one—the sophisticated Dining Room and a less-formal Bar Room. Split up into two rooms separated by frosted glass, both restaurants reside in The Museum of Modern Art, one of the most elegant buildings in New York. In fact, most seats afford great views of the MoMA sculpture garden next door, so don't be surprised to catch glimpses of a Miró or a Picasso as you dine. Still, chef Gabriel Kreuther—who took home the James Beard Award for Best Chef: New York City in 2009—tries his darndest to take your attention from the masterpieces outside to those on your plate with his bold, flavorful food, and he succeeds. The romantic, 85-seat Dining Room offers more elegant dishes such as chorizo-crusted codfish with white cocoa bean purée and harissa oil; roasted lobster with chanterelles, heart of palm and chamomile blossom nage; and a Pennsylvania duck breast with a black trumpet marmalade, fleischschnecke and banyuls jus. In the less-formal Bar Room, you can find an earthy menu emphasizing small plates with big tastes, such as a pasta dish elevated by chewy, salty escargots and fragrant wild mushrooms. A not-to-miss dessert is the pistachio dark-chocolate dome with pistachio ice cream and amaretto gelée. It's essentially edible art.

French, Contemporary American. Lunch (Monday-Friday), dinner. Closed Sunday. $36-85

★★★MONKEY BAR
Hotel Elysée, 60 E. 54th St., Midtown, 212-207-9085; www.elyseehotel.com

If it seems like everyone dining here has been plucked straight from the pages of *Vanity Fair*, it's because there is a good chance that they have. Monkey Bar is co-owned by Graydon Carter, editor of the trend-centric publication, and the dining clientele is predictably polished. From the doorman who greets you upon arrival to the doting waitstaff, service is impeccable—and it should be considering the prices. The menu is a mixed bag, offering everything from scrambled eggs to burgers to chicken paillard. Your best bet is to stick with the classics. The fish n' chips are surprisingly light and flavorful. Or just come for the cocktails, which include a very tasty (and potent) mango mojito. The interior is Art Deco cool with murals throughout and comfortable banquettes. Monkey Bar won't serve you the best meal of your life, but you may have the time of your life people-watching.

Contemporary American. Lunch (Monday-Friday), dinner. Closed Sunday. $36-85.

★★★SPARKS STEAK HOUSE
210 E. 46th St., Midtown East, 212-687-4855; www.sparkssteakhouse.com

A Manhattan mainstay since 1966, Sparks delivers the boys club style and brisk service often associated with old-school steak joints. Give or take the décor, this midtown behemoth delivers on flavor. The menu encompasses all the steakhouse standards: shrimp cocktail, creamed spinach, hash brown potatoes, and a surprisingly small array of beef cuts (don't come craving a ribeye.) But what is on the meat menu is excellent. The New York sirloin is the signature dish, slightly charred and salty on the outside, but still rare. No need for steak sauce, which is a good thing since the waitstaff doesn't take kindly to the request. The wine list is hefty and offers a nice range of vintages and prices.

Steak. Lunch (Monday-Friday), dinner. Closed Sunday. $36-85

★★★★SUGIYAMA
251 W. 55th St., Midtown West, 212-956-0670; www.sugiyama-nyc.com

This may be the closest you'll get to Japan without hopping on a plane. The minimalist Sugiyama (tiny bamboo lanterns offer minimal sparkle to an otherwise spartan, booth-filled space) offers innovative and interesting takes on traditional Japanese food that you won't find elsewhere in the city. It specializes in kaiseki, three-, five- or eight-course seasonal tasting menus that emphasize harmony in flavor, texture, color and shape. The menu typically progresses from cold dishes (mixed greens with Japanese mushrooms) to hot (beef tenderloin grilled on a hot stone), producing a taste bud-pleasing medley of flavors and sensations. A chef's choice kaiseki menu (called omakase) is also available.

Japanese. Dinner. Closed Sunday-Monday. $36-85

RECOMMENDED

CARNEGIE DELI

854 Seventh Ave., Midtown West, 800-334-5606; www.carnegiedeli.com

This is a Jewish deli on steroids—heaps of deliciously fatty pastrami piled between soft slices of rye bread are enough for at least two meals, and mile-high cheesecake wedges could double as door stops. Nothing says American excess like this New York institution, which boasts a personality as large as its portions. Try creatively named sandwiches such as Carnegie Haul (pastrami, tongue and salami with relish) or Bacon Whoopee (chicken salad BLT)—and enjoy these hulking sandwiches or a big bowl of matzo ball soup while gazing at the celebrity headshots lining the walls.

American. Breakfast, lunch, dinner. $16-35

TRIBECA/MEATPACKING DISTRICT
★★★★BOULEY

163 Duane St., Tribeca, 212-964-2525; www.davidbouley.com

David Bouley recently moved his acclaimed restaurant to a new Tribeca headquarters and the results are impressive. The dining room's vaulted gold-leafed ceiling is bold, his determination to serve high-end ingredients is fierce, and freebies like a lemon tea cake for ladies to take home for the next morning's breakfast are a godsend. You won't be able to restrain your glee at Bouley's classic-yet-unconventional French fare, including rosemary-crusted rack of lamb in a pool of zucchini-mint purée, and seafood dishes adorned with yuzu and Japanese pickles. The over-the-top mantra doesn't stop at the entrées: The Chocolate Frivolous dessert is an exercise in excess—a plate piled high with chocolate brûlée, chocolate parfait, chocolate-walnut spice bread, orange-cointreau ganache and a generous scoop of chocolate ice cream. You'll be on a sugar rush all evening.

French. Lunch (Tuesday-Sunday), dinner. Reservations recommended. $86 and up

★★★CORTON

239 W. Broadway, Tribeca, 212-219-2777; www.cortonnyc.com

White on white is the new black at this trendy Tribeca restaurant. The windowless space epitomizes modern simplicity with lightly stenciled whitewashed walls, white linen tablecloths and white Bernardaud china. Such sophistication is par for the course with old school chef Paul Liebrandt, who works his magic in a state-of-the-art kitchen visible from the dining room through a narrow slit in the wall. The three-course prix fixe menu ($85) may appear fussy at first glance—think foie gras with sour cherries, chioggia beet and marcona almonds, and Montauk cod over razor clam risotto and arugula chantilly—but Liebrandt delivers with exceptionally delicate flavors and farm fresh ingredients. Dessert keeps the culinary bar held high with French treats such as the black cherry clafoutis with sour plum and lemon verbena. At a time when

Manhattan foodies are turning their attention toward cheap burger joints and casual no-nonsense menus, Corton proves that exceptional food is always in vogue. Good luck getting a reservation less than a month in advance, but once you're in, you'll be very glad you came.

French. Dinner. Closed Sunday. Reservations recommended. $86 and up

★★★THE HARRISON
355 Greenwich St., Tribeca, 212-274-9310; www.theharrison.com

Since chef Amanda Freitag took the reins in January 2008, she has infused new life into The Harrison, whose sister restaurant, Chelsea's The Red Cat, also has that Mediterranean-American thing down pat. Freitag's menu is both familiar and imaginative—traditional offerings like lamb chops get punched up with anchovy and rosemary, and the seasonal salmon will clear your sinuses thanks to the horseradish crust and red mustard greens. Fries cooked in duck fat are both indulgent and addictive. The candlelit tables are a little too close for comfort, but the reliable food more than makes up for the tight surroundings. Sidewalk seating out front is ideal for enjoying a warm evening and fabulous people-watching in eternally trendy Tribeca.

Contemporary American. Dinner. $36-85

★★★LOCANDA VERDE
377 Greenwich St., Tribeca, 212-925-3797; www.locandaverdenyc.com

The newest incarnation in Robert De Niro's trendy Greenwich Hotel, Locanda Verde is a refreshingly casual and affordable eatery in a neighborhood of heavy hitters. The once cavernous space has become intimate with warm lighting, a charming granite bar and soaring French doors that open onto the sidewalk. The open kitchen allows diners to keep tabs on chef Andrew Carmellini as he churns out family-style Italian fare with little fluff and lots of taste. Small plates, known as cicchetti, start the evening off well. The blue crab crostino with jalapeño and tomato, and the sheep's milk ricotta are both excellent. The small theme carries throughout the menu with portion sizes ringing in well below average. Luckily size has nothing to do with flavor; the orecchiette with rabbit sausage, sweet peas and fiore sardo will have you wishing you lived next door.

Italian. Breakfast. Lunch (Monday-Friday), dinner, Saturday-Sunday brunch. $36-85

★★★NOBU
105 Hudson St., Tribeca, 212-219-0500; www.myriadrestaurantgroup.com

Chef Nobuyuki Matsuhisa solidified his darling status here when he opened this, the first of his New York City eateries, in 1994. The sleek restaurant backed by Robert De Niro broke traditional sushi rules with its pioneering Japanese-South American style, serving concoctions such as scallops drizzled with hot pepper sauce and slivers of velvety yellowtail studded with rounds of jalapeño. Nobu's miso-marinated black cod has inspired countless imitations, but it's gotten easier to try the real deal now that there are 17 Nobu restaurants around the world, from Miami to Milan. If you can't get a table at Nobu here in New York, try its sister spot Nobu Next Door (212-334-4445) one door down, where the menu is almost exactly the same but the no-reservations policy (except for dinner parties of five or more) makes it a good last-minute option.

Japanese. Lunch (Monday-Friday), dinner. $36-85

★★★THE STANDARD GRILL

The Standard Hotel, 848 Washington St., Meatpacking District, 212-645-4100;
www.thestandardgrill.com

Nestled under the High Line in the euro-chic Standard Hotel, The Standard
Grill is sexy, showy, and anything but, yes, standard. The kitchen is open from
7 a.m. to 4 a.m., catering to both neighborhood early birds and the party-hardy
night owls. Four separately managed dining rooms keep the madness under
control, but the atmosphere is still loud and slightly frenetic; if you can get a
table in the expansive outdoor garden, do so. Popular dishes include a green
bean salad accompanied by cinnamon and crispy shallots; a perfectly seasoned
Berkshire pork chop; and duck fat smashed potatoes. The cocktails are as
strong a draw as the food. Bartenders work at ludicrous speeds to pour out
inventive potables such as the penny drop (a vodka and ginger zinger) and the
housemade limoncello.

Contemporary American. Breakfast, lunch, dinner, late-night. $16-35

RECOMMENDED

ODEON

145 W. Broadway, Tribeca, 212-233-0507; www.theodeonrestaurant.com

Hot spots come and go but the crowds eventually come home to Odeon, the
original hipster restaurant in Tribeca (which used to serve the likes of Andy
Warhol back in the day). Odeon is refreshingly simple and straighforward,
offering well-executed bistro classics such as a rich and crispy croque monsieur,
a thick and juicy hamburger with cheese and bacon, and a nice omelet with
fries. Order one of the potent martinis and you pretty much have a meal that is
guaranteed to hit the spot.

Contemporary American. Lunch, dinner, late-night, Saturday-Sunday brunch. $16-35

UNION SQUARE/FLATIRON DISTRICT/GRAMERCY PARK/ MURRAY HILL

★★★CRAFT

43 E. 19th St., Flatiron District, 212-780-0880; www.craftrestaurant.com

Tom Colicchio of *Top Chef* obviously knows food. It shows at his restaurant
Craft (part of the Craft chain that includes Craftsteak, Craftbar and 'wichcraft),
which emphasizes fresh ingredients and cooking methods as so many other
restaurants do, but does so like no other. Diners build their own meals—an
exciting or daunting experience, depending on your sense of adventure and
food curiosity. First, select a preparation method (roasting, braising, raw),
and then the ingredient (halibut, sweetbreads, oysters) for the table. Servers
bring plates for everyone in the group to share. The diver scallops and braised
short ribs are standouts, while the restaurant's desserts have a deserved cult
following—the homemade Boston crème doughnuts with blueberry compote,
chocolate malted milk and cheesecake ice cream will not disappoint. The
elegantly industrial dining room emulates the menu's work-in-progress theme,
with dangling filament light bulbs and exposed brick and iron.

Contemporary American. Dinner. $36-85

★★★★★ELEVEN MADISON PARK

11 Madison Ave., Flatiron District, 212-889-0905; www.elevenmadisonpark.com

The large scale of the Art Deco dining room—think high ceilings, voluminous floral arrangements, hulking light fixtures—contrasts with the modestly-sized food portions. But what does adorn the plate is so thoughtfully conceived, gorgeously executed and alive with flavor that you won't mind. The French-influenced greenmarket cuisine by chef Daniel Humm includes such dishes as Muscovy duck glazed with lavender honey, and foie gras terrine with plums, umeboshi and bitter almonds. The restaurant recently dropped its à la carte menu in lieu of a four-course or five-course tasting menu. They also reduced the number of seats and the cooks themselves bring out the dishes. The menu (presented on little cards that simply list ingredients) is meant to provoke a conversation with your server about what you feel like eating. The result is an even more special experience that takes diners on a great culinary trip.

French, American. Lunch (Monday-Friday), dinner. Closed Sunday. $86 and up

★★★★GRAMERCY TAVERN

42 E. 20th St., Flatiron District, 212-477-0777; www.gramercytavern.com

Charming Gramercy Tavern is self-assured without being flashy and comfortable without being dull, making it a favorite upscale dining choice for everyone from expense-account suits to serious foodies wondering if the Chioggia beets came from the farmers market down the street (they probably did). Executive chef Michael Anthony has filled the big toque left behind by Tom Colicchio, and he has infused the classic menu with creative flourishes—from the hazelnut yogurt sauce and red cabbage complementing the halibut to the apple chutney on the foie gras custard—that keep you on your toes just when you think you've got the place pegged. Try a specialty such as the shrimp salad with grapefruit or rack of pork and braised belly, and for dessert, warm chocolate bread pudding. The long bar is a perfect perch from which to enjoy the à la carte menu, plates of cheese and wines by the glass.

Contemporary American. Lunch (Monday-Friday), dinner. Reservations recommended. $86 and up

★★★UNION SQUARE CAFÉ

21 E. 16th St., Union Square, 212-243-4020; www.unionsquarecafe.com

One of New York's most revered restaurants, Union Square Café set a new standard for seasonal greenmarket cuisine when it opened more than 25 years ago, and it continues to be a go-to spot for everyone from tourists to trendoids. The menu hasn't changed much since the start, but why mess with a good thing? Plus, the dishes feel timeless rather than dated due to the ever-changing seasonal touches on the menu, like sugar snap pea salad tagliatini and pan-roasted chicken atop asparagus bread pudding. The restaurant's creamy walls and warm wood floors and chairs are so comfortable that you might feel like you're eating at an old friend's house—in many ways, you are.

Contemporary American. Lunch, dinner. Reservations recommended. $36-85

★★★VERITAS

43 E. 20th St., Flatiron District, 212-353-3700; www.veritas-nyc.com

Wine, wine and more wine. With a list more than 192,000 bottles deep, thanks

HIGHLIGHT

WHAT ARE THE BEST BARBECUE RESTAURANTS IN NEW YORK CITY?

HILL COUNTRY
30 W. 26th St., 212-255-4544; www.hillcountryny.com

If you don't know where Hill Country is—think long horns and George W.—, you're sure to learn upon stepping inside this soaring Manhattan namesake. It is all about Texas barbecue here, where an enormous silver lone star hangs over the bar, photographs of deserted dusty roads decorate the walls and beef is what's for dinner (although you can get pork and chicken, too). Reminiscent of legendary Kreuz Market, Hill Country serves its dry-rubbed brisket, sausage and ribs by the pound cafeteria-style, each wrapped in authentic butcher paper. Opt for the marvelously tender brisket, choosing either lean or moist (fatty), and don't skimp on the sides. The sweet potato bourbon mash acts as a nice flavor contrast to the barbecue, while the green bean casserole ensures that you're getting your daily serving of greens. Two full bars and a live music stage draw a lively and refreshingly casual, nightlife crowd for Chelsea.

Barbecue. Lunch, dinner. $16-35

DAISY MAY'S
623 11th Ave., 212-977-1500; www.daisymaysbbq.com

After earning its stripes for its affordable and juicy pulled pork sandwiches served fresh from a midtown lunch cart, Daisy May's has enjoyed rock star status in New York City's barbecue circuit. The counter service and cafeteria atmosphere of the Hell's Kitchen homebase may not seem like a huge step up from sidewalk service, but there is a certain charm to the place—Big Ten pennants, beer signs, counter service and all. Touting authentic Southern barbecue, the menu is a carnivore's dream. Stick to the specials: Oklahoma jumbo beef ribs, Kansas City sweet pork ribs, and beef brisket. Of course any self-respecting barbecue joint is just as serious about its sides as its meat. The brown sugar sweet potatoes are a dream. The prices have slowly risen in recent years, but so have the portion sizes. Worth its weight in barbecue sauce? You decide.

Barbecue. Lunch, dinner. $15 and under

mainly to the Park B. Smith wine collection becoming available, wine is the keystone of any meal at Veritas. And what better accompaniment to award-winning wine than gourmet French fare? Black truffles, foie gras and frog legs all play a part in chef Gregory Pugin's sophisticated menu. The wagyu filet with béarnaise croquets and shishito peppers in a bordelaise sauce is perhaps the most memorable dish on the menu. Sidestep the sweets for the ever-changing assortment of cheeses. The interior is neutral and modern, leaving the focus entirely on the food and wine.

French. Lunch, dinner. $36-85.

RECOMMENDED

ARTISANAL FROMAGERIE & BISTRO

2 Park Ave., Murray Hill, 212-725-8585; www.artisanalbistro.com

If you love cheese, then you've found your paradise in this sprawling, dimly lit bistro with buttercream yellow walls and red-checkered floors. Couples nibble on baskets of airy gougères at the bar while cheese-savvy servers hustle pots of gooey fondue to tightly packed wooden tables. It's the quality of the French-style food, from hearty leg of lamb to charred hanger steak, that salvages Artisanal from becoming a kitschy fondue joint and instead makes it a delightful restaurant you will want to return to again and again. Weekend brunch isn't for the cholesterol conscious—the cinnamon sugar dusted beignets are impossible to refuse.

French. Lunch (Monday-Friday), dinner, Saturday-Sunday brunch. $16-35

BLUE SMOKE

116 E. 27th St., Murray Hill, 212-447-7733; www.bluesmoke.com

The smell of smoking meat wafts through the entire spacious, airy restaurant, priming your appetite for its stick-to-your-ribs food. Many regional barbecue styles are served here—so expect the likes of saucy Kansas City ribs and dry-rubbed Texas-style fare. While the barbecued ribs and brisket hit the spot, the side dishes are stars in their own right. Gooey macaroni and cheese, smoky baked beans and braised collard greens with bacon will have you licking your plate clean. The burger here is a double-fister, and it can be topped with smoked bacon. The jazz club downstairs and a late-night menu keep this place jumping past midnight.

American. Lunch, dinner, late-night. $16-35

THE BRESLIN

16 W. 29th St., Midtown, 212-679-1939; www.thebreslin.com

From the owners of the perennially packed Spotted Pig and fresh off the closing of their higher-end seafood experiment, the John Dory (rumor is it will be reopening at a newer location in the future), comes the Breslin, the cozy and eclectic restaurant and pub attached to the lobby of the hipper-than-thou Ace Hotel. Open all day for breakfast, lunch, dinner and cocktails, as well as late-night, there is really not a bad time to visit this carefully orchestrated, dark drinking and pig-eating den, but be prepared to wait as reservations are not accepted. From the artfully peeling tin ceiling to the taxidermy and pig paraphernalia reminiscent of its older West Village sibling, the environment at the Breslin is one that encourages convivial activity such as drinking hand-pulled cask beers and devouring chef April Bloomfield's down-home snacks such as peanuts fried in pork fat and pork scratchings. For a quick meal, the gamey lamb burger with feta and arguably the city's best fries is a good bet, but bring a friend and try to tackle the massive pig's foot built for two. Hearty main courses and seasonal vegetable sides round out the menu.

American. Breakfast, lunch, dinner, late-night. Daily. Bar. $36-85

CITY BAKERY

3 W. 18th St., Flatiron District, 212-366-1414; www.thecitybakery.com

Every neighborhood should have a City Bakery, where imaginative salads make vegetables exciting, soups are silky and flavorful, and chocoholics rejoice at the creamy, dreamy hot chocolate with homemade marshmallows. The caramelized French toast (available only on weekends) and pretzel croissant have legions of fans, as do the array of sweet baked treats. Seating in the boisterous, high-ceilinged café is limited, so if you're not the patient type, take your goods to go and sit in nearby Union Square to munch alfresco.

American. Breakfast, lunch. $15 and under

MESA GRILL

102 Fifth Ave., Flatiron District, 212-807-7400; www.mesagrill.com

Food Network fans know chef Bobby Flay as the red-haired chef who is a master of the grill. Today, he's practically an empire, with multiple restaurants under his helm, cookbooks and numerous television appearances. But Mesa Grill, which opened in 1991, was his first restaurant, and above all else, Flay is the king of all things spicy. Dishes like the shrimp and roasted garlic corn tamales, New Mexican spice-rubbed pork tenderloin with crushed pecan butter, and sixteen-spice duck breast with carrot-habanero sauce and a chorizo-goat cheese tamale with thyme, prove that his food keeps getting better and better. The service can be clunky, but your focus will be on the food.

Southwestern. Lunch (Monday-Friday), dinner, Saturday-Sunday brunch. $35-85

UPPER EAST SIDE

★★★CAFÉ BOULUD

20 E. 76th St., Upper East Side, 212-772-2600; www.danielnyc.com

The look of the dining room may have changed, thanks to a cosmetic renovation in 2009, but the same exceptional French cuisine continues to flow from the kitchen under the command of chef Gavin Kaysen. Daniel Boulud's more casual eatery, Café Boulud is reminiscent of a buzzing neighborhood brasserie with high ceilings, tightly packed tables and mirrors lining the walls. It's hard to resist getting traditional with the foie gras au torchon, or dipping into the summer season with Maine peekytoe crab over a carrot purée. For a good smattering of each, opt for the prix fixe lunch. Café Boulud is a popular destination for brunch as well. One look at the viennoiseries basket of pastries and you'll understand why.

French. Lunch, dinner, Sunday brunch. $36-85

★★★★★DANIEL

60 E. 65th St., Upper East Side, 212-288-0033; www.danielnyc.com

Chef Daniel Boulud is fastidious about details—like the clarity of his veal stock, the flower petals suspended in ice cubes in some of the cocktails and the complimentary basket of warm madeleines at meal's end. But this is what's kept Daniel firmly moored among New York's most elite and elegant restaurants. After a massive redesign in 2008 under the command of famed designer Adam Tihany, the space marries neo-classical sophistication and organic playfulness. Archways and balustrades are bisected by vine-like wrought iron sconces, Limoges chandeliers drape the dining room in warm light and understated leafy table arrangements stand out against otherwise neutral tones. Eating here, you'll happily part with stacks of greenbacks just to dig a fork into his legendary potato-coated sea bass or a dish of succulent veal prepared three ways. The very attentive staff is a highlight, expertly helping well-heeled diners navigate the 1,500-bottle wine list and graciously amending tasting menus to fit your preferences. Choose between a three-course prix fixe and six- or eight-course tasting menus, or dine à la carte in the lounge.

French. Dinner. Closed Sunday. Reservations recommended. $86 and up

★★★JOJO

160 E. 64th St., Upper East Side, 212-223-5656; www.jean-georges.com

Dining at Jojo's is more akin to a meal at a friend's apartment than a restaurant—as long as that friend has a palatial Upper East Side townhouse, a knack for cooking flawless French cuisine and goes by the name Jean-Georges. The interior can waver on overdone, but one bite of the ricotta ravioli with spring vegetables, and you'll hardly care. The poached lobster is unique with a tangy lemon risotto and caramelized fennel, while the duck is perfectly cooked in sweet and sour shallots. Desserts are extraordinary. Raspberry crisp, gooey chocolate cake, poached peaches, warm madeleines. Take your pick; they're all rich and satisfying.

French. Lunch, dinner, Saturday-Sunday brunch. $36-85

★★★SHUN LEE PALACE

155 E. 55th St., Upper East Side, 212-371-8844; www.shunleepalace.com

A favorite choice for Chinese-food-loving New Yorkers who want something a little more refined than some of the places in Chinatown, Shun Lee specializes in Hunan, Cantonese and Szechuan classics. Its following is not unfounded: The food here is flavorful and light, with many authentic, time-intensive dishes you won't find at neighborhood Chinese spots. The Beggar's Chicken, for example, is a vegetable-, pork- and seafood-stuffed chicken wrapped in lotus leaves and packed in clay soil before baking for several hours. Vegetarians who wrestle with the carnivore-craze, particularly the Peking duck variety, will find salvation in the Veggie Duck Pie, a tofu take on the famous delicacy, pancake, hoisin sauce and all. Shun Lee's sister restaurant, Shun Lee on the Upper West Side (*43 W. 65th St., 212-595-8895*), serves similar food and is a popular choice with the Lincoln Center crowd.

Chinese. Lunch, dinner. $16-35

RECOMMENDED

SERENDIPITY 3

225 E. 60th St., Upper East Side, 212-838-3531; www.serendipity3.com

Don't let the crush of people ogling knickknacks for sale dampen your desire to indulge in a signature frozen hot chocolate or three-scoop "drugstore" sundae at this Upper East Side sweet shop. There are few places in New York as playful as Serendipity, where both kids and kids-at-heart can unabashedly worship at the altar of sweets. Serendipity feels like an Alice in Wonderland tea party come to life, complete with multicolored Tiffany lamps (some of them real), a tiny space and larger-than-you-can-imagine sticky treats. "Serious" food is available, too, from burgers and hot dogs to meatloaf and pasta.

American. Lunch, dinner. $16-35

UPPER WEST SIDE

★★★★ASIATE

Mandarin Oriental, New York, 80 Columbus Circle, Upper West Side, 212-805-8881; www.mandarinoriental.com

French-Asian fare is nothing new, but it sure is something to write home about if it comes from this restaurant inside the Mandarin Oriental hotel. Asiate offers thoughtful, well-executed East-meets-West fare, like roasted foie gras and glazed eel atop braised daikon in an anise-pineapple broth, and black sea bass with stir-fried Asian vegetables in a ginger-lemongrass consommé. Indeed, everything about this restaurant is noteworthy, from the sweeping views of Central Park, courtesy of the 16-foot-high windows, to the glittering tree-branch sculpture hanging from the ceiling, to the beautiful china on your table and the wine collection, which fills up an entire wall. The chocolate fondant with raspberry granite is the perfect complement to your evening.

French, Asian. Breakfast, lunch (Monday-Friday), dinner, Saturday-Sunday brunch. $86 and up

★★★CESCA

164 W. 75th St., Upper West Side, 212-787-6300; www.cescanyc.com

Dependably delicious and cozy, the rustic Italian restaurant 'Cesca has been a favorite of Upper West Siders since it opened in 2003. Stenciled white walls, soft lighting and large, circular booths keep the mood relaxed. The open kitchen churns out hits such as parmesan and prosciutto fritters dusted with a surprising kick of cayenne, and orecchiette with crumbled pork sausage and broccoli rabe. A three-course pre-theater menu is available before 6:30 p.m. for crowds catching a show at nearby Lincoln Center. If you need a kickstart before the performance, swing by the long, granite-topped bar for a Tuscan Maple Sidecar with maple syrup and Grand Marnier or a tangy Via Veneto Spritz, bubbling over with Prosecco, Aperol and lemon.

Italian. Dinner, Sunday brunch. $36-85

★★★DOVETAIL

103 W. 77th St., Upper West Side, 212-362-3800; www.dovetailnyc.com

Neighboring the American Museum of Natural History, Central Park and Lincoln Center, Dovetail is a welcome addition to a tourist heavy, and restaurant-slim locale. Chef John Fraser honors fresh, local ingredients with simple dishes that emphasize flavor over fuss. The pistachio crusted duck with daikon, water greens and sweet and sour plums is succulent and tangy with an even balance of salty and sweet, while the truffle gnocchi alongside Serrano ham and chanterelles is light and airy. Come for the famed Sunday Suppa, an affordable prix fixe menu, or head down to the sherry cellar to watch the magic in the kitchen while you dine. The interior is sleek without being pretentious and modern without being uncomfortable. Brick columns and muslin-covered walls give the space a casual urban vibe, perfect for the Upper West Siders who frequent it.

Contemporary American. Lunch (Friday), dinner. Saturday-Sunday brunch. $36-85

★★★★★JEAN GEORGES

1 Central Park West (near Columbus Circle), Upper West Side, 212-299-3900;
www.jean-georges.com

So this is what fabulous looks and tastes like. The minimalist dining room is Grade-A sexy—it resembles an extra-large egg, thanks to the curved white seating, soft round lighting, pale white walls and sheer drapes. The soaring ceiling and windows and the dainty Spiegelau stemware contribute to the delicate, airy feeling, but that's as far as your attention will veer from the real star of the show: Jean-Georges Vongerichten's ethereal Asian-influenced French cuisine (roasted sweetbreads with pickled white asparagus and coriander; young garlic soup with frog's legs). Vongerichten is a master at layering flavor, making each bite a hit parade of taste—striking you first with smoky squab, chasing it with poignantly sweet summer peas, then following with a refreshing hint of peppermint. Savor his flawless technique in a three-course meal ($98) or a seven-course procession of signature dishes ($148). For a more casual rendezvous with Jean Georges' tantalizing cuisine, settle for a table at the outdoor Terrace or neighboring Nougatine.

French. Lunch (Monday-Saturday), dinner. Closed Sunday. Reservations recommended. $86 and up

★★★★★MASA

Time Warner Center, 10 Columbus Circle, Upper West Side, 212-823-9800; www.masanyc.com

When you surrender this much cash (at least $450 a head—or more, depending upon availability of ingredients—before drinks and tip) and power (the chef decides what you'll eat), the food better be flawless. Luckily, chef Masa Takayama's creations are, and when you put yourself entirely in his expert hands, he'll regale you with an array of five to six appetizers, 20 to 25 different types of fresh seafood and a dessert course. The chef is infatuated with high-end, luxury ingredients such as truffles (white truffle tempura; black truffles on oysters), caviar (a generous scoop of which tops tuna belly), Ohmi beef and foie gras. Seafood is flown in daily from Japan. There are just 26 seats; ask if you can sit at the sushi counter, composed of a single slab of Japanese cypress Hinoki wood, so you can watch Takayama and his team of chefs at work.

Japanese. Lunch (Tuesday-Friday), dinner. Closed Sunday. Reservations recommended. $86 and up

★★★★★PER SE

Time Warner Center, 10 Columbus Circle, Upper West Side, 212-823-9335; www.perseny.com

Per Se bears the same blue front doors as French Laundry (its country cousin in Napa Valley) and has similar high-end flourishes like nine varieties of salt, plus chef Thomas Keller's legendary "oysters and pearls" dish of Island Creek oysters, creamy tapioca and caviar. The 64-seat Per Se in the Time Warner Center, with its neutral brown palette and silver accents, feels more cosmopolitan and overtly ambitious in ways the pastoral French Laundry is not. Yet at its heart, Per Se offers the fine-dining indulgences fans worship Keller for (artisanal butter; a fierce focus on fresh ingredients), and it'll still take you five hours to stuff yourself silly on foie gras and truffles as a cavalcade of servers fawn over you. (The daily changing nine-course tasting menu—vegetarian option available—is $275, and a $175 five-course lunch menu is available Friday through Sunday.) So what if the East Coast setting is a bit more buttoned-up? You won't miss the original a bit.

Contemporary American. Lunch (Friday-Sunday), dinner. Jacket required. Reservations recommended. $86 and up

★★★★PICHOLINE

35 W. 64th St., Upper West Side, 212-724-8585; www.picholinenyc.com

Chef Terrance Brennan's French-Mediterranean cuisine continues to impress at Picholine, which opened in 1993 and seems to get more distinguished with age. The refined menu lacks the fussiness of some French restaurants—you won't find overly rich sauces and heavy, buttery entrées here—but it doesn't skimp on elegance. The fare is simple, seasonally driven and clean in construction: Hearty rabbit comes with fresh tagliatelle and wild snails, while wild striped bass is served with corn chorizo and chanterelle escabéche. Pull up to the bar and try the cheese flights, which are organized by country of origin, and make a good pre- or post-theater treat. The service is poised in the windowless lavender dining room, which gets its sparkle from an enormous chandelier overhead.

French. Dinner. Closed Sunday. Reservations recommended. $86 and up

ALSO RECOMMENDED

BARNEY GREENGRASS

541 Amsterdam Ave., Upper West Side, 212-724-4707; www.barneygreengrass.com

If you like your restaurants with a schmear of character and history, look no further than the 100-year-old Barney Greengrass. Known affectionately as "The Sturgeon King," this appetizing Jewish deli (which moved from its original Harlem location to its current spot in 1929) takes the nickname seriously: Sturgeon and velvety lox top bagels and bialys, and weave through fluffy scrambled eggs with onions for one of the most popular breakfasts on the Upper West Side. Other traditional fare such as herring, sable and whitefish salad have also understandably made this no-frills Formica haven with its surly counter staff a go-to eatery for generations of New Yorkers. Expect a long wait, especially on weekends, when you might bump elbows with the likes of Jerry Seinfeld.

Deli. Breakfast, lunch. Closed Monday. $16-35

SARABETH'S

423 Amsterdam Ave., Upper West Side, 212-496-6280; 1295 Madison Ave., Upper East Side, 212-410-7335; 40 Central Park South, Midtown West, 212-826-5959; Lord & Taylor, 424 Fifth Ave., Midtown, 212-827-5068; www.sarabeths.com

During the nearly inevitable hour-long wait for a table on Sunday mornings, you may wonder if pancakes and eggs are worth it. The answer? Absolutely. This brunch mainstay is favored by a J.Crew-clad, preppy set seeking other-worldly ricotta lemon pancakes and three-egg omelets in a faux-country setting. If you can't bear the wait, pick up a selection of scones and muffins and a jar of jewel-toned homemade jam (we like strawberry peach, mixed berry or plum cherry) from the bakery counter. Lunch and dinner offerings like chicken pot pie are just what you'd expect—hearty and homey.

American. Breakfast, lunch, dinner. Lord & Taylor location: lunch only. $16-35

HARLEM

★★★SYLVIA'S

328 Lenox Ave., Harlem, 212-996-0660; www.sylviasrestaurant.com

Critics may say that Sylvia's has lost some of its soul since it spawned cookbooks and a line of food products including canned black-eyed peas and jarred "Sassy Sauce." But this legendary Harlem soul-food eatery—which Sylvia Woods opened with her husband Herbert in 1962 in a luncheonette where she had formerly waitressed—is still a go-to spot for everything fried, smothered and sauced in the Southern comfort tradition. All of the usual faves are here: catfish, chicken livers, ribs, waffles and fried chicken, grits, collard greens, coconut cake, banana pudding—we could go on. President Barack Obama has been seen dropping in for fried chicken, as has former President Bill Clinton. Don't miss the Sunday gospel brunch; you'll leave with a spring in your step and your belly full.

American, Southern. Breakfast, lunch (Monday-Saturday), dinner, Sunday brunch. $16-35

BROOKLYN

★★★THE GROCERY

288 Smith St., Carroll Gardens, Brooklyn, 718-596-3335; www.thegroceryrestaurant.com

Located about 20 minutes from Manhattan in this pretty Brooklyn neighborhood, the Grocery is an unassuming-yet-overachieving eatery specializing in exceptional farmers market fare (roasted beets with goat cheese ravioli, slow-rendered duck breast with kasha) churned out by chefs Charles Kiely and Sharon Pachter, a low-key husband-and-wife team. The 30-seat restaurant feels quaint—with the chefs sometimes even serving the food. There's a positively lovely garden out back and sage-green walls inside, so anywhere you dine is a delight. But the prices ($130 for a six-course tasting menu with wine) remind you that Brooklyn is just a stone's throw from Manhattan.

Contemporary American. Lunch (Thursday-Saturday), dinner. Closed Sunday-Monday. $16-35

★★★PETER LUGER STEAK HOUSE

178 Broadway, Williamsburg, Brooklyn, 718-387-7400; www.peterluger.com

Just over the East River in a somewhat sketchy part of Brooklyn near the Williamsburg Bridge is the legendary Peter Luger's, whose dining room can only be described as beer-hall chic—weathered wooden tables, a few beer steins on the shelves and somewhat surly servers who seem like they've been here since the restaurant opened in 1887. The Forman family, which owns the venerable steakhouse, personally selects the prime beef and then dry ages it onsite, resulting in tasty cuts that go unrivaled by other steakhouses. Our advice: Skip the menu and simply explain whether you want steak for one, for two and so on. Sides are simple classics, like German fried potatoes and creamed spinach, intended to keep the buttery broiled porterhouse the deserved star of the meal. Unless you have a Peter Luger credit card (apply online at the restaurant's website), you must pay cash or risk the wrath of your waiter.

Steak. Lunch, dinner. $36-85

HIGHLIGHT

WHAT ARE NEW YORK CITY'S BEST BISTROS?

ARTISANAL FROMAGERIE & BISTRO
Couples nibble on baskets of airy gougères at the bar while cheese-savvy servers hustle pots of gooey fondue to tightly packed wooden tables.

BALTHAZAR
This warm, noisy French bistro has become a fixture in Soho for tourists and locals alike who come to dig into cheese plates, platters of oysters, burgers and more.

BLUE RIBBON BRASSERIE
Blue Ribbon is everything a good brasserie should be—woody and warm, with a menu that leans heavily on upgraded comfort classics like strip steak and fried chicken.

LOCANDA VERDE
Located in the Greenwich Hotel, Locanda Verde is a refreshingly casual and affordable eatery that offers crowd-pleasing specials such as buttermilk fried chicken.

THE RED CAT
From the moment you enter the warm red and white dining room to the moment you leave feeling perfectly satisfed from your dinner of chicken with garlicky soy beans or steak and potatoes, you will be happy.

RECOMMENDED

AL DI LÀ
248 Fifth Ave., Park Slope, Brooklyn, 718-783-4565; www.aldilatrattoria.com

Past the crush of hungry waiting diners and thick velvet drapes at the door lies a cozy dining room where a glassy chandelier suspends from the ceiling. You'll think you can hear gondoliers singing outside when you tuck into the authentic Northern Italian dishes like creamy cuttlefish risotto, braised rabbit and pillowy squash ravioli sautéed in brown butter and sage. Years of positive word of mouth and a no-reservations policy create painfully long waits on weekends, but the restaurant's wine bar around the corner is a colorful and comfortable spot to happily spend your wait.

Northern Italian. Lunch (Wednesday-Sunday), dinner. Closed Tuesday. $36-85

GRIMALDI'S PIZZERIA

19 Old Fulton St., Dumbo, Brooklyn, 718-858-4300; www.grimaldispizza.com

If the line snaking down the sidewalk for a red-and-white-checkered-table cloth-topped table doesn't tip you off, then we'll spell it out: The coal-oven pizzas here are sublime, from the creamy ricotta cheese topping down to the blistered crust underneath. A large pie is just $15 and toppings add a few dollars more, so if you can't get a table, order one to go—this pizza tastes just as good when you're eating it sitting on the stoop outside. Grimaldi's is near the base of the Brooklyn Bridge, in fashionable Dumbo, making the walk over the bridge and back to Manhattan easy as pie.

Pizza. Lunch, dinner. $15 and under.

SPAS

★★★CAUDALÍE VINOTHÉRAPIE SPA AT THE PLAZA

The Plaza, 1 W. 58th St., Upper East Side, 212-265-3182; www.caudalie-usa.com

Who would have thought that wine, massage and pampered relaxation go so well together? The powers behind Caudalíe Paris have brought the concept of vinotherapy stateside in the form of an immaculate new spa space at The Plaza. The wine theme carries throughout, from the French Paradox wine lounge to the vines hanging effortlessly on the walls to bowls of crisp cold grapes in the relaxation rooms. Even the treatments incorporate the fruit of the vine. The Honey and Wine Wrap works to fortify and hydrate aging skin by applying a warm mixture of wine yeast and honey before wrapping the body in toasty blankets, while the signature Caudalíe Massage uses grapeseed oils to resculpt any problem areas in the body. A post-treatment stop in the wine lounge, which serves blends from the Caudalíe family vineyard, is an intoxicating way to keep the relaxed vibe going into the evening hours.

★★★★LA PRAIRIE AT THE RITZ-CARLTON SPA

The Ritz-Carlton New York, Central Park, 50 Central Park South, Midtown, 212-308-9100; www.ritzcarlton.com

Services at this small hotel spa (with just six treatment rooms) use the La Prairie line of Swiss skincare products. Treatments include a long list of pleasures for the face, body and nails. The Caviar Firming Facial uses caviar extracts to transform your skin. The Jet Lag Therapy combines a 30-minute aromatherapy massage, 30 minutes of foot/hand reflexology and a 30-minute facial—leaving you perfectly pampered for your big adventure in the city. There's plenty of details to remind you that you're at the Ritz, too: The women's changing area has a steam room and all the personal amenities you might need, plus lockers with their own jewelry boxes. The men's area has a supersized steam room, which is said to have hosted more than one business meeting.

★★★★★THE PENINSULA SPA BY ESPA

The Peninsula New York, 700 Fifth Ave., Midtown, 212-903-3910; www.peninsula.com

When a superlative spa refuses to rest on its laurels by constantly adding improvements, you should plan on becoming a regular. This much-loved spa at the Peninsula has undergone a complete renovation in conjunction with spa consultants ESPA. It's part of a collaboration that began in 2006 with a swank re-do of the spa chain's flagship Hong Kong property. The sparkling new addition here is the only ESPA spa in the city, and the only place to try signature treatments like the Yin Uplifter, designed to rid you of chills with a stone massage and application of clay mixed with cinnamon, licorice and ginger before you're placed in a linen wrap. Meanwhile, the Yang Soother addresses overheated or sensitive skin with a body treatment that mixes chrysanthemum, black lychee and marine mud or algae that leaves skin as smooth as silk. (Both treatments last for two hours.) The commanding space on the 21st and 22nd floors of the hotel, with skyline views, 12 treatment rooms, one couples' suite and private lounges is as relaxing as it gets. Locker rooms offer aromatherapy showers plus steam, sauna and thermal suites.

★★★★THE SPA AT FOUR SEASONS HOTEL NEW YORK

Four Seasons Hotel New York, 57 E. 57th St., Midtown East, 212-758-5700; www.fourseasons.com

This subterranean spa reflects the Four Seasons' signature style with an unobtrusive-yet-attentive staff and a penchant for luxurious details. The quiet space located beneath the hotel lobby provides services inspired by international practices, but eschews New Age notions. You can schedule acupressure combined with back-walking here, but you'll have to go elsewhere if you want your chakras balanced. The Four Seasons New York Signature Therapeutic Massage, draws from four complementary traditions (shiatsu, Thai stretching, Swedish massage and reflexology) to ensure you're de-stressed and as loose-limbed as possible. Or go native with the Big Apple Antioxidant Body Treatment, which uses two apple-based preparations—an apple/brown sugar scrub with a Vichy shower followed by an apple body butter massage—and capitalizes on the natural enzymes in the fruit to leave your skin super soft and with a dewy glow.

★★★★★THE SPA AT MANDARIN ORIENTAL, NEW YORK

Mandarin Oriental, New York, 80 Columbus Circle, Columbus Circle, 212-805-8800; www.mandarinoriental.com

Sweeping views of Central Park and the Hudson River from floor-to-ceiling windows aren't the only thing that'll put this 35th-floor hotel spa at the top of your list of favorites. First, book a 90-minute block

---

WHICH NEW YORK CITY SPAS HAVE THE BEST MASSAGES?

The Spa at Four Seasons Hotel New York:
The skilled therapists will customize your massage; you also can't go wrong with the signature treatment, which incorporates four types of massage, including shiatsu, Thai, Swedish and reflexology.

The Spa at Mandarin Oriental, New York:
All of the massages here are highly effective; the Thai Yoga Massage is great when you are feeling especially tense.

of time, then consult with the top-notch staff to determine the best treatments to fill it. Asian-influenced services range from relaxing (the signature Thai Yoga Massage combines kneading with gentle yoga poses and assisted stretching) to rejuvenating (Ama Releasing Abhyanga loosens congestion and promises to free your body of toxins with a combination of exfoliation, cleansing and massage). While you're alleviating tension, take advantage of complimentary amenities, including an Oriental Tea Lounge, vitality pool and amethyst-crystal steam chamber, all awash in soothing beiges and golds.

WHERE TO SHOP

CHELSEA
LINGO
257 W. 19th St., Chelsea, 212-929-4676; www.lingonyc.com

The who-wore-it-better debate is a popular topic for celebutants across Manhattan who commonly lose sleep over whether someone else will be wearing the same outfit as them at a party. No such fear for Lingo patrons, as each piece is custom made by a local designer and stocked solely at this hidden Chelsea gem. The owner (and her well-behaved shepherd mix) provides an atmosphere that is more akin to a friend's fabulous closet than a chic department store dressing room. Lines like Fresh Meat and Sirius lead the charge from casual to evening wear, and accessories from purses to jewels are plentiful.
Tuesday-Saturday 1-8 p.m., Sunday 1-6 p.m.

MICHAEL ARAM
136 W. 18th St., Chelsea, 212-461-6903; www.michaelaram.com

Inspired by India's rich tradition of metalworking, this American home furnishings designer's first boutique offers a darkly handsome space for his elegant, handcrafted tableware and furniture. Black brick walls and gold displays let the shimmering stainless steel pitchers, gold-dipped bowls and silverplated tea kettles take center stage. Earthy types will gravitate toward the intricate leaf-shaped trays, vases cast to resemble the bark of white birch trees and twig-like serving spoons.
Monday-Saturday 11 a.m.-7 p.m., Sunday noon-6 p.m.

CHINATOWN/LITTLE ITALY/NOLITA
DUNCAN QUINN
8 Spring St., Nolita, 212-226-7030; www.duncanquinn.com

For dapper gents, this minuscule yet swank haberdashery jams in plenty of Savile Row style within its stripe-wallpapered walls. Known for its slim fit and rock 'n' roll sensibility, Quinn's signature suiting is cut from exceptional Scottish and British fabrics, and there's a smart bespoke collection when ready-made won't do. Elegant shirts, Italian ties, pocket squares, enamel cuff links and sterling-silver collar stays should please detail-oriented dandies.
Monday-Saturday noon-8 p.m., Sunday noon-6 p.m.

HIGHLIGHT

WHERE IS THE BEST SHOPPING IN MIDTOWN?

Home to Broadway theaters, media powerhouses and much of the city's commerce, Midtown is quite literally the center of New York City and boasts some of its toniest emporiums. Time-pressed office workers jostle for elbow room with gaggles of tourists on the well-trodden sidewalks of Fifth and Madison avenues.

Start your spree at **Bloomingdale's** sprawling flagship, which takes up an entire city block (*1000 Third Ave., 212-705-2000; www.bloomingdales.com*). Bloomies offers more democratically priced items than the next few department stores on your list. It also has a huge selection of jeans on the second floor, great men's formalwear and loads of shoes for brides.

Your next stop is hip department store **Barneys New York** (*660 Madison Ave., 212-826-8900; www.barneys.com*), where creative director Simon Doonan's over-the-top, often humorous windows have featured a live actor playing Sigmund Freud and a mannequin of Margaret Thatcher in dominatrix garb. Inside, the loot is less risqué but equally attention-grabbing, ranging from Stella McCartney to Manolo Blahnik. Don't even think about skipping the shoe department; locals love to lunch at Fred's, up on the ninth floor, where the chicken soup will keep you fortified.

Get ready to drop a bundle at luxe **Bergdorf Goodman** (*754 Fifth Ave. at East 58th Street, 212-753-7300; www.bergdorfgoodman.com*). Ladies can peruse Valentino gowns and Prada clutches or the pieces inside specialty designer boutiques within the store for Chanel, Armani and other high-end labels. Gents get their due just across the street at **Bergdorf Goodman Men's** (*745 Fifth Ave.*), three entire floors devoted to men with John Varvatos jackets and William Rast jeans.

Nearby lies a trinity of goodies for accessory fiends at leather-good icon **Louis Vuitton** (*1 E. 57th St., 212-758-8877; www.louisvuitton.com*), bastion of the iconic little blue box **Tiffany & Co.** (*727 Fifth Ave., 212-755-8000; www.tiffany.com*) and diamond king **Harry Winston** (*718 Fifth Ave., 212-245-2000; www.harrywinston.com*). Label hounds can then hit the Trump Tower for **Gucci** (*725 Fifth Ave., 212-826-2600; www.gucci.com*) before heading down to trendy **Henri Bendel** (*712 Fifth Ave., 212-247-1100; www.henribendel.com*), which draws in young ladies craving makeup, gorgeous lingerie and designs by the next big things in fashion. Bendel's also offers a slew of fun gifts up on the second floor, from picture frames to key chains.

Start praying to the retail gods for heavy markdowns as you head a block-and-a-half farther south to the name-sake flagship of **Saks Fifth Avenue** (*611 Fifth Ave., 212-753-4000; www.saksfifthavenue.com*), whose shoe department nearly boasts its own zip code. Then, walk the 11 blocks from Saks to mainstay **Lord & Taylor** (*424 Fifth Ave., 212-391-3344; www.lordandtaylor.com*).

End your day by heading five blocks further south and an avenue west to behemoth **Macy's** (*151 W. 34th St., Herald Square, 212-695-4400; www.macys.com*). The enormous department store stays open late on weekends.

RESURRECTION

217 Mott St., Nolita, 212-625-1374; www.resurrectionvintage.com

Nicolas Ghesquière, Marc Jacobs and Anna Sui have all rummaged through the racks of pristine pre-loved garb at this legendary vintage dealer. Perhaps it's because these designers know that fashion works in cycles; the latest trend can trace its design roots to some of the 20th-century finery neatly organized by item here. Though the stock in this crimson-hued store contains a preponderance of mod '60s styles including Courrèges dresses, there are also slinky Halston gowns from the disco era and '80s punk-rock trousers. Look, too, for enduring classics such as Chanel quilted purses and Hermès leather cuffs.

Monday-Saturday 11 a.m.-7 p.m., Sunday 1 p.m.-6 p.m.

EAST VILLAGE/LOWER EAST SIDE

OLIVER SPENCER

330 E. 11th St., East Village, 212-475-0079; www.oliverspencer.co.uk

With fans like the Rolling Stones and Scissor Sisters, you'd think this London-based designer would be known for skin-tight leather leggings, not well-tailored trench coats and other menswear. Opened in partnership with the owners of men's chain Odin, Spencer's first stateside boutique provides a clubby nook for his designs. Bell jars enclose silk ties, Bill Amberg carryalls rest on an antique apothecary, and a small selection of Sharps shaving creams keep men on the razor's edge.

Monday-Saturday noon-8 p.m., Sunday noon-7 p.m.

GREENWICH VILLAGE/SOHO/WEST VILLAGE

3.1 PHILLIP LIM

115 Mercer St., Soho, 212-334-1160; www.31philliplim.com

Beloved by fashionistas and celebrities for his clean-cut, casual aesthetic, designer Phillip Lim has claimed a piece of coveted Soho turf for his burgeoning empire's first flagship. Unlike other frenzied neighborhood stores pumping with loud soundtracks, this more serene spot draws on Lim's elegant but approachable style with a wall constructed of oak flooring and a chandelier fashioned from glass bocce balls. The fact that Lim's pared-down womenswear, menswear and accessories are all gathered under one roof should come as a relief to those used to running all over town to snap up his pieces.

Monday-Saturday 11 a.m.-7 p.m., Sunday noon-6 p.m.

AEDES DE VENUSTAS

9 Christopher St., West Village, 212-206-8674; www.aedes.com

Scent connoisseurs make a beeline to Aedes de Venustas for its passel of niche perfumes, skin-care lines and bathtime indulgences. Kitted out with a crystal chandelier and crimson carpet, the shop carries everything you need to surround yourself in a cloud of gardenia, white pepper or saffron, thanks to fragrances from Creed, Annick Goutal and obscure brands such as Escentric Molecules. Its array of Diptyque candles, Santa Maria Novella organic potpourri and Duchess Marden Damascena rose water also make luxe presents.

Monday-Saturday noon-8 p.m., Sunday 1-7 p.m.

HIGHLIGHT

WHERE ARE NEW YORK'S SAMPLE SALES?

Every season, agencies and designers descend on New York City's retail market with samples of what's to come. Once those retailers make their picks and place their orders, the samples are put on the seller's block to make room for next season's look books. The result: A sea of designer clothing at a fraction of its retail price.

Before learning how to get the most out of a sample sale, let's clear up some misconceptions. You don't have to be a celebrity to get in. And every piece of clothing is not a tiny size two. The more digging you're willing to do, the more treasures you're apt to find.

The best way to ensure admittance is to call ahead and make an appointment if you can. Know where you're going. These sales often are in random loft spaces or office buildings, and don't come with two-story signs and neon arrows pointing you in the right direction. Something else they don't come with: dressing rooms.

Sample sales are much like liquidation events: Everything must go, and it will, eventually. If you want the best selection, show up early. If you want the best price, sneak in toward the end. Whatever you do, just don't show up at lunchtime unless you're more inclined to crowd-surf than shop. And bring cash, as many sample sales don't accept credit or debit cards, or personal checks.

Before your trip, scout out which sample sales are taking place by checking out magazines such as New York and Time Out New York or online at *www.dailycandy.com* or *www.topbutton.com*. There's always a good sample sale going on somewhere.

MOSS

150 Greene St., Soho, 212-204-7100; www.mossonline.com

Don't be fooled by the striking museum-quality pieces behind the glass here: Murray Moss' temple of high-end housewares may feel like MoMA for the domestic set, but virtually everything is for sale. With reproductions of Wiener Werkstätte champagne coupes and 18th-century Meissen porcelain, the stock offers a brief history of tableware. This is Moss, remember—not Macy's or Martha Stewart—so you'll find contemporary, noteworthy pieces such as Fernando and Humberto Campana's whimsical chairs amassed from stuffed animals, Maarten Baas's neon-green clay side tables, and Tom Dixon's polished metal orb-shaped pendant lights.

Monday-Saturday 11 a.m.-7 p.m.

MUJI

455 Broadway, Soho, 212-334-2002; 620 Eighth Ave., Midtown, 212-382-2300; 16 W. 19th St., 212-414-9024, Chelsea; www.muji.us

Its name is shortened from the Japanese phrase for "no-brand goods," and the Tokyo-based chain churns out everything from stationery and furniture to clothing and umbrellas—all with a no-frills charm that has made Muji a favorite of design purists. Basics here are affordable and thoughtfully designed, like popular portable

HIGHLIGHT

WHERE ARE THE BEST BARGAINS IN NEW YORK?

New Yorkers are always looking for a deal, and there are many to be found, even in this expensive city. Everyone's favorite **Century 21** (*22 Cortlandt St., 212-227-9092; www.c21stores.com*) is beloved for its deep discounts on designer pieces. Another bargain treasure trove for designer labels on the cheap is the Chelsea flagship of **Loehmann's** (*101 Seventh Ave., 212-352-0856; www.loehmanns.com*). Its "Back Room" is renowned for gems from the likes of D&G, Prada and Marc Jacobs. Clothingline (*261 W. 36th St., 212-947-8748; www.clothingline.com*) is only open when there's a sale—usually for 40 weeks out of the year, when you can score knocked-down prices on direct-from-the-showroom Tocca, Kate Spade, Helmut Lang and more. Eco-chic shoppers can save the earth and some green at the sustainably minded Samples for **(eco)mpassion** (*2 Great Jones St., 917-226-9765; www.greenfinds.com*). Snap up pieces like 7 for All Mankind jeans at a steal and five percent of your purchase will be donated to such charities as Trees for the Future. A 10-minute walk south, Soho's doubleheader, **Topshop** (*478 Broadway, 212-966-9555; www.topshopnyc.com*)—a longtime British favorite and **Mango** (*561 Broadway, 212-343-7012; www.mango.com*) is a savvy stylista's home run, thanks to ultra-trendy pieces that may just last a season, but that's the point.

New Yorkers go to **Pearl River Mart** (*477 Broadway, 212-431-4770; www.pearlriver.com*) for ceramics, pretty Chinese slippers, stationary and lots more. And no trip to New York is complete without a visit to the epicenter for thrifty finds—**Chinatown**. Here, open-air stalls packed with bags, jewelry, scarves, hats and clothing line Canal Street from Broadway to the Bowery. Though the police have been cracking down on creators of Gucci, Dolce & Gabbana and other knock-offs—not to mention bootleg DVDs (save yourself a headache at the airport and skip buying these poorly filmed, pirated blockbusters)—there are still plenty of vendors to be found on the bustling strip. Most salespeople are open to some haggling, so don't be afraid to talk down a price. To help seal the deal, tell them you saw the same item for less down the street.

speakers that arrive flat and easily fold out to pop into action. You won't see any logos or flashy patterns splashed on the cereal bowls, notebooks, or bedroom slippers; instead, you'll find neutral-hued staples with a minimalist aesthetic. *Monday-Saturday 11 a.m.-9 p.m., Sunday 11 a.m.-8 p.m. Chelsea: Monday-Saturday 11 a.m.- 8 p.m., Sunday 11 a.m.-6:30 p.m.*

MZ WALLACE

93 Crosby St., Soho, 212-431-8252; 102 Christopher St., West Village, 212-206-1192; www.mzwallace.com

It's no surprise that mixing a chic fashion stylist and an experienced accessories editor and designer is a recipe for success. The true feat of MZ Wallace has been its staying power in the fierce handbag-eat-handbag world of Soho fashion. Since opening its doors nearly a decade ago, this small white-washed boutique is all about functionality and classic style. You're unlikely to find any in-today-out-tomorrow designs. Instead, owners Monica Zwirner and Lucy Wallace Eustice employ lightweight, durable materials and versatile sizes and colors to give women a tote they can actually tote everywhere, from an afternoon play date to an evening at Carnegie. The store also stocks a variety of accessories including wallets and cosmetic bags, in case there's no more room in your luggage for yet another handbag.

Monday-Saturday 11 a.m.-7 p.m., Sunday noon-6 p.m.

ODIN

199 Lafayette St., Soho, 212-966-0026; 328 E. 11th St., East Village, 212-475-0666; 750 Greenwich St., West Village, 212-420-8446; www.odinnewyork.com

This slick men's chain might be named after a Norse god, but its well-curated casual threads are assuredly for mere mortals. Nautically themed T-shirts by Rogues Gallery, Engineered Garments plaid shirts and Stetson fedoras exude an everyman vibe, albeit a smartly dressed one. Cult accoutrements such as Comme des Garçons wallets and Shane bejeweled belt buckles round out the mix.

Soho store: Monday-Saturday 11 a.m.-8 p.m., Sunday noon-7 p.m. East Village store: Monday-Saturday noon-9 p.m., Sunday noon-8 p.m.

OPENING CEREMONY

35 Howard St., Soho, 212-219-2688; Ace Hotel, 1190-1192 Broadway, Midtown, 646-695-5680; www.openingceremony.us

Known as the United Nations of fashion, the premise behind this ultra-creative boutique/gallery/showroom is to shine the spotlight on a visiting city for one year, gathering together the styles from established and upcoming designers, vintage items and select pieces from open-air markets. Since its opening, the store has focused on Hong Kong, Brazil, Germany, England, Sweden and Japan, each time entering into exclusive agreements with top retailers in those countries—for example, when they were highlighting the UK back in 2005, Opening Cermony was the only place to buy pieces from Topshop. World travelers and owners Humberto Leon and Carol Lim have also expanded the minimally embellished store's focus to also include a collaboration with Chloë Sevigny, and periodically offer special lines from retailers such as Tretorn created exclusively for the shop. You'll also find designs from Rachel Comey, Rodarte, Proenza Schouler and others. The store in the Ace Hotel offers lots of cool travel accessories.

Monday-Saturday 11 a.m.-8 p.m., Sunday noon-7 p.m.

SEIZE SUR VINGT

78 Greene St., Soho, 212-625-1620; The Plaza Retail Collection, 1 West 58th St., 212-832-1620; www.16sur20.com

Prepare for a shirt storm at Sieze sur Vingt. Having recently moved into a new space and incorporating its spin-off Group16SUR20 into one store, Sieze sur Vingt offers made-to-measure shirts and tailored clothing. Made from silky Egyptian cotton or crisp broadcloth, the traditional, well-tailored button-downs here are painstakingly custom-made from European fabrics, earning them raves from investment bankers and fashion editors alike. Browse through the bulky binders bursting with swatches of checks, stripes and plaids to create a made-to-order Oxford wardrobe for either gender, as well as men's suits and cashmere

sweaters. Fellas in need of quick gratification can grab off-the-rack graphic T-shirts from United Boroughs of New York, who mixes fashion with politics.
Monday-Saturday 11 a.m.-7 p.m., Sunday noon-6 p.m.

UNIQLO

546 Broadway, Soho, 917-237-8811; www.uniqlo.com

Japan's version of Gap has landed stateside, and its Soho outpost is Uniqlo's largest anywhere, brimming from floor to ceiling with casual sportswear—some sold only at this location. A wall near the entrance showcases artful tees, while cashmere sweaters get their due with a Crayola-box-like array of hues near the back. Everything from button-down shirts and blazers to socks and gym shorts are stocked in the tri-level space. One-off capsule lines by designers like Alexander Wang and Alice Roi up the fashion quotient.
Monday-Saturday 10 a.m.-9 p.m., Sunday 11 a.m.-8 p.m.

TRIBECA/MEATPACKING DISTRICT

DIANE VON FURSTENBERG

874 Washington St., Meatpacking District, 646-486-4800; www.dvf.com

Sure, von Furstenberg might be the president of the Council of Fashion Designers of America, but first and foremost, she'll always be queen of the wrap dress. Located on a prime corner in the Meatpacking District, her glittering flagship exudes a girly, futuristic vibe via fuchsia couches, white walls and a sprinkling of circular mirrors on the ceilings. DVF's ultrafemme pieces abound, including signature curve-skimming frocks along with chunky bracelets and jawbreaker-sized cocktail rings, the result of a collaboration with H. Stern jewelry. A slightly hidden set of stairs leads to a VIP dressing room, where you just might meet the diva herself (her studio is above the shop). Another store in Soho opened in mid-2010 at 135 Wooster Street.
Monday-Wednesday, Friday-Saturday 11 a.m.-7 p.m., Thursday 11 a.m.-8 p.m., Sunday noon-6 p.m.

EARNEST SEWN

821 Washington St., Meatpacking District, 212-242-3414; 90 Orchard St., Lower East Side, 212-979-5120; www.earnestsewn.com

Urban cowboys and city slickers alike are devoted to this local denim company's rustic emporium. Modeled after an old-fashioned general store with copper ceilings and roughed-up floorboards, the selvage haven proffers stacks of ready-made, pre-distressed jeans that look as if they were smuggled out of Clint Eastwood's wardrobe from The Good, the Bad and the Ugly. Folks afraid of style doppelgängers can choose from a range of pocket silhouettes and upscale fabrics to whip up a custom pair. A new line, Lit'l Earnie, features adorable jeans, jackets and skirts for kids. The back room houses an ever-changing array of pop-up shops, which carry limited edition goods like sunglasses from Moscot and rugged outerwear from Filson.
Meatpacking District: Monday-Saturday 11 a.m.-7 p.m., Sunday noon-
6 p.m. Lower East Side: Monday-Saturday noon-8 p.m., Sunday noon-7 p.m.

JEFFREY NEW YORK

449 W. 14th St., Meatpacking District, 212-206-1272; www.jeffreynewyork.com

A former footwear buyer for Barneys, Jeffrey Kalinsky established his department store in 1999 as a low-key yet high-end alternative to uptown bastions such as Bergdorf Goodman, Saks and his previous employer. Today, the rehabbed warehouse space contains a finely tuned assortment of runway-fresh clothing by Prada, Chloé, Gucci, Missoni and Dsquared, sold by a sweet, low pressure sales staff who won't spritz you to death in the perfume section (a rare find in New York). Don't miss the store's treasure trove of on-trend shoes and accessories, including hard-to-find VBH (V. Bruce Hoeksema) leather clutches.

Monday-Wednesday, Friday 10 a.m.-8 p.m., Thursday 10 a.m.-9 p.m., Saturday 10 a.m.-7 p.m., Sunday 12:30 p.m.-6 p.m.

STEVEN ALAN

103 Franklin St., Tribeca, 212-343-0692; 229 Elizabeth St., Nolita, 212-226-7482; 69 Eighth Ave., West Village, 212-242-2677; Outlet, 465 Amsterdam Ave., Upper West Side, 212-595-8451; 349 Atlantic Ave., Brooklyn, 718-852-3257; www.stevenalan.com

If Brooks Brothers had a love child with Barneys, it might resemble this stronghold of classic style. Alan's eponymous line of artfully rumpled button-down shirts subtly tweaks the basics for both genders, and his well-edited picks from a slew of other up-and-coming labels such as Engineered Garments, Mayle and Lyell follow suit. The well-worn, airy shops are just small enough to be manageable, and the payoff for your closet can be immense, especially if your visit coincides with Alan's legendary biannual sample sales in mid-May and the first week of November. If you can't make the markdown fest, the Upper West Side outlet brims year-round with discounted blasts from past seasons.

Tribeca: Monday-Saturday 11 a.m.-7 p.m., Sunday noon-6 p.m. West Village: Monday-Saturday 11:30 a.m.-7 p.m., Thursday 11:30 a.m.-8 p.m., Sunday noon-6 p.m. Nolita: Monday-Saturday 11:30 a.m.-7 p.m., Sunday noon-6 p.m. Upper West Side: Monday-Saturday 11 a.m.-7 p.m., Sunday 11 a.m.-6 p.m. Brooklyn: Monday-Saturday 11 a.m.- 7 p.m., Sunday noon-6 p.m.

THOM BROWNE

100 Hudson St., Tribeca, 212-633-1197; www.thombrowne.com

The New York designer has earned both snickers and cheers for his snug, shrunken men's suits that dare to bare ankles. His first eponymous showroom feels like the set of *Mad Men* and veers from his more adventurous runway looks (think feather-trimmed trousers and plaid skirts for men). Call ahead to make an appointment to try on tailored basics such as gray three-button jackets, preppy cashmere sweaters and snappy dress shoes, or to get measured for a bespoke pair of those trademark short pants.

Tuesday-Saturday 11 a.m.-7 p.m. or by appointment.

YOHJI YAMAMOTO/Y-3

1 Gansevoort St., Meatpacking District, 212-966-3615; www.yohjiyamamoto.co.jp

The Japanese designer's minimalist, deconstructed designs might just be as artful as his unusually shaped pair of boutiques. A handful of gorgeously constructed, asymmetric garments in a mostly black palette are exhibited like sartorial sculptures in the light-flooded, triangular storefront. (Don't worry about the sparse stock on hand; a storage room lies across the courtyard.) Across the street at Y-3 (*317 W. 13th St., Meatpacking District, 917-546-8677; www.adidas.com/y-3*), you'll find scads of sleek sneakers, polos, track pants and

the like from Yamamoto's sporty collaboration with athletics giant Adidas.
Tuesday-Saturday 11 a.m.-7 p.m.

UPPER EAST SIDE
SHANGHAI TANG
600 Madison Ave., Upper East Side, 212-888-0111; www.shanghaitang.com

Putting the East in East Coast, this small Chinese department store special-izes in eye-popping Asian treasures. Roaring dragons perch on wine stoppers, silver-plated chopsticks nestle into lime-fabric-lined cases, and Chinese char-acters adorn jacquard-covered photo albums. Vivid colors punch up Shanghai Tang's traditionally inspired clothing, which runs the gamut from relaxed-fit silk pajamas and curvy cheongsam dresses to modern mandarin-collar men's jackets and beaded cocktail frocks that wouldn't seem out of place on the red carpet. New parents can snag baby slippers that come in a cute, coordinating drawstring purse, and cuddly pandas dressed in Tang suits.
Monday-Wednesday, Friday-Saturday 10:30 a.m.-7 p.m., Thursday 10:30 a.m.-8 p.m., Sunday noon-6 p.m.

BROOKLYN
BIRD
220 Smith St., Cobble Hill, Brooklyn, 718-797-3774; 316 Fifth Ave., Park Slope, Brooklyn, 718-768-4940; 203 Grand St., Williamsburg St., 718-388-1655; www.shopbird.com

Brooklyn's retail scene has taken flight, and this breezy womenswear emporium is one of the borough's style pioneers. Known for its carefully honed range of on-the-cusp designers, Bird sells charming dresses, edgy ankle boots and slouchy leather hobo bags from local talents such as Lily Raskind of Sunshine & Shadow and Caitlin Mociun. Adorned with vintage-looking floral-print wallpaper and a tin ceiling, the Smith Street outpost also offers a comfy spot to sort through an international array of labels like Burkman Brothers, Tsumori Chisato and Paul Smith.
Monday-Friday noon-8 p.m., Saturday noon-7 pm., Sunday noon-6 p.m.

ZOË
68 Washington St., Dumbo, Brooklyn, 718-237-4002; www.shopzoeonline.com

Though Brooklyn has made a name for itself as a haven for indie brands, this 3,500-square-foot temple to big-ticket European fashion houses means you can still get your Jimmy Choos on this side of the East River. The white-walled, industrial-looking spot dishes up clothes and accessories for both genders, from the likes of Lanvin, Marni, Burberry and James Perse. You can also stock up on down-to-earth staples such as Splendid tees, J Brand jeans.,and cozy and cool Rag & Bone cardigans.
Monday 11 a.m.-7 p.m., Tuesday-Thursday, Saturday 11 a.m.-8 p.m., Friday 11 a.m.-9 p.m., Sunday noon-6 p.m.

THE FUTURE PERFECT
115 N. Sixth St., Williamsburg, Brooklyn, 718-599-6278; www.thefutureperfect.com

Forward-thinking David Alhadeff fills his design stronghold with quirky home décor for the Surface-reading set. Irony is a strong theme here with mainstays like Jason Miller's ceramic antler chandeliers, Sarah Cihat's recycled and

HIGHLIGHT

HOW FAR IS ATLANTIC CITY FROM NEW YORK?

Atlantic City is about 130 miles from New York. It will take you about 2 ½ hours to get there, which makes it a little hard to swing as a day trip, but with all that is changing in this city (and a new express train that makes nine round trips over the weekend from Penn Station), you might want to consider staying a night or two. **The Borgata Hotel Casino & Spa** (*1 Borgata Way, Atlantic City, New Jersey, 609-317-1000; www.theborgata.com*) currently reigns as the hotel-of-the-moment and is setting out to chart a sophisticated new direction for the city. The 161,000-square-foot casino, 12 restaurants (including three from celebrity chefs Bobby Flay, Michael Mina and Wolfgang Puck), four nightclubs, swank spa, and surround-sound event center definitely up the luxury factor in Atlantic City. For a more private affair, check out **The Water Club**, Borgata's chic boutique hotel within a hotel. Of course, Trump also has a few star-worthy properties here including **Trump Plaza** (*Boardwalk at Mississippi Ave., Atlantic City, New Jersey, 609-441-6000; www.trumpplaza.com*), **Trump Marina** (*Huron and Brigantine Blvd., Atlantic City, New Jersey, 609-441-2000; www.trumpmarina. com*) and **Trump Taj Mahal** (*1000 Boardwalk at Virginia Ave., Atlantic City, New Jersey, 609-449-1000; www.trumptaj.com*).

The famed **Atlantic City Boardwalk** dates back to 1870—built to appease hoteliers who complained of beach sand in their hotel lobbies—and once stretched more than seven miles. Today it totals only four, but has become more upscale in recent years, with high-end shops and restaurants replacing kitschy stores and fast-food joints. **The Pier Shops at Caesars** (*One Atlantic Ocean, at Arkansas, Atlantic City, New Jersey, 609-345-3100; www.thepiershopsatcaesars. com*) has more than 70 retail stores, including Gucci, Louis Vuitton and Burberry, and several restaurants, namely Stephen Starr's Buddakan and The Continental.

Upscale restaurants aside, no trip to Atlantic City is complete without a bag of sticky saltwater taffy. You can find this Atlantic City original at numerous shops lining the boardwalk. Other famous Atlantic City eats include the city's best raw bar and fresh seafood samplers at **Dock's Oyster House** (*2405 Atlantic Ave., Atlantic City, New Jersey, 609-345-0092; www.docksoysterhouse.com*). Around since 1897, there are rarely less than eight oyster varieties to choose from, and Dock's pan-sautéed crab cakes are as good as (and far cheaper than) any you'll find in Manhattan. **White House Sub Shop** (*2301 Arctic Ave., Atlantic City, New Jersey, 609-345-1564*) is another solid option, and a valuable reminder that New York isn't the only proximate metropolis. Philadelphia hoagies (that's "subs" to Garden Staters) have found their way down the shore. The sandwiches are enormous, piled high with meats, cheeses and loads of toppings. Celebrities such as Frank Sinatra and the Beatles chowed at this low-key haunt back in the day, and some say that Bill Cosby has had White House's subs flown to him in California on occasion.

rehabilitated tea sets and unique candelabras from various artists. You'll also find tongue-in-cheek toile du Jouy wallpaper with urban embellishments, and gifts such as Kelly Lamb's geometric birdhouse and Kristin Victoria Barron's sterling silver Taxicab Receipt Necklace. A free gallery space downstairs hosts a rotating roster of art.

Daily noon-7 p.m.

NIAGARA FALLS

Higher falls exist, but Niagara is an impressive and must-see natural wonder. On the border with Canada, the American Falls are 184 feet high, the Canadian Horseshoe, 176 feet. The two are separated by Goat Island. For several hours in the evening, the beauty of the falls continues in a display of colored lights playing over the water.

Originally, after the glacial period, the falls were seven miles downstream at the Niagara escarpment. Rocks have crashed from top to bottom, causing the falls to retreat at a rate averaging about one foot per year. With a flow of more than 200,000 cubic feet of water per second, Niagara has a power potential of about 4 million horsepower. Electrical production is controlled by agreements between the United States and Canada so that each receives a full share while the beauty of the cascading water is preserved. Kitschy souvenir shops and amusement parks surround the area.

WHAT TO SEE

AQUARIUM OF NIAGARA

701 Whirlpool St., Niagara Falls, 716-285-3575, 800-500-4609; www.aquariumofniagara.org

See more than 1,500 aquatic animals from around the world here, including sharks, otters, piranha, endangered Peruvian penguins and exotic fish. There is a free outdoor sea lion pool with shows every 90 minutes and shark feedings on alternate days.

Admission: adults $9.50, seniors $7.50, children 4-12 $6, children under 3 free. Daily 9 a.m.-5 p.m.

ARTPARK

450 S. Fourth St., Lewiston, 716-754-4375, 800-659-7275; www.artpark.net

This 150-acre state park and summer theater is devoted to the visual and performing arts. Events at the 2,300-seat theater with lawn seating include musicals, classical concerts by the Buffalo Philharmonic Orchestra, dance programs, jazz and pop music concerts. During the summer, free Tuesday night concerts draw large crowds.

Prices and show times vary.

CASTELLANI ART MUSEUM

Niagara University, 5795 Lewiston Road, Niagara Falls, 716-286-8200; www.niagara.edu

The more than 3,700 artworks at this museum range from the Hudson River School to contemporary sculpture. It boasts a first-rate folk arts program, including exhibits, artist demonstrations and performances. The collection of mid-20th-century pieces by artists such as De Kooning, Rauschenberg and Bearden is of particular interest.

Admission: free. Tuesday-Saturday 11 a.m.-5 p.m., Sunday 1-5 p.m.

CAVE OF THE WINDS

2153 Juron Drive, Niagara Falls, 716-278-1770; www.niagarafallslive.com

Elevators from Goat Island take you 175 feet deep into the Niagara Gorge. From the elevator, go through a series of wooden walkways to Hurricane Bridge, where you'll feel the spray at the base of the American Falls. Waterproof garments (including shoes) are supplied.

Admission: adults $10, children 6-12 $7, children under 6 free. May-October, daily 9 a.m.-7:30 p.m.

DEVIL'S HOLE STATE PARK

Robert Moses Parkway N., Niagara Falls, 716-284-4691; www.nysparks.state.ny.us

Enjoy views of the lower Whirlpool rapids and power authority generating plant, with a walkway leading along the Niagara River. There is also fishing, nature trails and picnicking. In the winter, Devil's Hole is a prime spot for snowshoeing and cross-country skiing.

Admission: free. Daily.

GOAT ISLAND

Niagara Falls, 716-278-1762; www.niagarafallslive.com

Goat Island separates the Canadian Horseshoe and American Falls. Drives and walks in a 70-acre park offer the closest possible views of the falls and upper rapids. Smaller Luna Island and Three Sister Islands can be reached by a footbridge.

Admission: free. Daily.

MAID OF THE MIST BOAT TOUR

Prospect Point Niagara Falls, 716-284-4233; www.maidofthemist.com

Maid of the Mist debarks from the base of the Observation Tower at Prospect Point and takes passengers on a 30-minute boat tour near the base of the American and Horseshoe Falls. Waterproof gear is supplied, but you should expect to get wet anyway.

Admission: adults $13.50, children 6-12 $8.30, children under 6 free. June-September, daily 10 a.m.-8 p.m.

NIAGARA FALLS STATE PARK

Robert Moses Parkway, Niagara Falls, 716-278-1770; www.nysparks.state.ny.us

This park, the oldest state park in the nation, provides many views of Niagara Falls and the rapids above and below the cataract from Prospect and Terrapin points, Luna Island and other locations. It was designed by Frederick Law Olmsted, who also laid out New York's Central Park. The 282-foot Prospect Park Observation Tower offers peerless views of each of the falls.

Admission: free. Daily.

NIAGARA GORGE DISCOVERY CENTER

Robert Moses Parkway, Niagara Falls

This educational center showcases geological formations and the history of the falls. There is a great 180-degree multiscreen theater and audiovisual presentation as well as a rock garden and gorge overlook.

Admission: $5. June-October, daily.

NIAGARA POWER PROJECT VISITOR CENTER

5777 Lewiston Road, Lewiston, 866-697-2386; www.nypa.gov

All that water goes to good use at the Niagara plant, one of the largest hydro-electric power outposts in the world. Tour the glass-enclosed observation building and be sure to step onto the outdoor balcony for spectacular views of the Niagara River Gorge. For those interested in seeing how the whole system works, there is a nice hands-on exhibit with a functioning hydropower turbine model.

Admission: free. Daily 9 a.m.-5 p.m.

NIAGARA SCENIC TROLLEY

139 Niagara St., Niagara Falls, 716-278-1796; www.niagarafallsstatepark.com

This three-hour, eco-friendly guided train ride travels from Prospect Point to Goat Island and back. It has seven stopovers, including the Cave of the Winds, the Maid of the Mist, Terrapin Point and Three Sister Islands. Ride all day for one price.

Admission: adults $2, children 6-12 $1, children under 6 free. April-October, daily.

OLD FORT NIAGARA STATE HISTORIC SITE

Robert Moses Parkway, Youngstown, 716-745-7611; www.oldfortniagara.org

This restored fort, which dates back to 1679 and has been held by France, Great Britain and the United States, played an important role in the French and Indian War and in the War of 1812. The buildings on the site are the oldest in the Great Lakes region and include the French Castle, constructed by the French in 1726. Living history programs and reenactments occur frequently.

Admission: adults $10, children 6-12 $6, children under 6 free. September-June, daily 9 a.m.-5 p.m.; July-August, daily 9 a.m.-7 p.m.

WHIRLPOOL STATE PARK

Robert Moses Parkway and Niagara Rapids Blvd., Niagara Falls, 716-284-4691; www.nysparks.state.ny.us

Take in splendid views of the famous Niagara River Gorge whirlpool and rapids. Ongiara Trail brings you down into the gorge for great fishing opportunities.

Admission: free. Daily.

WHERE TO STAY

★★★CROWNE PLAZA NIAGARA FALLS

300 Third St., Niagara Falls, 716-285-3361, 888-444-0401; www.ichotelsgroup.com

This property is a refreshing change from the more touristy hotels that pervade Niagara Falls. Rooms are cheerfully decorated with duvet-topped beds. The well-equipped fitness center is open 24 hours while the Old Falls Sports Bar & Grille is a prime spot for a burger or a brew while catching a sports game.

391 rooms. Restaurant, bar. Fitness center. Pool. Casino. $251-350

★★★THE RED COACH INN

2 Buffalo Ave., Niagara Falls, 716-282-1459, 866-719-2070; www.redcoach.com

Modeled after the Old Bell Inn in England, the Red Coach Inn has welcomed guests since 1923. Situated just 1,500 feet from the falls and near many other attractions, the English Tudor house has antique furniture, floral curtains and

HIGHLIGHT

WHAT ARE THE BEST SPOTS TO SEE THE FALLS?

CAVE OF THE WINDS
Take an elevator 175 feet deep into the Niagara Gorge. Walkways will take you to near the base of the American Falls, and you'll feel the spray hit your face.

GOAT ISLAND
This island, which separates the Canadian Horseshoe and American Falls, gives you the closest possible view of the cascading waters and upper rapids.

MAID OF THE MIST BOAT TOUR
Sail right to the bases of the American and Horseshoe Falls during this 30-minute boat tour that will leave you soaked.

NIAGARA FALL STATE PARK
You'll have your choice of vistas above and below the falls at this park. To see both of the falls, go to the top of the Prospect Park Observation Tower.

NIAGARA POWER PROJECT VISITOR CENTER
Admire a breathtaking view of the falls from the center's balcony, then head inside to learn how the hydroelectric power plant works.

linens, whirlpool tubs and amazing views in its guest accommodations. Most suites have kitchens and fireplaces. Continental breakfast is included and champagne, fruit and cheese await you upon arrival.
19 rooms. Restaurant, bar. Complimentary breakfast. $151-250

ALSO RECOMMENDED
COMFORT INN, THE POINTE
1 Prospect Pointe, Niagara Falls, 716-284-6835, 800-284-6835; www.choicehotels.com
This hotel is at the point of the American side of the falls, and you can hear the roar of the rushing water as you approach the entrance. Like any Comfort Inn, this outlet in the chain doesn't offer a lot of amenities, but its terrific location and no-frills price make it worth consideration if you're in town to see one of America's most amazing natural wonders.
118 rooms. Complimentary breakfast. Fitness center. $61-150

HOLIDAY INN GRAND ISLAND
100 Whitehaven Road, Grand Island, 716-773-1111; www.holidayinn.com

This hotel is located 12 miles from Niagara Falls and 10 miles from Buffalo. It offers an indoor/outdoor pool, a children's pool, a game room, a tennis court and more. A golf course and marina are adjacent to the hotel.

263 rooms. Restaurant, bar. Business center. Fitness center. Pool. Tennis. $61-150

WHERE TO EAT

RECOMMENDED
COMO RESTAURANT
2220 Pine Ave., Niagara Falls, 716-285-9341; www.comorestaurant.com

This little gem of a restaurant is located in Niagara Falls' Little Italy. Family-owned and operated since 1927, the Como Restaurant is popular with locals who come for traditional and tasty Italian fare like spaghetti with housemade sausage or pork-stuffed mushroom caps with a white wine gravy. If you're eating on the run, the onsite deli offers a selection of pasta dinners and luncheon plates as well as soups, sandwiches and pizzas.

Italian. Lunch, dinner. Reservations recommended. Children's menu. Bar. $16-35

HONEY'S NIAGARA FALLS
2002 Military Road, Niagara Falls, 716-297-7900; www.gohoneys.com

With its red-and-yellow-striped awning, Honey's is hard to miss. Located at the Prime Outlet Mall of Niagara Falls, this restaurant is great for a post-shopping meal with the family. Sample the unusual charred wing flavors, like barbecue raspberry.

American. Lunch, dinner, late-night. Outdoor seating. Children's menu. Bar. $15 and under

THE RED COACH INN
2 Buffalo Ave., Niagara Falls, 716-282-1459; www.redcoachinn.com

Exposed beams, upholstered banquettes and chairs, and dark wood create a cozy, Old World atmosphere at The Red Coach Inn restaurant. Signature dishes include juicy Black Angus filet mignon and Australian lobster tail. In warm weather, opt to sit on the patio.

Continental. Lunch, dinner. Reservations recommended. Outdoor seating. Children's menu. $16-35

GREATER NIAGARA

The Greater Niagara area is nicely nestled along Lake Ontario and Lake Erie, which provide gorgeous scenery. But don't just camp out along the waterfront; the region is peppered with eclectic small towns with lots of personality. Buffalo, at the eastern end of Lake Erie, is New York's second-largest city and one of the largest railroad centers in America. The city is as well known for its brutal winters, namesake chicken wings and tenacious NFL team, the Buffalo Bills.

Buffalo is attractive for its architectural stunners, such as its $7 million Art Deco City Hall; it's 1895 Prudential Building, recognized as the world's first skyscraper; and several Frank Lloyd Wright houses. Public parks also appear throughout the city, many of which were designed by Frederick Law Olmsted, father of American landscape architecture. The Buffalo Philharmonic Orchestra, Albright-Knox Art

Gallery and many cultural nightclubs cater to the varied interests of residents and visitors, and the six colleges and universities in the area inspire a youthful vibe.

The town of Lockport was originally settled around a series of locks of the Erie Canal, now the New York State Barge Canal. The historic downtown district sits right on the canal and affords great views of the action.

East Aurora lies very close to the large industrial center of Buffalo. In the early 1900s, Elbert Hubbard, author of "A Message to Garcia," lived here and made it the home of the Roycroft, a handicraft community known for making fine books, copper and leather ware and furniture. The Roycroft Campus is still operating, and it is the only continuous operation of its kind in America today. East Aurora is also the headquarters of Fisher-Price toys.

WHAT TO SEE

BUFFALO
ALBRIGHT-KNOX ART GALLERY
1285 Elmwood Ave., Buffalo, 716-882-8700; www.albrightknox.org

One of the oldest arts organizations in the United States, the gallery has a varied collection, including extensive works from 18th-century English, 19th-century French and 20th-century American and European painters. Pieces by Picasso, Matisse, Monet, Renoir and Van Gogh are on display, as well as sculpture from 3000 B.C. to the present.

Admission: adults $12, seniors and students $8, children under 12 free. Wednesday 10 a.m.-5 p.m., Thursday-Friday 10 a.m.-10 p.m., Saturday-Sunday 10 a.m.-5 p.m.

BUFFALO AND ERIE COUNTY BOTANICAL GARDENS
Olmsted's South Park, 2655 S. Park Ave., Buffalo, 716-827-1584;www.buffalogardens.com

Boasting a Victorian conservatory and gardens, this 156-acre park is teeming with plants in its 11 greenhouses and desert, rainforest and Mediterranean collections.

Admission: adults $6, seniors and students $5, children 6-13 $3, children under 6 free. Daily 10 a.m.-5 p.m.

BUFFALO AND ERIE COUNTY NAVAL & MILITARY PARK
1 Naval Park Cove, Buffalo, 716-847-1773; www.buffalonavalpark.org

The largest inland naval park in the nation displays ships, aircraft and tanks, including cruiser *USS Little Rock*, destroyer *USS The Sullivans* and submarine *USS Croaker*. There are also exhibits on women in the military, Vietnam veterans and Marine Corps memorabilia from World War I to the present.

Admission: adults $9, seniors and children 6-16 $6. April-October, daily 10 a.m.-5 p.m.; November, Saturday-Sunday 10 a.m.-4 p.m. Closed December-March.

BUFFALO MUSEUM OF SCIENCE
1020 Humboldt Parkway, Buffalo, 716-896-5200, 866-291-6660; www.buffalomuseumofscience.org

Explore exhibits on astronomy, botany, geology, zoology, anthropology and natural sciences in one of the region's premier museums, which also contains a research library. Kids will love Camp-In, a program that lets them spend a night in the museum.

HIGHLIGHT

WHAT ARE THE TOP THINGS TO DO IN GREATER NIAGRA?

VISIT THE BUFFALO AND ERIE COUNTY NAVAL & MILITARY PARK
Military buffs will want to check out this place, the largest inland naval park in the country. There are ships, aircraft, tanks and exhibits on military personnel.

GET A LESSON AT THE BUFFALO MUSEUM OF SCIENCE
One of the premier museums in the region, the BMS makes science accessible and fun with exhibits on mummies, space and scientific illustrators.

SEE SOME FRANK LLOYD WRIGHT HOUSES
The celebrated architect designed several homes in Buffalo. Take a tour of his work, and be sure to stop by the Martin House, which shows off Wright's Prairie style.

CHECK OUT THE PRUDENTIAL BUILDING
This structure was designed by Dankmar Adler and Louis Sullivan and is considered to be one of the first skyscrapers in America.

HIT THE SLOPES AT KISSING BRIDGE SKI AREA
If you are heading to this region for its snowy slopes, this 700-acre ski area provides some of the best runs in the Colden Snowbelt of western New York.

Admission: adults $7, seniors $6, military and students $5, children 3-18 $5, children under 3 free. July-August, Monday-Saturday 10 a.m.-5 p.m.; September-July, Wednesday-Saturday 10 a.m.-5 p.m., Sunday noon-5 p.m.

BUFFALO ZOOLOGICAL GARDENS
Delaware Park, 300 Parkside Ave., Buffalo, 716-837-3900; www.buffalozoo.org

More than 2,200 animals roam in this 23½-acre park. It features indoor and outdoor exhibits, a gallery of Boehm wildlife porcelains, a tropical gorilla habitat, outdoor lion and tiger exhibits and a children's zoo. Be sure to visit the newest member of the Buffalo Zoo, a baby Indian Rhinoceros named Clover.

Admission: adults $9.50, seniors and students $7, children 2-14 $6, children under 2 free. July-August, daily 10 a.m.-5 p.m.; September-June, 10 a.m.-4 p.m. Closed January-February, Monday-Tuesday.

CITY HALL/OBSERVATION TOWER

65 Niagara Square, Buffalo, 716-851-4200; www.ci.buffalo.ny.us

City Hall is an exceptional example of Art Deco architecture. Enjoy panoramic views of western New York, Lake Erie, and Ontario, Canada, from the observation deck.

Admission: free. Monday-Friday 8 a.m.-4 p.m.

FRANK LLOYD WRIGHT HOUSES

Buffalo, 716-856-3858; www.darwinmartinhouse.org

The famed American architect designed several buildings in Buffalo. They include the Darwin D. Martin house (*125 Jewett Parkway*); George Barton House (*118 Summit Ave.*); Gardener's Cottage (*285 Woodward Ave.*); Walter V. Davidson House (*57 Tillinghast Place*) and William Heath House (*76 Soldiers Place*). The Martin House is perhaps the best example of Wright's famed Prairie style, characterized by horizontally oriented structures, prominent foundations and organic materials.

Admission: Varies by location. Hours vary.

PRUDENTIAL BUILDING

28 Church St., Buffalo, 716-854-0003

Designed by Dankmar Adler and Louis Sullivan and completed in 1896, the Prudential (formerly Guaranty) Building is an outstanding example of Sullivan's famed functional design and terracotta ornament. It was declared a National Historic Landmark in 1975.

Admission: free. Daily.

SHEA'S PERFORMING ARTS CENTER

646 Main St., Buffalo, 716-847-1410; www.sheas.org

Two theaters make up Buffalo's premier performing arts center. Shea's Buffalo Theatre and Shea's Smith Theatre (right next door) both showcase a constant influx of Broadway shows, dance performances, operas, musical acts and family programs.

Admission: Prices vary. Ticket office: Monday-Friday 10 a.m.-5 p.m., Saturday 10 a.m.-2 p.m.

STUDIO ARENA THEATRE

710 Main St., Buffalo, 716-856-8025, 800-777-8243; www.studioarena.org

This regional professional theater presents world premieres, musicals, classic dramas and contemporary works. It's a great spot to scout fresh talent; Kelsey Grammer graced the Studio Arena stage before making it big with *Cheers* and *Frasier*.

Admission: Prices vary. Showtimes vary

WILCOX MANSION: THEODORE ROOSEVELT INAUGURAL NATIONAL HISTORIC SITE

641 Delaware Ave., Buffalo, 716-884-0095; www.nps.gov

Theodore Roosevelt was inaugurated in this classic Greek Revival mansion in 1901 following the assassination of President McKinley. The site underwent massive renovations to upgrade the aging mansion and create a reconstructed carriage house addition.

Admission: adults $5, seniors and students $3, children 6-14 $1, children under 5 free. Monday-Friday 9 a.m.-5 p.m., Saturday-Sunday noon-5 p.m.

EAST AURORA

THE ELBERT HUBBARD ROYCROFT MUSEUM

363 Oakwood Ave., East Aurora, 716-652-4735; www.roycrofter.com

This five-bedroom, 1910 Craftsman period home built by and for the Roycrofters is a testament to their handiwork. It contains Roycroft furniture, modeled leather, hammered metal, leaded glass, books, pamphlets and other artifacts from 1895 to 1938. There's also material on Elbert Hubbard, author of the famous essay "A Message to Garcia".

Admission: $5. June-October, Wednesday, Saturday-Sunday 1-4 p.m.

KISSING BRIDGE SKI AREA

10296 State Road, Glenwood, 716-592-4963; www.kbski.com

With 700 acres of terrain at its disposal, Kissing Bridge offers some of the best ski runs in the Colden Snowbelt of western New York. The trails run from beginner to expert, and most are lit for night skiing. There are also rail and terrain parks to practice your latest tricks.

Admission: adults $16-52, children under 14 $16-42. December-March, daily.

MILLARD FILLMORE MUSEUM

24 Shearer Ave., East Aurora, 716-652-8875

This is the house President Millard Fillmore built for his wife in 1825, though he only lived here for four years. It contains memorabilia, furnishings and an 1830s herb and rose garden. The Carriage house, built in 1830 of lumber from the former Nathaniel Fillmore farm, contains antique tools and a Fillmore sleigh.

Admission: adults $5. June-October, Wednesday, Saturday-Sunday 1-4 p.m.

LOCKPORT

CANAL BRIDGE

Cottage Street, Lockport

Claimed to be one of the widest single-span bridges in the world at 399½ feet, the Canal Bridge offers unparalleled views of the locks' operation, raising and lowering barges and pleasure crafts more than 60 feet.

Daily.

COLONEL WILLIAM BOND HOUSE

143 Ontario St., Lockport, 716-434-7433; www.niagarahistory.org

This pre-Victorian home was built with bricks made onsite. Dating back to 1824, the restored house has 12 furnished rooms open to the public. The kitchen and children's garret are particularly interesting.

Admission: free. May-December, Thursday, Saturday-Sunday 1-5 p.m.

KENAN CENTER

433 Locust St., Lockport, 716-433-2617; www.kenancenter.org

Occupying 25 acres, the center encompasses a sports arena, a converted carriage house theater, recreation fields, a community meeting space and the Kenan house, a 19th-century Victorian mansion with an art gallery and formal gardens. Exhibits change frequently in the gallery, but they showcase painting, sculpture, photography and textiles, all set against the backdrop of carved mahogany entrances, Italian marble floors and stunning Victorian fireplaces.

Admission: free. September-May, Monday-Friday noon-5 p.m., Saturday-Sunday 2-5 p.m.; June-August, Monday-Friday noon-5 p.m., Sunday 2-5 p.m.

NIAGARA COUNTY HISTORICAL CENTER

215 Niagara St., Lockport, 716-434-7433;
www.niagarahistory.org

The historical center occupies an 1860 brick house filled with antiques, Erie Canal artifacts and 19th-century farming equipment. Also on display are the Niagara Fire Company No. 1 fire engine with pumpers from 1834 and 1836 as well as 19th-century farming equipment.

Admission: free. Monday-Saturday 9 a.m.-5 p.m.

WHERE TO STAY

BUFFALO

★★★ASA RANSOM HOUSE

10529 Main St., Clarence, 716-759-2315, 800-841-2340;
www.asaransom.com

This charming bed and breakfast is surrounded by gardens and offers nine rooms, each with a distinct character and charm. Rooms are furnished with antiques and period reproductions, and several have both fireplace and private balconies. Don't miss the full country breakfast served at your leisure every morning.

9 rooms. Restaurant. Complimentary breakfast. Closed January. $151-250

★★★BUFFALO MARRIOTT NIAGARA

1340 Millersport Highway, Amherst, 716-689-6900,
800-334-4040; www.buffaloniagaramarriott.com

Although situated in a quiet suburban location, the Buffalo Marriott Niagara is close to the Buffalo Airport, downtown Buffalo and Niagara Falls. Rooms are bright, elegant and spacious. Amenities include a complimentary airport shuttle, an indoor/outdoor pool and a 24-hour health club. There are also numerous golf courses nearby in case you want to work on your swing.

356 rooms. Restaurant, bar. Business center. Fitness center. Pool. $151-250

★★★HYATT REGENCY BUFFALO

2 Fountain Plaza, Buffalo, 716-856-1234; www.buffalo.hyatt.com

This hotel is located downtown and connected to the Buffalo Convention Center. It is also on the metro rail and within walking distance of shopping,

WHICH GREATER NIAGRA HOTEL HAS THE BEST DESIGN?

The Arts and Crafts movement began in East Aurora, and you can see an example of it at the **Roycroft Inn.** Opened in 1905, the National Landmark still showcases the amazing handcraftsmanship of the original hotel furniture and fixtures.

WHAT IS THE BEST ITALIAN RESTAURANT IN GREATER NIAGRA?

Salvatore's Italian Gardens is the best place around for delectable Italian eats. Get one of the "dinner for two" meals with your sweetheart or keep the steak Joseph, a filet with lumb crab meat doused in a sherry-lobster sauce, for yourself.

restaurants, theaters, cultural and sports entertainment and other attractions. Guest rooms are spacious and include Hyatt Grand beds and work desks. Request a room with a view of Lake Erie and the Peace Bridge to Canada.

396 rooms. Restaurant, bar. Business center. Fitness center. Pool. $151-250

EAST AURORA
★★★ROYCROFT INN

40 S. Grove St., East Aurora, 716-652-5552, 800-267-0525; www.roycroftinn.com

Visit this birthplace of the New York Arts and Crafts movement, located just 30 minutes from Buffalo. The grounds, called the Roycroft Campus, originally housed 500 craftsmen and their shops and now are a national landmark. Rooms are showcases of original furniture and fixtures.

28 rooms. Restaurant, bar. Complimentary breakfast. $151-250

RECOMMENDED

BUFFALO
COMFORT SUITES DOWNTOWN

601 Main St., Buffalo, 716-854-5500, 877-424-6423; www.comfortsuites.com

Business travelers come for the convenience this hotel provides, including a location within walking distance of the Buffalo Niagara Convention Center and downtown business district. The hotel also offers free airport transportation.

146 rooms. Restaurant, bar. Complimentary breakfast. $61-150

WHERE TO EAT

BUFFALO
★★★ASA RANSOM HOUSE

10529 Main St., Clarence, 716-759-2315, 800-841-2340; www.asaransom.com

Sample fare like the Asa chicken pot pie loaded with homegrown vegetables or the grilled apple butter salmon at this romantic, country-style retreat. Choose your ambience: Enjoy the formal Ransom Room or head for the more casual Clarence Hollow Room, should you wish to leave the sport coat behind. The same menu is offered in all dining areas.

American. Breakfast, lunch, dinner. Closed January-mid-February. Outdoor seating. Children's menu. $36-85

★★★SALVATORE'S ITALIAN GARDENS
6461 Transit Road, Buffalo, 716-683-7990, 800-999-8082; www.salvatores.net

One of Buffalo's finest Italian eateries, Salvatore's is renowned for its "dinner for two" meals as well as its seafood medley and several varieties of veal. The house garlic bread is buttery and delicious and the steak Joseph, a tender filet topped with lump crab meat and finished in sherry-lobster sauce, will have you coming back next time you're in town.

American, Italian. Dinner. Children's menu. Bar. $36-85

EAST AURORA
★★★ROYCROFT INN
40 S. Grove St., East Aurora, 716-652-5552; www.roycroftinn.com

This inn originally opened in 1905 to accommodate the thousands of visitors to the thriving Roycroft Arts and Crafts Community, a large, self-contained group of writers and craftspeople. Today, the restaurant is a popular gathering place for locals and serves creative and fresh cuisine with continental influences, including French onion soup au gratin, rack of lamb and sesame-encrusted tuna.

American. Lunch, dinner, Sunday brunch. Reservations recommended. Outdoor seating. Children's menu. Bar. $16-35

RECOMMENDED

EAST AURORA
OLD ORCHARD INN
2095 Blakeley Corners Road, East Aurora, 716-652-4664; www.oldorchardny.com

A century-old rustic country inn, this former hunting lodge offers hearty food in a warm atmosphere. During the summer months, enjoy its covered patio seating or wander through the property's 25 wooded acres. The macadamia sea bass topped with a warm wildberry sauce is fantastic.

American. Lunch, dinner. Closed Monday-Tuesday; also January-April. Outdoor seating. Bar. $36-85

LOCKPORT
GARLOCK'S
35 S. Transit Road, Lockport, 716-433-5595; www.garlocksrestaurant.com

Originally constructed to house canal laborers, this 1821 building is packed with antiques. Simple American dishes are served with loads of taste. Steak is the specialty; you can get everything from prime rib au jus to a thick porterhouse.

Seafood, steak. Dinner. Children's menu. Bar. $16-35

HUDSON VALLEY

In the Hudson Valley, you'll find panoramic views of the Hudson River and a number of historical mansions and spots. Hyde Park, noted for the varying scenery—from rock outcroppings to scenic water views—is best known as the site of Springwood, the country estate of Franklin Roosevelt. It's also home to the Culinary Institute of America.

Many people know the Hudson River town Poughkeepsie as the site of Vassar College, founded in 1861 by a brewer named Matthew Vassar. The Smith Brothers also helped put it on the map with their cough drops, once made here. For a brief time during the Revolutionary War, this town was the state capital. It was here in 1788 that New York ratified the Constitution.

Rhinebeck was once known as "violet town" because it claimed to produce more hothouse violets than any other city in the United States. Today, Rhinebeck is better known for its charming boutiques and restaurants as well as beautifully restored historic homes.

The village of Tarrytown and the neighboring villages of Irvington and Sleepy Hollow were made famous by the writings of Washington Irving, particularly *The Legend of Sleepy Hollow*, from which this region takes its name.

West Point has been of military importance since Revolutionary days, when it was one of four points on the mid-Hudson River fortified against the British. The military academy was founded by an act of Congress in 1802. The barracks, academic and administration buildings are closed to visitors, but there is still plenty to explore.

If you're searching for the quintessential small-town atmosphere, Cold Spring is a good choice. The Main Street shopping district attracts shoppers and visitors who just want to stroll the charming roads. The surrounding area offers opportunities for outdoor recreation, including hiking, boating and kayaking. Don't miss the unique Hudson Fjord.

In October 1776, Gen. George Washington outfoxed General Lord Howe in White Plains. But today, White Plains is a popular suburb to New York City.

WHAT TO SEE

COLD SPRING
FOUNDRY SCHOOL MUSEUM
63 Chestnut St., Cold Spring, 845-265-4010; www.pchs-fsm.org

You can learn a lot from this old-fashioned schoolroom, which contains West Point Foundry memorabilia, paintings, Native American artifacts and antiques. Maintained by the Putnam County Historical Society, the museum contains a genealogy and historical research library and rotating exhibits.

Admission: adults $5, seniors and children 7-12 $2, children under 7 free. Wednesday-Sunday 11 a.m.-5 p.m.

RIVERFRONT DOCK AND BANDSTAND
Lower Main Street and the Hudson River, Cold Spring

This 100-foot dock offers views of the Hudson Highlands as well as Bear Mountain and Crow's Nest. Fishing draws locals and visitors to the area. You're in for a special experience on Sunday nights in July and August, when free concerts are put on at the bandstand.

Admission: free. July-August, Sunday.

HYDE PARK
ELEANOR ROOSEVELT NATIONAL HISTORIC SITE AT VAL-KILL
56 Val-Kill Park Drive, Hyde Park, 845-229-9115, 800-967-2283; www.nps.gov

Dedicated as a memorial to Eleanor Roosevelt on October 11, 1984, the 100th anniversary of her birth, Val-Kill was her country residence from the 1920s until her death. The original house on the property, Stone Cottage, is now a conference center. Her second house at Val-Kill was originally a furniture and crafts factory that Roosevelt sponsored in an effort to stimulate rural economic development. After closing Val-Kill Industries, she had the factory remodeled to reflect her tastes and humanitarian concerns. She used the space to entertain family, friends and heads of state from around the world.

Admission: adults $8, children under 16 free. May-October, daily 9 a.m.-5 p.m.; November-April, Thursday-Monday 9 a.m.-5 p.m.

FRANKLIN D. ROOSEVELT PRESIDENTIAL LIBRARY AND MUSEUM

4079 Albany Post Road, Hyde Park, 845-486-7770, 800-337-8474; www.fdrlibrary.marist.edu

First of the public presidential libraries, it has exhibits covering the private lives and public careers of Franklin and Eleanor Roosevelt. The research library contains family artifacts and documents as well as the presidential archives.

Admission: adults $7, children under 16 free. November-April, daily 9 a.m.-5 p.m.; May-October, daily 9 a.m.-6 p.m.

HOME OF FRANKLIN D. ROOSEVELT NATIONAL HISTORIC SITE

4097 Albany Post Road, Hyde Park, 845-229-9115; www.nps.gov

This Hyde Park estate, Springwood, was President Roosevelt's birthplace and lifelong residence. The central part of the building and oldest section dates from about 1826. The house was bought in 1867 by FDR's father and was extensively remodeled and expanded in 1915 by FDR and his mother, Sara Delano Roosevelt. At that time, the frame Victorian house took on its present brick and stone, neo-Georgian form. The interior is furnished exactly as it was when FDR died. Roosevelt and his wife's graves are in the rose garden.

Admission: adults $14, children under 16 free. Daily 9 a.m.-5 p.m.

MILLS MANSION STATE HISTORIC SITE

Highway 9 and Old Post Road, Staatsburg, 845-889-8851; www.staatsburgh.org

Built for Ogden Mills in 1896 by prominent architect Stanford White, this Greek Revival mansion includes 65 rooms furnished in Louis XIV, Louis XV and Louis XVI styles, with tapestries, art objects, marble fireplaces and gilded plasterwork. The surrounding park affords beautiful views of the Hudson River.

Admission: adults $5, seniors and students $4, children under 13 free. January-March, Saturday-Sunday 11 a.m.-4 p.m.; April-October, Tuesday-Saturday 10 a.m.-5 p.m., Sunday noon-5 p.m.

VANDERBILT MANSION NATIONAL HISTORIC SITE

Highway 9, Hyde Park, 845-229-9115; www.nps.gov

This 1898 Beaux-Arts home designed by McKim, Mead & White for Frederick W. Vanderbilt is a prime example of the mansions typical of the period. The interior retains most of the original furnishings as designed by turn-of-the-century decorators. The grounds offer superb views up and down the Hudson River.

Admission: adults $8, children under 16 free. Daily 9 a.m.-5 p.m.

POUGHKEEPSIE

BARDAVON OPERA HOUSE

35 Market St., Poughkeepsie, 845-473-5288; www.bardavon.org

This 1869 building is the oldest operating theater in the state, and one of the top performance houses in the Hudson Valley. It presents various dance, theatrical and musical performances, as well as Hudson Valley Philharmonic concerts. Check the website for performance schedules.

Prices and showtimes vary.

JAMES BAIRD STATE PARK

14 Maintenance Lane, Pleasant Valley, 845-452-1489; www.nysparks.state.ny.us

This 590-acre park has a championship 18-hole golf course and driving range, tennis, hiking trails, cross-country skiing, a playground and a nature center. If you get hungry, there is a restaurant overlooking the golf course and numerous picnic areas.

Daily dawn-dusk.

LOCUST GROVE

2683 South Road, Poughkeepsie, 845-454-4500; www.lgny.org

Formerly the house of Samuel F. B. Morse, inventor of the telegraph, it was remodeled into a Tuscan villa in 1847. Many of his possessions still remain onsite, including telegraph equipment and various paintings by Morse. The house also has alternating exhibits of dolls, fans, costumes, books and souvenirs acquired by the Young family (the owners following Morse); paintings, art objects and American furnishings. There is also a 180-acre wildlife sanctuary and park with hiking trails and picnic area.

Admission: adults $10, children 6-18 $6. March-December, daily 10 a.m.-5 p.m.

MID-HUDSON CHILDREN'S MUSEUM

75 N. Water St., Poughkeepsie, 845-471-0589; www.mhcm.org

This interactive children's museum features more than 50 exhibits, including a life-size mouse trap-like structure where you shoot a ball along copper railings to illustrate gravity, Da Vinci 16th-century inventions and a machine that will put your little one inside of a humongous bubble. The Hudson Valley is also examined through the Hudson River mural and Diving Bell exhibit.

Admission: adults and children 2-18 $6.50, children under 1 free. Tuesday-Friday 9:30 a.m.-5 p.m., Saturday-Sunday 11 a.m.-5 p.m.

VASSAR COLLEGE

124 Raymond Ave., Poughkeepsie, 845-437-7000; www.vassar.edu

Vassar was started as a women's college in 1865, but has since gone coed. The 1,000-acre campus was the first to have an art gallery onsite, the Frances Lehman Loeb Art Center, and continues to boast an impressive and diverse collection of works. Be sure to stroll by the chapel to see the intact Tiffany windows.

Daily.

RHINEBECK
HUDSON RIVER NATIONAL ESTUARINE RESEARCH RESERVE
Highway 9G, Annandale, 845-889-4745; www.dec.ny.gov

The Hudson River is an estuary, running from Manhattan to Troy, N.Y. More than 5,000 acres of this estuarine land have been reserved for the study of its life and ecosystems. The reserve includes Piermont Marsh and Iona Island in Rockland County, Tivoli Bays in Dutchess County and Stockport Flats in Columbia County. The headquarters have lectures, workshops, special exhibits and public field programs.

Admission: free. Daily.

MONTGOMERY PLACE
55 Montgomery place, Annandale, 845-758-5461; www.hudsonriverheritage.org

This 1805 mansion estate along the Hudson River was remodeled in the mid-1800s in the classical-revival style. The grounds contain a coach house; visitor center; greenhouse with rose, herb, perennial and woodland gardens; museum; and garden shop. Bring your walking shoes, as there are numerous scenic trails with views of the cataracts that meet the Hudson.

Admission: adults $5, children 5-17 $3, children under 5 free. May-October, Saturday-Sunday 10 a.m.-5 p.m.

OLD RHINEBECK AERODROME
42 Stone Church Road, Rhinebeck, 845-752-3500; www.oldrhinebeck.org

This self-proclaimed "living" museum of aviation boasts one of the largest collections of antique airplanes and engines in the world. Automobiles, motor-cycles and paraphernalia from the Lindbergh era are also on display. Planes from World War I and earlier are flown in air shows on weekends. Biplane air rides are also available.

Admission: adults $10-20, seniors and children 13-17 $8-15, children 6-12 $3-5, children under 5 free. Mid-May-October, daily 10 a.m.-5 p.m.

TARRYTOWN
KYKUIT, THE ROCKEFELLER ESTATE
Highway 9 N. and N. Broadway, Sleepy Hollow, 914-631-3992; www.hudsonvalley.org

This six-story stone mansion was home to three generations of the Rockefeller family. Sitting atop a hill, the name means "lookout" in Dutch and befittingly affords sweeping views of the Hudson River. Today, the house is awash with antiques and period furnishings. The property also includes extensive gardens featuring an important collection of 20th-century sculpture acquired by Gov. Nelson A. Rockefeller, including works by Alexander Calder, Constantin Brancusi and Pablo Picasso. Scheduled tours running 2½ hours depart approximately every 15 minutes from Philipsburg Manor. Children under five are not permitted.

Admission: adults $23, seniors and children 5-18 $21. May-October, Wednesday-Monday 9 a.m.-5 p.m.

LYNDHURST
635 S. Broadway, Tarrytown, 914-631-4481; www.lyndhurst.org

Considered one of the best examples of the Gothic-Revival style in the United States, this marble mansion built in 1838 for William Paulding, mayor of New

York City, sits on 67 landscaped acres overlooking the Hudson River. The interior includes exquisite stained-glass windows, soaring arched ceilings and intricate period furniture, like canopy beds and writing desks.

Admission: adults $12, seniors $11, children 6-16 $5, children under 6 free. Mid-April-October, Tuesday-Sunday 10 a.m.-5 p.m.; November-mid-April, Saturday-Sunday 10 a.m.-4 p.m.

MUSIC HALL THEATER
13 Main St., Tarrytown, 914-631-3390; www.tarrytownmusichall.org

One of the oldest-remaining theaters in the county, this 1885 structure now serves as a center for the arts. Big-name performers like Wynton Marsalis and Tony Bennett have performed here, and it also has hosted an impressive share of movie premieres.

Prices and showtimes vary.

OLD DUTCH CHURCH OF SLEEPY HOLLOW
42 N. Broadway, Tarrytown, 914-631-1123; www.olddutchburyingground.org

This 1685 church structure of Dutch origins was built on what was the manor of Frederick Philipse and is widely considered the oldest church in New York State. The stone and wood structure has been restored and showcases a replica of the original pulpit inside. Sleepy Hollow Cemetery surrounds the church and free tours are given of both sites on Sunday at 2 p.m.

Admission: free. June-August, Monday, Wednesday-Thursday 1-4 p.m., Saturday-Sunday 2-4 p.m.; September-October, Saturday-Sunday 2-4 p.m.

PHILIPSBURG MANOR
381 N. Broadway, Sleepy Hollow, 914-631-3992; www.hudsonvalley.org

Head back in time with a visit to this colonial farm and trading site from the mid-1700s. Tour the 300-year-old manor house and a restored operating gristmill. A highlight is the exhibit on slavery in the colonial north. There is also a wooden millpond bridge across the Pocantico River.

Admission: adults $12, seniors $10, children 5-17 $6, children under 5 free. April-October, Wednesday-Monday 10 a.m.-6 p.m.; November-December, Saturday-Sunday 10 a.m.-4 p.m.

SLEEPY HOLLOW CEMETERY
540 N. Broadway, Sleepy Hollow, 914-631-0081; www.sleepyhollowcemetery.org

Surrounding the Old Dutch Church, the burial grounds contain graves of Washington Irving, Andrew Carnegie and William Rockefeller, among others. Legend has it that Irving used this cemetery to gain inspiration for character names in famous novel.

Monday-Friday 8 a.m.-4:30 p.m., Saturday-Sunday 8:30 a.m.-4:30 p.m.

SUNNYSIDE
W. Sunnyside Lane, Tarrytown, 914-631-8200; www.hudsonvalley.org

Washington Irving's Hudson River estate contains much of his furnishings, personal property and library. A guide in traditional period dress will lead you through the 1830s residence, explaining Irving's eclectic architectural decisions in designing Sunnyside and its grounds.

Admission: adults $12, seniors $10, children 5-17 $6, children under 5 free. April-October, Wednesday-Monday 11 a.m.-6 p.m.; November-December, Saturday-Sunday 10 a.m.-4 p.m.

HIGHLIGHT

WHAT ARE THE TOP THINGS TO DO IN THE HUDSON VALLEY?

LEARN ABOUT FDR AT THE FRANKLIN D. ROOSEVELT PRESIDENTIAL MUSEUM

Find out more about our 32nd president at this museum, which showcases family artifacts and documents. The structure also houses a presidential library.

VISIT THE HOME OF FRANKLIN D. ROOSEVELT

This brick Hyde Park estate was FDR's birthplace and lifelong residence. Go to the rose garden to see Roosevelt and his wife's graves.

BRING JUNIOR TO THE MID-HUDSON CHILDREN'S MUSEUM

Your little one can shoot a ball through a Mouse Trap-like maze and get encased in a giant bubble at this interactive museum.

TAKE FLIGHT AT THE OLD RHINEBECK AERODOME

Plane aficionados will have to add this place to their itineraries; the aerodrome has one of the largest collections of airplanes and engines in the world.

VAN CORTLANDT MANOR

500 S. Riverside Ave., Croton on Hudson, 914-631-8200; www.hudsonvalley.org

Explore this post-Revolutionary War estate of the prominent Van Cortlandt family. A highlight is the 18th-century tavern onsite. Frequent demonstrations of open-hearth cooking, brickmaking and weaving are held in the nearby tenant house.

Admission: adults $12, seniors $10, children 5-17 $6, children under 5 free. June-August, Thursday-Sunday 11 a.m.-6 p.m.; November-December, Saturday-Sunday 10 a.m.-4 p.m.

WEST POINT
BATTLE MONUMENT

Thayer and Washington roads, West Point, 845-938-4011; www.usma.army.mil

One of the most prominent monuments at the academy, this memorial was dedicated in 1897 to the 2,230 officers and men of the Regular Army who died in action during the Civil War. Nearby are some links from the chain used to block the river from 1778 to 1782.

Admission: free. Daily.

CADET CHAPEL

Ruger Road and Cadet Drive, West Point, 845-938-4011; www.usma.army.mil

On a hill overlooking the campus, this large edifice was constructed entirely in native granite and has Gothic and Medieval influences in its architectural style. The Cadet Chapel organ, dating back to 1911, is now the largest church organ in the world. Don't miss the Sanctuary Window with the inscription "Duty, Honor, Country."

Admission: free. Daily.

MICHIE STADIUM

700 Mills Road, West Point, 845-938-4011

This 42,000-seat stadium sits directly alongside the Hudson River and boasts spectacular views of the waterway and the field from nearly every seat. Home football games are a sight to see.

Prices and hours vary.

WEST POINT MUSEUM

Pershing Center, West Point, 845-938-2638; www.usma.edu

With exhibits on everything from the evolution of warfare to the storied history of West Point, this museum is generally considered the oldest and largest military museum in the nation. Collections include weapons, artwork, uniforms and propaganda.

Admission: free. Daily 10:30 a.m.-4:15 p.m.

WHITE PLAINS

MONUMENT

S. Broadway and Mitchell Place, White Plains

The Declaration of Independence was adopted at this site on July 1776, and the State of New York was formally organized.

Admission: free. Daily.

WASHINGTON'S HEADQUARTERS

140 Virginia Road, North White Plains, 914-949-1236; www.westchestergov.com

This 18th-century farmhouse once served as Washington's command post during the Battle of White Plains. The converted museum now showcases Revolutionary War relics, colonial artifacts and original furniture used by Washington himself.

Admission: free. Third Sunday of the month, noon-3 p.m.

YONKERS

BILL OF RIGHTS MUSEUM

897 S. Columbus Ave., Mount Vernon, 914-667-4116

Exhibits include a working model of an 18th-century printing press and dioramas depicting John Peter Zenger, whose trial and acquittal for seditious libel in 1735 helped establish freedom of the press in America.

Admission: free. Monday-Friday 9 a.m.-5 p.m.

ST. PAUL'S CHURCH NATIONAL HISTORIC SITE

897 S. Columbus Ave., Mount Vernon, 914-667-4116; www.nps.gov

This storied church was the setting for historical events that established the basic freedoms outlined in the Bill of Rights. The stone-and-brick Georgian structure was started in 1763 but not completed until after the Revolutionary War. It served not only as a church but also as a meetinghouse and courtroom where Aaron Burr once practiced law.

Admission: free. Monday-Friday 9 a.m.-5 p.m.

WHERE TO STAY

COLD SPRING

★★★HUDSON HOUSE INN

2 Main St., Cold Spring, 845-265-9355; www.hudsonhouseinn.com

This circa-1832 country inn on the banks of the Hudson River offers 11 guest rooms and two suites. Guest rooms are charming, brimming with French-country furnishings and antiques. Be sure to ask for a room with a private balcony or terrace for exceptional views of the Hudson. After settling in, head downstairs to dine in the country-style restaurant or sup alfresco on the front porch with its terrific river vistas.

13 rooms. Restaurant, bar. Complimentary breakfast. $151-250

POUGHKEEPSIE

★★★OLD DROVERS INN

196 E. Duncan Hill Road, Dover Plains, 845-832-9311; www.olddroversinn.com

This historic inn was built in 1750 and is arguably the oldest continuously operated inn in the United States. Each room is decorated with fine antiques. The service is top-notch, too, and the setting is sublime. The onsite restaurant, The Tap Room, is a must-visit.

7 rooms. Restaurant. Complimentary breakfast. $151-250

★★★POUGHKEEPSIE GRAND HOTEL

40 Civic Center Plaza, Poughkeepsie, 845-485-5300, 800-216-1034; ww.pokgrand.com

Located adjacent to the civic center in the heart of the Hudson Valley, this hotel boasts plenty of meeting space and caters to a business-traveler crowd and wedding parties. For those who are traveling for work purposes, wireless Internet is free throughout the hotel, plus the executive suites are stocked with office supplies and have a lot of room if you need to spread out with your reports.

195 rooms. Restaurant, bar. Complimentary breakfast. Fitness center. $61-150

★★★TROUTBECK INN

515 Leedsville Road, Amenia, 845-373-9681, 800-978-7688; www.troutbeck.com

This English country-style inn and conference center sits on 600 acres near the Berkshire foothills and features rooms beautifully appointed with overstuffed furnishings and elegant fabrics. Try for a room with a fireplace and whirlpool bath in the wonderful Garden House, which overlooks the formal walled English garden.

42 rooms. Restaurant, bar. Complimentary breakfast. Fitness center. Pool. Spa. Tennis. $151-250

WHICH HUDSON VALLEY HOTEL IS BEST FOR AN ESCAPE FROM THE CITY?

When you need a quick getaway from the city that never sleeps, head to **The Ritz-Carlton, Westchester**, which is only minutes from Manhattan. Bike nearby trails, stroll the forest preserves or just hide out in your luxe room.

RHINEBECK

★★★BEEKMAN ARMS

6387 Mill St., Rhinebeck, 845-876-7077, 800-361-6517; www.beekmandelamaterinn.com

This historic inn—America's oldest continually run inn—is the perfect weekend escape. Guest rooms vary in size greatly, so be sure to request a larger room when booking, but all have country décor and include private baths, TVs and a complimentary decanter of sherry. Savor fine cuisine onsite or visit many local attractions, including the Roosevelt and Vanderbilt estates, the Culinary Institute of America and the Rhinebeck Aerodrome's World War I Air Show. Many of the rooms feature fireplaces.

23 rooms. Restaurant, bar. $151-250

TARRYTOWN

★★★CASTLE ON THE HUDSON

400 Benedict Ave., Tarrytown, 914-631-1980, 800-616-4487; www.castleattarrytown.com

Built between 1897 and 1910, this hotel has panoramic views of the Hudson River and the historic Hudson Valley. The rooms and suites are romantically furnished with four-poster or canopied beds. The grounds are meticulously maintained and feature tennis courts and a pool. Equus restaurant is a destination in its own right, and its three rooms suit a variety of moods. The Tapestry and Oak rooms resemble a European castle with stone fireplaces and beamed ceilings while the conservatory style of the Garden Room has scenic river views.

31 rooms. Restaurant, bar. Fitness center. Pool. Spa. Tennis. $251-350

★★★DOUBLETREE HOTEL TARRYTOWN

455 S. Broadway, Tarrytown, 914-631-5700; www.doubletree.com

This hotel features comfortable rooms with complimentary wireless Internet access and flat-screen TVs. The public area is impressive with Adirondack-style beamed ceilings and detailed stonework. If you need to work up a sweat, the fitness center is a nice perk.

247 rooms. Restaurant, bar. Business center. Fitness center. Pool. Tennis. $251-350

★★★TARRYTOWN HOUSE ESTATE AND CONFERENCE CENTER

49 E. Sunnyside Lane, Tarrytown, 914-591-8200, 800-553-8118;www.tarrytownhouseestate.com

Located only 24 miles from Manhattan, this lovely estate was built in the late 1800s and has views overlooking the Hudson River Valley. The comfortable rooms mix country touches with a modern sensibility. Dine in the hotel's Sleepy Hollow Pub with its billiards table, fireplace and numerous wines by the glass.

212 rooms. Restaurant. Complimentary breakfast. Business center. Fitness center. Pool. Tennis.
$151-250

WHITE PLAINS

★★★HILTON RYE TOWN
699 Westchester Ave., Rye Brook, 914-939-6300; www.hilton.com

Spacious and well-appointed guest rooms await at this hotel in suburban Rye Brook. Accommodations feature Hilton's signature Serenity Beds with plush mattress-toppers and down comforters and pillows, as well as CD players, alarm clock radios with MP3 docks, minibars and work desks with lamps. A fitness center and pool help keep guests fit, and three onsite restaurants provide dining options for every taste.

437 rooms. Restaurant, bar. Business center. Fitness center. Pool. Pets accepted. Tennis.
$151-250

★★★RENAISSANCE WESTCHESTER HOTEL
80 W. Red Oak Lane, White Plains, 914-694-5400, 800-891-2696; www.marriott.com

Rooms at this hotel offer both comfort and luxury with rich fabrics, down comforters, plush pillows and views of the surrounding countryside. Fitness fanatics will have a field day with the exercise offerings: There's an indoor pool, as well as indoor tennis courts, volleyball courts and a fitness center with cardio equipment and free weights.

350 rooms. Restaurant, bar. Business center. Fitness center. Pool. Tennis. $151-250

★★★THE RITZ-CARLTON, WESTCHESTER
3 Renaissance Square, White Plains, 914-946-5500; www.ritzcarlton.com

Whether it's to avoid the 24-hour honking of New York City or to get closer to nature with nearby bike trails and forest preserves, you'll find plenty of reasons to extend a stay at this elegant hotel. Guest rooms are sizeable and contemporary with neutral tones and modern amenities, including flat-screen TVs and wireless Internet. If you can, opt for a room on the club level, which awards you a personal concierge, decadent treats throughout the day and access to a complimentary business center. No need to go into the city for dinner; just book a table at BLT Steak, where famed chef Laurent Tourondel whips up tasty French bistro fare in a chic urbane setting.

118 rooms. Restaurant, bar. Business center. Fitness center. Pool. Spa. $351 and up

RECOMMENDED

POUGHKEEPSIE
COURTYARD POUGHKEEPSIE
2641 South Road/Route 9, Poughkeepsie, 845-485-6336; www.marriott.com

Only a few miles from the Vassar campus, this hotel is ideal for visiting parents and business travelers. The spacious rooms have desks and high-speed Internet.

149 rooms. Restaurant, bar. Fitness center. Pool. $61-150

HOLIDAY INN EXPRESS

2750 South Road, Poughkeepsie, 845-473-1151; www.holiday-inn.com

This chain property has comfortable rooms and a 24-hour business center, which are helpful if you're in town for work. Relax by the outdoor pool in summer.

121 rooms. Complimentary breakfast. Business center. Fitness center. Pool. $61-150

TARRYTOWN
COURTYARD TARRYTOWN GREENBURGH

475 White Plains Road, Tarrytown, 914-631-1122, 800-589-8720; www.courtyard.com

The best thing about this chain hotel is the easy access it provides to many of the surrounding tourist attractions, like Kykuit and the Sunnyside Estate. Rooms are clean and basic, but include high-speed Internet and ergonomically designed work spaces.

139 rooms. Restaurant, bar. Business center. Fitness center. Pool. $151-250

WEST POINT
THE THAYER HOTEL

674 Thayer Road, West Point, 845-446-4731, 800-247-5047; www.thethayerhotel.com

Located in the heart of the Hudson Valley and on the grounds of the Academy, this historic hotel is both sprawling and intimate. The granite-and-brick structure was originally built to accommodate military personnel in 1926, and carries the name of one of the Academy's early superintendents, Colonel Sylvanius Thayer. Marble floors, detailed chandeliers and soaring ceilings outfit the lobby, while guest rooms boast rich wood furnishings and prints of historic military scenes. Ask for a room with a view of the Hudson, unless you're more inclined to enjoy a vantage toward the Academy and surroundings hillsides. The onsite restaurant serves a spectacular Sunday brunch.

151 rooms. Restaurant, bar. Fitness center. $151-250

WHITE PLAINS
LA QUINTA INN AND SUITES

94 Business Park Drive, Armonk, 914-273-9090; www.lq.com

A fitness center, free wireless Internet access and complimentary breakfast are just some of the amenities at this suburban chain property. Business travelers will like the close proximity to numerous company headquarters, including IBM. The Marc Charles Steakhouse downstairs is a notch above your typical hotel restaurant.

179 rooms. Restaurant, bar. Complimentary breakfast. Business center. Fitness center. Pets accepted. $61-150

WHERE TO EAT

COLD SPRING
★★★BRASSERIE LE BOUCHON

76 Main St., Cold Spring, 845-265-7676

This adorable French restaurant is as authentic as it gets in the Hudson Valley. The menu reads like a greatest hits of classic French cooking, from escargot kissed with garlic butter to hearty cassoulet. Don't leave without ordering the profiteroles.

French. Dinner. Reservations recommended. Outdoor seating. Bar. $16-35

★★★PLUMBUSH INN
1656 Route 9D, Cold Spring, 845-265-3904; www.plumbushinn.net

Just across the Hudson River from West Point, this Victorian inn offers elegant dinners in a romantic waterfront setting. You have your choice of eating in one of the oak-paneled dining rooms, the bright airy garden room or on the terrace overlooking the manicured grounds.

American. Lunch, dinner, Sunday brunch. Closed Monday-Tuesday. Bar. $36-85

HYDE PARK
★★★THE ESCOFFIER
433 Albany Post Road, Hyde Park, 845-471-6608;
www.ciachef.edu

Student chefs of the Culinary Institute of America prepare dishes that their peers serve in this classic French eatery that presents a lighter, more contemporary take on the cooking of Auguste Escoffier (think Asian-style braised veal cheeks with gratin potatoes). The seared sea scallops are exceptional.

French. Lunch, dinner. Closed Sunday-Monday; also three weeks in July, two weeks in December. $16-35

★★★RISTORANTE CATERINA DE MEDICI
433 Albany Post Road, Hyde Park, 845-471-6608; www.ciachef.edu

With its five distinct dining areas—from the more casual to the formal—the Culinary Institute of America's flagship restaurant will carry you to Tuscany thanks to dishes like branzino con guazza verde, a Mediterranean sea bass shallow poached in an herb broth with fingerling potatoes.

American. Lunch, dinner. Closed Saturday-Sunday. Reservations recommended. Bar. $36-85

POUGHKEEPSIE
★★★CHRISTOS
155 Wilbur Blvd., Poughkeepsie, 845-471-3400; www.christoscatering.com

Internationally influenced American cuisine is served in this elegant, wood-paneled dining room, where sparkling chandeliers, smooth service from tuxedo-clad waiters and a golf course view combine for a relaxing ambience. To make the mood even better, order the twin filet mignons Diane flamed with cognac and mustard sauce or the pan-roasted pork loin with coriander-madeira sauce. The wine list includes excellent selections for all price ranges.

American. Lunch, dinner. Closed Sunday-Monday. Reservations recommended. Bar. $16-35

TARRYTOWN
★★★★BLUE HILL AT STONE BARNS
630 Bedford Road, Pocantico Hills, 914-366-9600; www.bluehillstonebarns.com

An extension of Blue Hill restaurant in Manhattan, Blue Hill at Stone Barns is not only a restaurant but also a working farm and educational center dedicated to sustainable food production. The dining room is a former dairy barn that has been converted into a lofty, modern space with vaulted ceilings, dark wood accents and earthy tones. Instead of a menu, diners are presented with a simple list of ingredients, which detail the freshest offerings from the farm and market for that day. Diners can choose from a five-course or an eight-course Farmer's Feast Menu. The Farmer's Feast menu is created around that day's harvest. The desserts are freshly made and hard to resist.

WHAT ARE THE BEST FRENCH RESTAURANTS IN THE HUDSON VALLEY?

Brasserie Le Bouchon:
When you crave authentic French eats, go to this brasserie. You'll find all of the French standbys, but the don't-miss-dish is the profiteroles.

Equus:
This restaurant offers a charming atmosphere alongside flavorful dishes like bacon-wrapped chicken roulade with sweet corn pudding.

The Escoffier:
Sure, this French eatery is run by students of the Culinary Institute of America, but you just might have a meal from the next Daniel Boulud.

American. Dinner, Sunday lunch. Closed Monday-Tuesday. Reservations recommended. Bar. $85 and up.

★★★EQUUS

400 Benedict Ave., Tarrytown, 914-631-3646; www.castleattarrytown.com

Choose from three charming dining rooms at this restaurant within the Castle on the Hudson. The menu includes standouts such as bacon-wrapped chicken roulade with sweet corn pudding and pistachio-crusted tuna with grape tomatoes and arugula.

French, American. Breakfast, lunch, dinner, brunch. Jacket required. Bar. $36-85

RECOMMENDED

COLD SPRING
HUDSON HOUSE INN

2 Main St., Cold Spring, 845-265-9355; www.hudsonhouseinn.com

Set in the picturesque Hudson House Inn, this restaurant provides a win-win combination of inventive contemporary cuisine and outstanding alfresco dining on the riverside veranda. Locals pack the place on Sunday for the generous prix fixe brunch.

American. Lunch, dinner, Sunday brunch. Reservations recommended. Outdoor seating. Children's menu. Bar. $36-85

HYDE PARK
AMERICAN BOUNTY

433 Albany Post Road, Hyde Park, 845-471-6608; www.ciachef.edu/restaurants/bounty

From the Culinary Institute of America, this student-run restaurant occupies a stunning room in Roth Hall, once part of an old Jesuit seminary. Everything on this regional American menu is fresh and tasty. Go for the Maine lobster "Burgoo" with lobster claws, chanterelles and carrot froth, or the house-smoked Long Island duck with curried onions, spinach and preserved mango.

American. Lunch, dinner. Closed Sunday-Monday; also three weeks in July, two weeks in December. Bar. $16-35

POUGHKEEPSIE
AROMA OSTERIA

114 Old Post Road, Wappingers, 845-298-6790; www.aromaosteriarestaurant.com

You can't miss this Tuscan farmhouse-inspired canary-yellow building. Classic Italian cuisine is served with aplomb, and on warm days, the outdoor patio is a great spot to sit and while away the afternoon with a cappuccino. You can't go wrong with any of the pasta dishes.

Italian. Lunch (Tuesday-Saturday), dinner. Closed Monday. Reservations recommended. Outdoor seating. Bar. $16-35

BEECH TREE GRILL

1 Collegeview Ave., Poughkeepsie, 845-471-7279; www.beechtreegrill.com

This casual eatery continues to draw locals with its friendly service and reasonably priced fare. The beer selection is extensive and many say the juicy Angus burgers are second to none in the Hudson Valley.

American. Lunch (Tuesday-Saturday), dinner, Sunday brunch. Reservations recommended. Bar. $16-35

COSIMO'S TRATTORIA & BAR

120 Delafield St., Poughkeepsie, 845-485-7172; www.cosimospoughkeepsie.com

While the restaurant is large with five separate dining rooms, the atmosphere is cozy and intimate with a wood-fired brick oven and rustic Tuscan décor accenting the space. Regulars swear by the chicken penne. No matter what your entrée, don't leave without tasting the cannoli stuffed with a rich housemade filling and chocolate chips.

American, Italian. Lunch, dinner. Reservations recommended. Outdoor seating. Children's menu. Bar. $16-35

COYOTE GRILL

2629 South Road, Poughkeepsie, 845-471-0600; www.coyotegrillny.com

Come for the drinks, but stay for the food at this hip downtown Poughkeepsie restaurant. The cocktail menu is overwhelming, but if you stick to one of the mojitos, you're in for a treat. The Texas bleu crab cakes are a nice starter, and the seafood paella doesn't disappoint.

American, Mexican. Lunch, dinner, Sunday brunch. Reservations recommended. Children's menu. Bar. $16-35

LE PAVILLON

230 Salt Point Turnpike, Poughkeepsie, 845-473-2525; www.lepavillonrestaurant.com

Head back in time as you step into this 200-year-old farmhouse with classic French accents and aromas. Escargot is a popular choice, as is the coq au vin. Request a table on the patio if the weather allows.

French. Dinner. Closed Sunday-Monday. Reservations recommended. Outdoor seating. Bar. $16-35

RHINEBECK

CALICO RESTAURANT AND PATISSERIE

6384 Mills St., Rhinebeck, 845-876-2749; www.calicorhinebeck.com

This cozy neighborhood bistro serves delicious American fare with a French twist. Regardless of whether you choose to nosh on pork tenderloin or vegetable Napoleon, save room for dessert; the pastry chef works wonders with the likes of brown butter tarts, Milanese macaroons and truffle cakes.

American, French. Lunch, dinner, Sunday brunch. Closed Monday-Tuesday. Reservations recommended. Bar. $36-85

GIGI TRATTORIA

6422 Montgomery St., Rhinebeck, 845-876-1007; www.gigihudsonvalley.com

With rich tangerine tones and loft-like detailing, this Hudson Valley restaurant presents an inventive menu of pastas, seafood and cheeses. For a quick bite, try one of the signature flatbreads; the rustica with farm fennel sausage, broccoli rabe and red chili flakes is an excellent choice. The wine list is also reasonable and varied.

Italian, Mediterranean. Lunch, dinner. Reservations recommended. Outdoor seating. Bar. $16-35

TARRYTOWN

CARAVELA

53 N. Broadway, Tarrytown, 914-631-1863; www.caravelarestaurant.com

The paella is the thing to order at this intimate Brazilian restaurant with a friendly staff and local appeal. It's also a smart idea to bring friends along, since servings of this aromatic dish, packed with everything from sausage to chicken to clams, are generous.

Brazilian, Portuguese. Lunch, dinner. Reservations recommended. Outdoor seating. Bar. $16-35

SANTA FE

5 Main St., Tarrytown, 914-332-4452; www.santaferestaurant.com

A favorite with locals, this bright Southwestern spot offers good food, a friendly waitstaff and more than 30 premium tequilas from which to choose. Try the enchiladas Santa Fe, blue corn tortillas stuffed with shrimp and crab with tomatillo sauce and Monterey Jack cheese, or the cochinita pibil, pork marinated in orange juice and achiote and slow roasted in banana leaves. Be sure to specify if you aren't a fan of hot and spicy.

Mexican, Southwestern. Lunch, dinner. Bar. $16-35

WEST POINT

CANTERBURY BROOK INN

331 Main St., Cornwall, 845-534-9658; www.thecanterburybrookinn.com

Exposed-wood ceiling beams, brick walls and two fireplaces lend a rustic appeal to the interior of this restaurant, while the kitchen churns out decidedly Swiss fare. The oven-baked French onion soup and grilled Swiss bratwurst are perfect indulgences on a chilly afternoon. In warmer weather, the terrace is a great spot to enjoy wiener schnitzel alongside the meandering brook.

Swiss. Lunch, dinner. Closed Sunday-Monday. Outdoor seating. Bar $16-35

PAINTER'S

266 Hudson St., Cornwall-on-Hudson, 845-534-2109; www.painters-restaurant.com

The menu is eclectic, with influences from Italy to Mexico to Japan, but no matter which culinary route you take, your taste buds will be rewarded with fresh flavors. The signature focaccia with red peppers, garlic, mushrooms and provolone is outstanding as is the sesame tuna with sweet Chinese mustard and wasabi cream.

International. Lunch, dinner, Sunday brunch. Reservations recommended. Outdoor seating. Children's menu. Bar. $16-35

WHITE PLAINS

BLT STEAK

The Ritz-Carlton, Westchester, 3 Renaissance Square, White Plains, 914-946-5500;
www.bltsteak.com

Notable chef Laurent Tourondel cooks up French bistro fare in his take of a
sophisticated American steak house. Take a seat in the airy, bright dining
room and you'll get the fluffy signature popovers to nosh on while you decide
whether you want braised short ribs or a porterhouse. You'll be happy either
way.

Steak, French. Dinner. Bar. $36-85

SPA

★★★★THE RITZ-CARLTON SPA, WESTCHESTER

The Ritz-Carlton, Westchester, 3 Renaissance Square, White Plains, 914-467-5888,
800-241-3333; www.ritzcarlton.com

This gorgeous spa offers a getaway from New York City. The 10,000-square-
foot complex features a gym and an indoor rooftop pool, but if you really want
to relax, head for one of the four massage rooms. Opt for seasonal signature
services, such as summertime's Liquid Gold treatment, which includes a
cleanse of lemon and chamomile, a warm wrap of jojoba butter and a massage.
Or if you want to put your best face forward when you return home, get the
Derma Lift Facial, which uses a skin-lifting massage and marine-based products
to brighten the skin. Wrap up your trip to the spa with the half-hour New York
Minute manicure—the closest you'll get to the hustle and bustle of the Big
Apple at this sanctuary.

INDEX

NEW YORK CITY: OVERVIEW

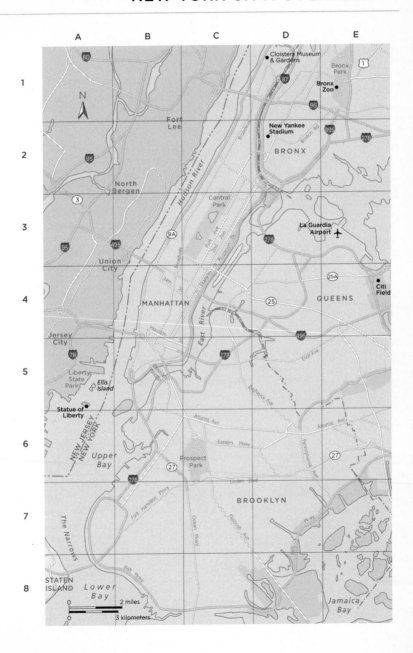

NEW YORK CITY: UPPER WEST SIDE

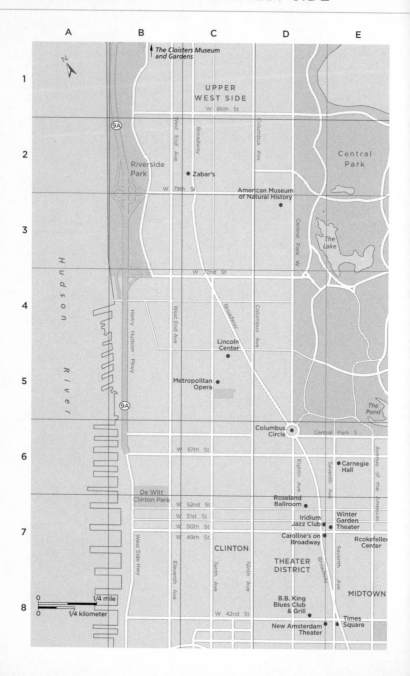

The Cloisters Museum and Gardens

UPPER WEST SIDE

W 86th St

Riverside Park

Zabar's

W 79th St

American Museum of Natural History

Hudson River

W 72nd St

Lincoln Center

Metropolitan Opera

Columbus Circle

Central Park S

W 57th St

Carnegie Hall

De Witt Clinton Park

W 52nd St

Roseland Ballroom

W 51st St

W 50th St

Iridium Jazz Club

Winter Garden Theater

W 49th St

Caroline's on Broadway

Rcokefeller Center

CLINTON

THEATER DISTRICT

MIDTOWN

B.B. King Blues Club & Grill

W 42nd St

Times Square

New Amsterdam Theater

Central Park

The Lake

The Pond

0 ___ 1/4 mile
0 ___ 1/4 kilometer

NEW YORK CITY: UPPER EAST SIDE

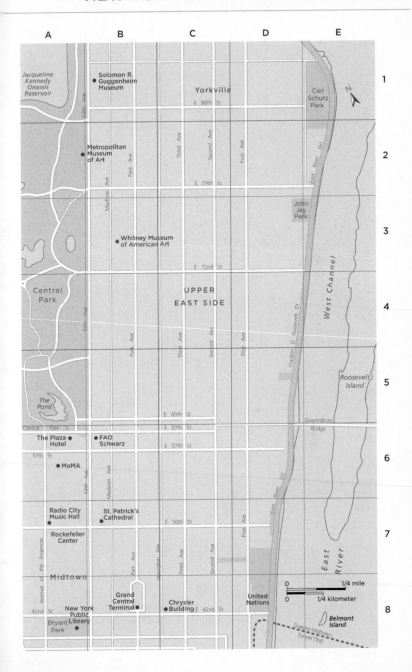

Jacqueline Kennedy Onassis Reservoir

Solomon R. Guggenheim Museum

Yorkville

E 86th St

Carl Schurz Park

Fifth Ave

Metropolitan Museum of Art

Park Ave

Third Ave

Second Ave

First Ave

East River Dr

E 79th St

John Jay Park

Madison Ave

Whitney Museum of American Art

E 72nd St

West Channel

Central Park

UPPER EAST SIDE

Fifth Ave

Park Ave

Third Ave

Second Ave

First Ave

Franklin D. Roosevelt Dr

Roosevelt Island

The Pond

E 60th St

Central Park S

E 59th St

Queensboro Bridge

The Plaza Hotel

FAO Schwarz

E 57th St

57th St

MoMA

Madison Ave

Fifth Ave

Radio City Music Hall

St. Patrick's Cathedral

E 50th St

Rockefeller Center

Avenue of the Americas

Midtown

Park Ave

Lexington Ave

Third Ave

Second Ave

First Ave

East River

East River Dr

Grand Central Terminal

Chrysler Building

United Nations

E 42nd St

42nd St

New York Public Library

Bryant Park

0 1/4 mile
0 1/4 kilometer

Belmont Island

Queens-Midtown Tunnel (Toll)

NEW YORK CITY: LOWER MANHATTAN

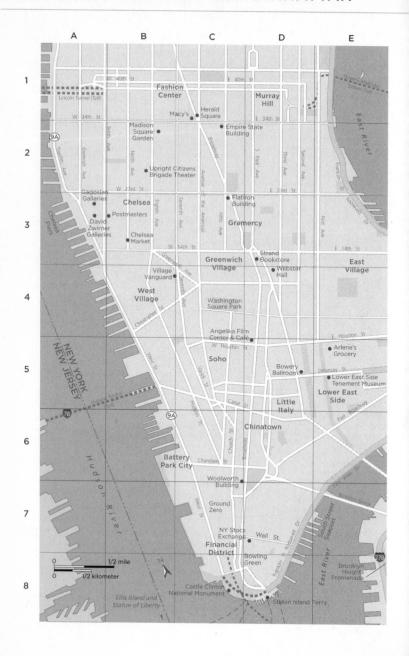

NEW YORK CITY: MIDTOWN SHOPPING

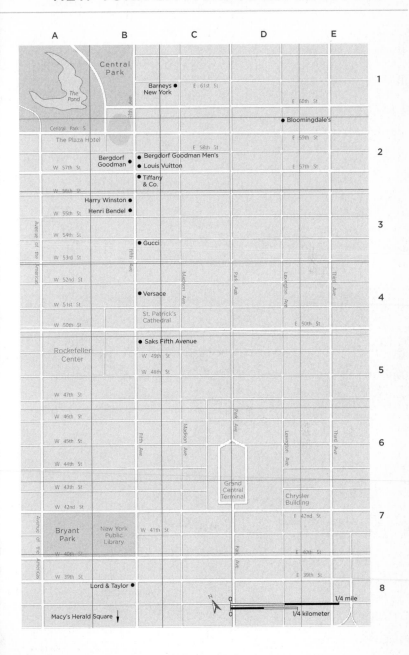

NEW YORK STATE

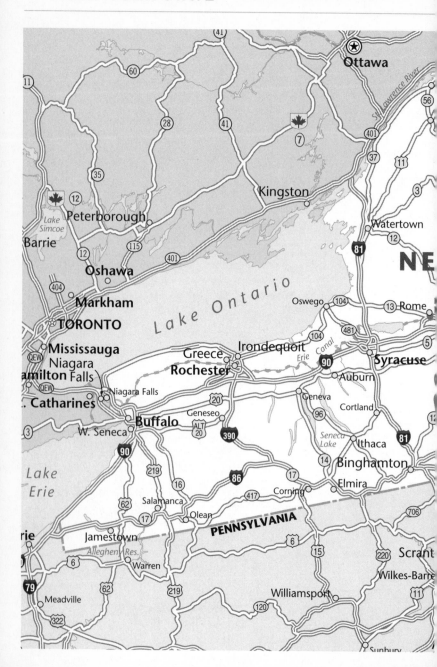